CHET

CHET

KING PICKER AND PIONEER OF THE NASHVILLE SOUND

MARK RIBOWSKY

Published by Chicago Review Press Incorporated
814 North Franklin Street
Chicago, Illinois 60610
ISBN 978-0-89733-692-5

Library of Congress Control Number: 2025938239

Typesetting: Jonathan Hahn

Printed in the United States of America

5 4 3 2 1

CONTENTS

Introduction

A COUNTRY GENTLEMAN

Talking to Chet Atkins is a distracting experience. He plays the guitar as he converses. While this may be unnerving at first, and brings about a feeling of inattention, one quickly realizes that every word is getting through. The guitar is more than a facade; it is a form of hearing aid.

—*Billboard*, June 3, 1967

I still like to hold my guitar. It's a familiar comfort to cradle it. I pluck the strings and feel the vibrations against my chest. I know the life I feel buzzing inside me is my own.

—Chet Atkins, 2000

I had that burning desire to play pretty tuned on a guitar, and I worked my ass off to do it. . . . I've spread the gospel of fingerpicking, and when I was playing guitar nobody did it . . . and now the whole fucking world is playing finger style. . . . Kids forget—they say, Chet Atkins, who the hell was that, you know. I think when history is written in the music business, somebody will remember and realize I did that and I'm proud of it.

—Chet Atkins, 1976

If Schopenhauer was right, that genius hits a target no one else can see, the premise of this book is that it can definitely be *heard*. And as it pertains to the baffling idiom of country music, all it takes is the spin of a record made under the watch of Chet Atkins. Known by name to almost all who know music, yet mostly unknown under the surface, this understated, mystifying legend of the guitar who had a fifty-year reign as the man who ran Nashville was, as *Rolling Stone* once branded him, "King Picker," a Band-Aid-like plectrum wrapped around his right thumb on the top strings, three-inch fingernails strumming below it, left hand frittering around on the fretboard with blinding speed. He recorded instrumentals that revealed every shade of every note, proving this was how they were meant to be heard, so full of depth and emotion they seemed haptic. How he did this is something that has obsessed guitar geeks forever, yet non-geeks—one of them being yours truly, a music biographer for three decades who doesn't know or give a tinker's damn about arpeggios, open tuning, or pickups and pull-offs—can become lost in Atkins's pentatonic scales (whatever those are) for hours, and as deeply as in any rock 'n' roll banger.

Despite his Promethean glow, he was as humble as the law allows, which surely composed an image of down-home simplicity. He once admitted that "if people knew how far I've come they'd be amazed," yet insisted, "I don't know how the hell I did it. I was shy and backward. I got fired a lot. I was original—my style sounded like two bad guitar players." In reality, he was playing what he called "a pseudo-classical style. Eventually I was playing arpeggios nobody'd done before. Octaves and thirds." Because he shunned semiotics of this sort, he indeed existed as an abstract, appealing to both highbrow musical adventurers and just plain folks. Branded by one writer as "a master of informality" with a "nonchalant brilliance," he seemed to enjoy being anything other than a guy of impeccable artistry that musicians defined with arcane specificity; to himself, he was a commoner with simple visions.

He never craved being recognized for any philosophical or social slants, keeping any of those to himself, though racial insularity bugged him to no end, quietly leading country music to divest at least some of its inherent bigotry with his status. Indeed, he never stopped moving upward, and it is nearly impossible to equate his influence with any other music figure of post-1950s vintage except perhaps his polar opposite,

Phil Spector, a malevolent urban-bred braggart who would hold on to his song rights until the day he died in prison for murder. Atkins was by contrast a man with a droll, sometimes cutting wit and salty tongue who dabbled in business because he was asked to, not knowing it would take a toll on his financial, mental, and possibly physical health. As such, he was keeping the bargain he had with RCA but also anyone who could elevate Nashville. And like Bogart's Rick Blaine in *Casablanca*, in Music City, USA, everyone came to see Chet Atkins.

It's now over two decades since he died, and Nashville remains his not-so-humble-anymore duchy; he is still the Country Gentleman, as he dubbed himself and was stamped on the most famous of the Gretsch guitars he endorsed for three decades. True enough is that the state of country music became big and overstuffed with money and egos—everything he feared he was helping to turn it into by making it *too* big. It was the irony he lived and died with, and didn't hesitate speaking about. After Atkins donated one of those sacred Country Gentleman guitars to the Smithsonian Institution in 1980, the *Washington Post* confided that Atkins, who the same day played for President Ronald Reagan, as he did for four other presidents at the White House, "felt a little sorry that he changed the face of country music." He had no compunction saying why, having gone on record years before that he had taken country too far astray, and that it had become "a parody of itself," and "I'm to blame for a lot of that myself. Country music moved uptown and it doesn't exist much any more in the old form. I don't know if it ever will."

These self-recriminations didn't stop there. In his time he claimed his own legacy as "an accident. I knew a good song, that's all it really takes. And I was kind of square. That helped [but] I don't ever listen to my records, don't like 'em, can't stand to hear 'em." He even predicted that the whole world would hold him accountable for his subversions. "Nobody'll remember me 15 years from now." Just to make it burn a little more on the wick, he added that country music was "a little half-assed anyway." He wasn't wrong, and because in truth he actually made it worthwhile, even transcendent at times, his confessions were overlooked; it was just Chet being Chet, a guy who had a way with a good-hearted put-down and included himself as a target. All it took to be a regular guy again was his Delphic grin and the turn of a good tale.

Then, too, he could say what he damn well wanted, because he *could.* We can certainly conclude that many of Atkins's remarks were wrong. Let's not mince words. Classical guitarist Rick Foster, one of Atkins's many disciples, once said, "Chet's tone, like that of Andrés Segovia, was magical," which made Atkins's guest appearances with the classical guitar godhead precious art. And contrary to his prediction, he has been remembered profusely, including by himself, in a tepidly ghostwritten 1974 memoir, *Country Gentleman.* Today music geeks can find the tabs and sheet music of many of his songs online and in books like John McClellan and Deyan Bratic's two volumes of *Chet Atkins in Three Dimensions* (the title spun from Atkins's 1955 album of that name) and Mark S. Reinhart's *Chet Atkins: The Greatest Songs of Mister Guitar.* But on a deeper, revealing level, the much broader human context was left untold for around fifty years. Don't ask why you hold it in your hands only now. There's no good answer.

He was more important than he looked, and a bit odd. Living in luxury, and so famous that on his sixty-sixth birthday he received a call from President George H. W. Bush, he bought himself a rooster, which he named Hotshot, because he liked to rise early as if on a farm. Seeming more like a CPA than a CGP—the initialism he mirthfully gave himself as a "certified guitar player"—he signed and produced the aboriginal outlaws Willie Nelson and Waylon Jennings, but he was no outlaw. But Atkins was an outlaw in one sense: he lived with risk. A Southern man with no tolerance for racism and old stereotypes promoted by the Grand Ole Opry, he was no less discomfited by the country establishment than Hank Williams, for whom he was a backing musician just before Hank checked out in the back seat of his Cadillac.

As the author of a Hank Williams biography, I could see the similarities. Both had a smirk that signaled their inner limited tolerance for butt-kissers. In fact, Atkins bore a facial resemblance to another famous smirker, George W. Bush. But Chet was smarter and more refined than Hank. He liked his bourbon and cigars but avoided drugs, didn't screw around on his wife, and stayed alive for seventy-seven overly productive years, working both ends of the fence as a working musician and a reliable corporate soldier, a clash that nearly wasted him. In the end, though, he was, he liked to say, just a guitar player who knew a good song when he heard it. Though his creaky voice precluded him from singing much, turning him almost exclusively to instrumentals, he leveraged that undernoticed niche into the best mirror of human emotion and variegated moods; and when he produced singers, he required himself and his session players to memorize the words before playing a note, so as to catch the "feel" of all the nuances.

He once said, "I can play anything I want to, on records or in concert, from foot-stompers to things that will please the symphony crowd," and "The only reason I'm considered country is that I'm from the country." But that, too, sold himself short. As a mountain Mozart, he was touched by something that cannot really be explained by music technicity but understood immediately upon being heard, which this book encourages one to do while living through the timeline of his life and learning how driven he was. Atkins, for instance, wore gloves in all weather to protect his witchlike nails, which he painted and filed and rubbed against a building or a sidewalk for the right texture, or dabbed under his nose to lubricate them so as not to cause fretboard squeaking. But the main vine of his life is more epic: he recaptured and updated the country idiom's African folk roots in the name of keeping the hits coming when rock 'n' roll was borrowing the best of country—rockabilly—and leaving the rest of it buried in a tomb of self-mocking drinking, cheating, and celebrating Jim Crow exclusion.

Because he had no affinity for inane or racist tropes, he brought blackness into the tempest, and only his extraordinarily popularity kept that wheel turning. It's why country music still exists, and lives well. It might not have, had Chet Atkins never come to Nashville. The story goes that someone once told him, "Man, that guitar sure sounds good!" Chet set the guitar down on a chair and slyly asked, "OK, how does it sound now?" Because if he wasn't playing it, it sounded less than perfect. Another time, when someone asked how in the world he played two different songs at the same time, he clarified, "When I'm playin' two tunes at once, I'm usually thinkin' about washing my car, too, so I'm really doing three things." He was never as haughty as he could have been. Indeed, he could admit that "I lose confidence every time I step in front of an audience, I suppose because I'm such an emotional person. I tend to freeze. My technique is hampered. It becomes mechanical." To counter that, he would never make a set list, instead letting it all happen on the spot, which "help[ed] me get more feeling." But he also once said, just as honestly, "I knew I could produce records because I was working with a lot of people who couldn't. I knew I could do a lot better than they were doing."

His work is proof. His skill, instincts, and idealism seemed more like eight or nine dimensions (on his Caribbean-influenced album *Sails*, he incorporated into country sitar and bouzouki), and his hauteur clashed with other strong-willed men, most famously the primordial outlaw Waylon Jennings, who admittedly was semi-insane. Signed by Chet to RCA when he was a singing bartender in Arizona, Waylon found fame through Atkins but grew to detest his all-controlling dictatorship, and the two had a battle of wills over song selection and backing musicians, which Waylon would win without ever publicly badmouthing Chet—a smart move, outlaw notwithstanding, since Chet could be one tough sonofabitch. Although he preferred to defuse any bad vibes, his demeanor rigidly pleasant and bland, this was also a buffer against getting too close to anyone outside the family and his close circle of musicians, mainly Jerry Reed. Rather than signing autographs, he would hand out guitar picks, which he said was more meaningful, but also less engaging.

His kindness was real, and his generosity, primarily to musicians he bonded with. The Nashville "A-Team" musicians, his boys, did quite well, constantly working at his beck and call, and few ever left that sanctuary. When he died in 2001, it felt like everyone in Nashville lost a family member, even if few ever really got to know him personally. Indeed, loved as he was, he had a standoffishness that people could take for arrogance. He saved his emotions for his music and often hid behind a cutting wit people learned to laugh along with. He once noted that "despite being shy, I've always been bossy," and that "I know more than most of the people I work with, and I hate to see them screw up and just sit there and not say anything." Being "talked to" by Chet Atkins meant learning a little more about making hits and melodies. It put you inside the kingdom.

Today, all along Music Row, the fabled if seedy boulevard of bravura and bourbon that at its peak housed thirty-five music studios, he lives as a street-sign saint on Chet Atkins Place, which went up while he was still alive. The avenue meanders from Music Square East to 20th Avenue South, with RCA's Studio A and Studio B preserved at 30 Music Square West, the latter identifiable by giant faux guitars with "Roy Orbison" painted on one and "Heartbreak Hotel," along with Elvis's image, on the other. Steps away are the rebuilt hull of Owen Bradley's Quonset Hut Studio B, the old Columbia shop where Bob Dylan—whom Joni Mitchell thought she was slagging by saying he "borrowed his voice from old hillbillies"—recorded *Nashville Skyline*. A few blocks east, on Gay Street, Russell Faxon's eight-hundred-pound bronze statue of Atkins strumming a guitar, dedicated just before he died, sits outside one of many places where he is honored, the Musicians Hall of Fame and Museum.

Atkins and Bradley not only built those studios but later, when Nashville's onetime pillars were being torn down, saved them from the wrecker's ball. Atkins surveyed Nashville's turf and foresaw profit. The great Nashville songwriter Boudleaux Bryant, Atkins's first writing collaborator, once said, with admiration, "Chet knew to buy up half of Nashville's Music Row before the dirt turned to diamonds." One can hardly look at any street on Music Row and not see an office or studio that Atkins had bought the property rights to when they were residential brownstones and sold them for many times more to speculators. Once, asked what the proverbial "Nashville Sound" was, Atkins mused, "It's the sound of money." But he was also frugal, living with Leona and their daughter Merle, named after his plucker hero Merle Travis, in the same split-level on Lynnwood Boulevard from 1957 on, an amp-shaped swimming pool outside and a basement studio inside, and a separate room for his sixty or so guitars, all designed by him and treated like members of *his* family.

The most famous of them was his number-one "son"—that Gretsch Chet Atkins 6120, the legendary orange Country Gentleman, created for him in 1955 and the top-line of the endorsement line he had with the company that endured until the 1980s, when he switched allegiance—a very big deal—to Gibson. The first Gretsch he owned is now enshrined in the Country Hall of Fame, and the 6120's history includes being played by Eddie Cochran, Duane Eddy, George Harrison (as can be seen in the old films of the Beatles' Ed Sullivan gigs, and he played an Atkins Tennessean model on several Beatles records), and Pete Townshend. Those Gretsches have obsessed guitar freaks and inspired such volumes as *Gretsch 6120: The History of a Legendary Guitar*. Atkins himself fetishized his collection in a book, *Me and My Guitars*, and in his 1964 album *My Favorite Guitars* (reissued in 1995 as *It's a Guitar World*, which for him was a truism). For most musicians, his guitars were as close as they came to meeting him, and to do the latter, Paul McCartney flew to Nashville just to cut two tracks, "Walking in the Park with Eloise"—written years before by Paul's father Jim and brother Joe"—and "Bridge on the River Suite," with Chet, his longtime partner Floyd Cramer, and Wings' Denny Laine, released in 1974 as singles under the mock name of the Country Hams, and included on the 2014 rerelease of Wings' *Venus and Mars*. Though the two giants in fact seemed from different planets, when they met at Nashville's Loveless Cafe and Paul told him of the song, Chet suggested they record it as a tribute to their somewhat estranged fathers, taking the Country Hams moniker from a sign in the bar.

Atkins recorded innumerable tracks in his basement studio and workshop, a virtual mad scientist's lab, refusing entry to all others, including his wife of fifty-five years and their daughter Merle. Wherever he was, however, a guitar went with him. Even as an old man, he was still playing himself to sleep, as he had as a child. Paul Simon once said the guitar is "like a universe—you can never come to the end of what you can learn from it." Atkins spent his life trying, while insisting "Everything I've ever done was out of fear of being mediocre." It may have sounded like a joke, but when he routinely deadpanned to his backing bands after concerts, "Well, fooled 'em again," he was more serious than they ever knew.

He was the introverted son of a music man by trade and an adulterer by choice who disappeared from sight for long periods in the backwoods of the Tennessee hills and walked out on Chet's mother, creating feelings of rejection that always hounded his youngest son. But two of James Arlie Atkins's sons reached the big top of music: Chet and his older half-brother Jimmy, who played guitar and sang with the Les Paul Trio and the Fred Waring Orchestra. Music was the only thing Chet had to comfort him, and then, in small steps, it liberated him, to the point that he would compose songs that became his sobriquets—both "The Country Gentleman" and the 1951 album it was on, *Mister Guitar*, became virtual identities as the volume of his work grew, and grew.

And the numbers are insane. The all-but-incalculable discography of songs he wrote, produced, and/or played on reaches to over a thousand, including 113 singles under his name and a frieze of titles by everyone who was anyone in country—to name a *very* few, Willie Nelson's "The Party's Over," Waylon Jennings's "Only Daddy That'll Walk the Line," Skeeter Davis's "The End of the World," Jim Reeves's "Four Walls,"

Don Gibson's "Oh, Lonesome Me," Bobby Bare's "Abilene," Eddy Arnold's "Turn the World Around," Porter Wagoner's "Misery Loves Company," Jerry Reed's "Amos Moses," and Boots Randolph's "Yakety Sax," which led to his own hit called "Yakety Axe." There are some fascinating tidbits, such as Bob Callaway and the Chicks' "Lookout for the Clothesline," Don Bowman featuring the Tijuana Drum and Bugle Corps' "Spanish Weed," and Atkins's version of the satirical genius Shel Silverstein's "A Boy Named Sue," written for Johnny Cash.

Atkins produced an astonishing 382 records alone for his longtime crony Floyd Cramer, and his sixty-plus studio albums and twenty-plus collaborative albums are chapter and verse in the American songbook. The Everly Brothers, whom he discovered, insisted that they sang differently with Atkins in the studio, by rote, and that went for everyone who was ever in that position, including his biggest influences, who later made haste to Nashville to record with him, like Les Paul, Merle Travis, Doc Watson, his goombah Jerry Reed, and favored pickers Paul Yandell, Tommy Emmanuel, Lenny Breau, and Suzy Bogguss. His 1980 *The Best of Chet on the Road* was partly recorded in Paris. Retrocon Atkins packages pop up regularly, the most copious being the fifty-track, double CD from Buddah Records in 2000, *Guitar Legend: The RCA Years*; the forty-track *The Essential Chet Atkins* double CD from Legacy Records in 2007; and for those inclined to do little else but listen to his work, the 2004 four-CD, 216-track Italian release box set *High Rockin' Swing*, culled from 1946 to 1954, and the 215-track, seven-CD *Mister Guitar: The Complete Recordings 1955–1960* from Germany in 2004. Not to be overlooked either are his side ventures, like the Nashville String Band and the Million Dollar Band, which classed up the hillbilly TV series *Hee Haw*.

To make a point of clarification, it is virtually impossible to include every song he ever brought to fruition, including even some of his own songs; a complete discography of known Atkins works would consume endless pages and still likely not capture them all. A further point: for readability and conciseness, this book has omitted some stray Atkins album tracks, with the full awareness that someone somewhere might have a favorite lost treasure among them. This alone is a tell about how history clings to him, and about his everywhere man influence. He was elemental when Elvis recorded "Heartbreak Hotel" and produced the first number one country song on the pop chart, "The Three Bells" by the Browns in 1959. Cramer's "Last Date" was kept from the top spot only by Elvis's "Are You Lonesome Tonight?" Atkins's first Grammy nomination, his production of Homer and Jethro's sendup of "The Battle of New Orleans," "The Battle of Kookamonga," won a Grammy for comedy.

Atkins's first performance Grammy was not for country but for Best Rock & Roll Recording, *Teen Scene*, and a later nomination was for Best Pop Instrumental for his second album with Les Paul, *Guitar Monsters*. In 1964 his production of Dottie West's "Here Comes My Baby" won the first female country Grammy. Another of his own, *Chet Atkins Picks On the Beatles*, was a chance to play the funky, flattened-seventh mixolydian chords that Harrison copied so melodiously on many Fab Four records (which George said were subconsciously written with Chet in mind). Those who may not know Atkins heard him when his last record, the jaunty "Jam Man," was used in a TV commercial for Esurance, and his jangly licks amped up on the Everly Brothers' "All I Have to Do Is Dream" were used by both Airbnb and CarGurus.

He went into the Country Music Hall of Fame at thirty-four (the youngest ever to be inducted) and the Rock & Roll Hall of Fame posthumously, won a record ten Country Music Association awards as Instrumentalist of the Year (nominated nineteen years is a row) and fourteen straight times in *Cash Box*, and won fourteen Grammys (bettered on the country end only by Alison Krauss, Vince Gill, and Ricky Skaggs) out of forty nominations, the last one in 1997, at age seventy-three, for "Jam Man." (Another Grammy relevant to him was from his protégé Steve Wariner's 2009 *My Tribute to Chet Atkins* album, "Producer's Medley," which won Best Country Instrumental.) He also notched the Grammy Lifetime Achievement Award and the *Billboard* Century Award. The Atkins-produced Eddy Arnold LP *My World*, which topped the country chart for seventeen straight weeks in 1965, is in the Library of Congress's National Recording Registry, as is the stunning "Amazing Grace" from the 1962 album *Chet Atkins Plays Back Home Hymns*. And this is just a taste.

His judgment could be wrong sometimes. They laughed about it later, but when Dolly Parton arrived in Nashville, he told her that her "gaudy" look wouldn't sell. He also got into petty arguments with Les Paul when they combined for two thorny albums, not that the work was compromised; their first album, *Chester & Lester*, won a Grammy. But the "square," tersely spoken, and seemingly distant Atkins played that role well, unconcerned with personal glory. Back in his day, such coolness was what one saw in Charles Aznavour, Dave Brubeck, Nina Simone, Thelonious Monk, and Chet Baker. Emergent rockers took to Atkins; the Kinks' Ray Davies said his influences were Atkins and Big Bill Broonzy, both country-blues guitarists, one White, one Black. When Dire Straits' fingerpicking Scottish frontman Mark Knopfler—whose collaboration with Atkins spawned three Grammys and another nomination for the 1990 *Neck and Neck* album—first heard an Atkins record, he was fourteen or fifteen. "I just assumed it was multitracking and that it was impossible to play all those notes at one time," he said. "I just thought, 'Well, that's [from] another planet. You don't ever get to play like that.'"

As if Atkins's usual workload wasn't enough, he played all manner of outside gigs, such as popping up on Garrison Keillor's *A Prairie Home Companion* and composing music for the 1977 German flick *Stroszek* and the PBS series *About Us*. Today, YouTube videos preserve him on big and small TV shows, on the Elvis TV specials, and on Opry shows—something he had to do despite having contempt for the Opry and its cultural retardation, though, having been fired by the Opry as a young performer, he was never sure it wouldn't happen again, even as Opry crowds idolized him, which gave him the sway to make cultural and musical changes. Not least of all, he paved the entry for Charley Pride, whom he had signed to RCA as the first modern Black country singer, to be accepted at the Opry, where he became only the second Black member. And Atkins also got the first Latin American country singer, Johnny Rodriguez, into the Ryman Auditorium. As Pride often said, "I thank God for Chet Atkins."

To many, that is a redundancy. When people spoke of the Nashville Sound (or the Countrypolitan Sound), they meant the Chet Atkins Sound. But when Atkins was asked what the Nashville Sound was, he was typically reasonable, calling it a "label" or "sales tag," and saying that "the studios in Nashville are like the studios anywhere else." He claimed he never even knew how to tune a guitar properly. Paying no attention to company hype, he said his albums "stunk" and were "sort of half-assed because I was involved in producing other artists." He said he could only read enough music to keep from getting in the way of his playing. His method of production was strikingly loose, by design, keeping everyone relaxed. "If it's good," he said, "it's completely lacking in pretense." Song arrangements were made from a simple numbers system still used today. One of Atkins's long-running cronies, the lighthearted singer Ray Stevens, said the intent was "Don't try to hit a home run. Sometimes a base hit is all you want."

Of course, there were times when the vibe became strained. Waylon Jennings fell out with Atkins for prohibiting him from smoking weed in the studio. When recording an album with the monstrously talented but cursed guitarist Lenny Breau in 1981, sessions stretched for over a year while failing to keep Breau off heroin. And Atkins was not immune from critique, which hardly bothered him, such as electro-pop country crooner Dwight Yoakam, who once went rogue and accused him of making country "bland," though he took so much blowback that he backtracked, saying he "went too far." The critics generally were slavish, but *MOJO*'s Fred Dellar wrote that Atkins "wasn't the most accomplished guitarist in country music," and, inanely, that "there were those in Nashville who could fashion half a dozen great licks in the time that Chet came up with one." But Dellar acknowledged that Atkins "had the edge" because "he knew what was right at the time [and] could make the most unlikely material eminently saleable."

Which is really all Atkins ever sought to do. And he did it by tailoring his forebears' styles to pop, not country. As the Statler Brothers sang in their 1981 song "Chet Atkins' Hand," "Thank you Les Paul, thank you Django, thank you Merle . . . You set that bashful boy from Nashville all aglow." He would make albums with all those influences except Reinhardt. But he also often sat in with symphony orchestras, had a real jazz fix, and composed a piece of dance music for the Tennessee Dance Theatre. Onstage, he could seamlessly follow Tampa Red's "Black Angel Blues" with Francisco Tárrega's "Recuerdos de la Alhambra." His legacy is wide but boils down to one signpost—his elevation of the guitar as something far more valuable than a rhythm instrument. As the veteran guitarist Pat Kirtley, who in 2008 released two DVDs called *Pickin' Like Chet*, said, "Chet made it OK to be a solo guitar player." He could rock it too. On his 1973 cover of the Cousin Emmy bluegrass banjo tune "Ruby, Are You Mad at Your Man?," his feedback riffs are as bracing as John Lennon's on "I Feel Fine" and Keith Richards's on "Satisfaction." To do all this required, as music journalist Bob Doershuck put it, a "technical revolutionary who built on Merle Travis' fingerstyle approach to reach a level of sophistication previously accessible only to classical guitarists." But not even encomiums like that could ease his worried mind.

He was a survivor, brushing off colon cancer, lung cancer, and brain cancer before he couldn't fight any longer. He was a remarkable conquistador. If only he could have been *happier* about himself and not the embodiment of his early song "Mister Misery." Steve Sholes, RCA's Nashville boss, who hired him in 1947, was once asked what the most profitable thing he ever did was. He replied, "Finding Chet Atkins." But despite earning around $5 million for himself, Atkins would say, "I feel like a damn prisoner." He would liberate himself, align with archrival

Columbia, defect from Gretsch to Gibson, and find a new niche with jazz and rock top-enders like Knopfler, George Benson, Earl Klugh, and Toto's Steve Lukather, winning three of his Grammys with Knopfler, for "Cosmic Square Dance" and two songs on *Neck and Neck*, "Poor Boy Blues" and "So Soft, Your Goodbye." He also bared some long knives cowriting "Would Jesus Wear a Rolex?" for Ray Stevens, a song confronting avaricious televangelists. He could poke fun at himself too, as with his "Certified Guitar Players" shtick, led by him and Jerry Reed.

He never spoke of it, but he seemed to have been agnostic about religion, politics, and music; his historic PBS and pay-TV shows bridging country, jazz, and rock; and his most favored music based outside Nashville. Even so, an Atkins tribute concert four years before his death held at the Ryman Auditorium featured an astounding *seventy* acts. His final album defined his greatest wish—*The Day the Finger Pickers Took Over the World*. But while crushed at not being able to play his instrument of life itself, his creed was expressed by another song: "I Still Can't Say Goodbye." But on June 30, 2001, ten days after his seventy-seventh birthday, he quietly died. With thousands of mourners inside and outside the Ryman, Garrison Keillor eulogized him by saying, "He was not a saint. He was a restless man. He'd be in a room and then he'd need to be somewhere else." Keillor noted that Chet had written him a letter that said, "I'm 70 and still don't know anything about life," but he was actually a man who knew too much to process, and "he had deep moods that came and went and that he couldn't enunciate." In the end, "he had a certain harmless vanity to him."

But was he so harmless? As crazy as it sounds, this author's research turned up that the Country Gentleman is on a government watchlist, dating back to the '50s, of people someone considered a "threat." His name appears alongside hundreds of others, notorious and otherwise, some as famous as Martin Luther King Jr., Che Guevara, and Woody Guthrie but also Barry Goldwater and Moses himself, Charlton Heston! Atkins, a mainly apolitical man who kept away from message songs, did rankle old-line Southerners with his integration of their music. But a FOIA request filed during the writing of this book brought only a letter on FBI letterhead denying that any relevant records about Atkins exist. Yet this anomaly reveals a jagged contour to the legacy of a man whose life and genius are not completely linear. Not that it blurs anything about his art and why everybody came to see Chet Atkins. In Jeffersonian terms, whatever else he was, King Picker was a man of his time and frame. And that's forever.

1

DUST BOWL BLUES

Chet Atkins once told, with that puckish grin and unending sense of wonder, about when Elvis Presley first recorded in Nashville, on January 10, 1956. That happened when RCA Records' Nashville boss, Steve Sholes, brought the still-emergent Elvis to the city specifically to work with the thirty-two-year-old Atkins, who got a taste of the future of pop music culture by seeing what Presley was wearing. "Elvis," he said, "had on a pair of bright pink britches and when he was singing 'Heartbreak Hotel' he split 'em . . . right down the back. He had to take them off and put on another pair and threw the old ones outside the studios. One of the girls who worked right there at the studios asked who they belonged to. I told her Elvis and said 'pick 'em up and keep 'em, they'll be worth a fortune soon.' She didn't believe me then, but ten years later she tried to get on *I've Got a Secret* because she had a pair of Elvis's pants!"

There were, of course, very broad social implications to Elvis, which became all too clear when the song he had really come to record, "Heartbreak Hotel," gave rock its raw animal instinct, with three verses of desperation and a middle eight of guitar heat. Decades later, Tom Petty, whose band name came from that song, would call it "really sensual" and "very spooky" and say that "it could have been the national anthem." For Atkins, though, the session seemed to be a stitch in time and Elvis perhaps a passing fad, requiring more work than perhaps necessary.

"We had a lot of pressure," he would say, "because everyone said RCA would destroy him, he'd be no good, we couldn't get that Sun sound. We got it, but I think we overdid it a bit."

That in a nutshell was Chet Atkins, who never thought he had gotten it quite right, yet when the song broke out like an overinflated beach ball, believed that the record might foment the end of country music altogether, the same consequence he would fret about for the rest of his life. Country fans, he would say, were nostalgic people who "don't want to analyze lyrics. Just hit 'em in the face with it." But his conflict was that his job was to create a soothing yet piquant sound that John Sebastian, in "Nashville Cats," his canon to Atkins, wrote was "clean as country water, wild as mountain air."

Doing so demanded much from him, too much, and there was only one reason why he got through it for so long, so thoroughly and brilliantly: by being what he once denied he was—"excessively obsessed." He had to be, since only someone excessive and obsessed would have believed, as he did, that guitars had human feelings—if left unplayed for three days, he said with perfect seriousness, it wouldn't remember he had ever played it when he picked it up again. And so it was that, with near religious commitment, he picked up a guitar almost every day, ever since he first flicked his fingers across a cheap secondhand guitar back in the Tennessee hills that sucked up so many other poor kids and left them no way out.

The 1968 Boudleaux and Felice Bryant song "Rocky Top," which has been sung by about every country singer on the earth, romanticizes the craggy, unadorned Tennessee terrain of Chet Atkins's youth so romantically that it was made the state song, the lyrics boasting that there "ain't no smoggy smoke on Rocky Top, ain't no telephone bills," and that it will always be "home sweet home to me." But for Atkins, who often played the song as an instrumental, "good old Rocky Top" may have been home but never was it sweet.

Born Chester Burton Atkins on June 20, 1924, he was delivered by kerosene light in a barely upright wooden shack on a fifty-acre tobacco farm in a town measuring less than four square miles. Because no one had bothered to name the town, which still had no electricity, the state informally extended the border of the closest place on the map of Union County—Luttrell, named after James Churchwell Luttrell II, a proslavery governor of nearby Knoxville, Kentucky, during the Civil War era. But when the census takers found the place nestled in the gulch at the base of the smoky Clinch Mountains, they filled in the location as only "Civil District No. 2," Union County, Tennessee, and in the margin, where street names go, "dirt road."

Those roads there today are mainly paved, though some still aren't. The Norfolk Southern Railroad still runs through it twice a day, en route to bigger and better locales than one in which the median family income is only $22,000 and the population barely over a thousand. It was, then and now, a place time has forgotten. But it was where the most famous musician ever to distinguish Nashville—which, while only two hundred miles to the east on Interstate 40, seemed more like light years away—entered. Delivered into the world that hot summer day in Dixie, he was the youngest child of thirty-six-year-old James Arlie Atkins, who was born in 1888 and lived on that same farm, bordering on miles of coal mines, cotton, or other tobacco fields where slaves used to be herded only sixty years before.

These humble habitats were called "hollers" by the locals, and though they sat forlornly on more dirt than soil, the Atkinses grew their own food, and weary cows and pigs stumbled around, and in the back forty, James and his children put in long hours in brutal heat or damp humidity tending to tobacco and corn crops. Remarkably, although the old house and side shed where James kept the milk and butter from spoiling were long ago torn down when the property was sold and a new home built, a door from the Atkinses' ramshackle corn crib does survive—in the house, the owner having built it into a wall, over a piano, knowing that the initials "CBA" carved into it by a young Chester Burton Atkins made it a real keepsake, the sole surviving vestige of his life in Luttrell.

As for James Arlie Atkins, he was a farmer only by family tradition, not choice. Fancying himself more intellectual and artistic than anyone else in town, he had learned to play piano, guitar, and violin as a young man and offered his services as a tutor, word of mouth gaining him work, at which time he would tear himself from the farm, put on his Sunday clothes, and get in his Model T headed for wherever. Still, he had no choice running the farm, which had been handed down from previous generations of Atkinses since the eighteenth century, when the first ancestors who migrated from England wound up in Luttrell—though Chet Atkins once speculated that his lineage had some "Cherokee blood," accounting for his high cheekbones.

The farm originally was much larger, before being subdivided, leaving only a quarter of it for James Arlie. But James was no gentleman farmer. He was much like his father, Wesley Sylvester Atkins, who was born in 1836 and as a young man studied music and became a popular fiddler and fiddle-maker, needing no persuasion to grab his fiddle and play at gatherings at which the natives would sing and dance to the Scottish folk tunes that inched toward the formative development of "mountain music." Among the Atkins clan, it was said that he was born with a streak of boldness and quirky individuality. His grandson Chet, who was born eight years after Wes died, would later speak of him by repeating homespun tales that made Wesley Sylvester Atkins seem like a character from a Southern novel, a proud Southern man who had fathered James Arlie in 1889, when Wes was fifty-two and his second wife, a hardy woman named Nancy Jane, forty. Wesley in his day had walked the same unpaved dirt roads of Luttrell that the family had dating back to antebellum days, and played the fiddle when not doing farm work.

For many in town, he was something of a dandy, who amused neighbors with his give-'em-hell attitude and stubborn streak, which the family preferred to call his free will. As Chet told it, Wesley had no compunction about voicing his own opinions, loudly, even during the Civil War, when he chose not to enlist in the Confederate Army or adopt Johnny Reb. This of course was considered heresy, which was fine with Wes. His head held high and his pride intact, he marched himself into the town's general store and announced to his neighbors and friends, "Hooray for Abe Lincoln and all that he stands for!" To make his point, he unfurled a hunting knife and slammed it into the front door. The men were stunned and word got around quickly about him. When Confederate soldiers came through town, so the story goes, they took Wes into custody, but, noted his grandson, "he would escape and come right back home." Nancy Atkins, who supplied much of this lore, would say, "Why, landsakes, he would march right down Main Street as if he was a returning hero."

This may have been apocryphal, but such lore likely had a role in Chet Atkins's attitudes about race in the pit of American apartheid, an attribute that had made many in Luttrell stare at Wes when he stuck up for Abe Lincoln and emancipation. And to be sure, Wesley was unforgettable. A photo of him from early in the twentieth century shows him in a dress suit holding his trusty fiddle, staring a little frighteningly into the camera and looking like the violin-playing comedian of the 1950s, Professor Irwin Corey, his hair long and unkempt, seeming like he had escaped from a rubber room. But for his grandson, strong-willed men like Wesley and his son James Arlie provided clues about how to survive the unkind slings of life—with independent attitudes that could sometimes be cryptic but got them to where they were going, and of course with music as a prime weapon of advancement. For the young Chet Atkins, this formula would run deep in his soul before he ever played a note.

James Arlie Atkins, the youngest of five children Wesley had fathered in two marriages, followed him into music and multiple marriages and children, but he was clearly not the character that Wes was. Wesley had encouraged him to find a real trade beyond the farm, and music was his escape route. He became so effortlessly talented on piano and fiddle that he quit high school after one year to hit the road. Prim and proper, neat as a pin and sharp as a tack, he was the anti-yahoo, his main impulse seeming to be his wanderlust, with music tied to simple freedom and a way to attract women to spend the night with. All gussied up, he made sure to play piano at the local churches and sing with the choir, a pretty good advertisement for his tutoring. He would also find work traveling with evangelists who needed music to swath their spiels at tent shows about delivering the gospel of Jesus to poor souls while passing the plate around for their spare change.

In 1910, when he was twenty-two, he abandoned the farm and moved in with his brother Charles in Cincinnati. It was there that he found a wife, Ella May Archer, who gave birth in 1913 to his firstborn, James Clarence Atkins, after James Sr. and Charles had relocated in the small town of Nichols, Nebraska. Two years later, after James Sr. took them back to live in Luttrell, Ella May tragically died at only twenty-one. This was part of a spell of heartbreak for James, who also had to bury both Wesley and Nancy Jane Atkins in successive years, 1916 and 1917, Wes in Kelly Cemetery in Luttrell. James, once again out on the road, made it back to Ohio, where he married again, to a short, pretty brunette, Ida Sharp, on August 19, 1918—a shotgun marriage, since Ida had given birth to their daughter, Nancy Niona, a few months before, making a wedding necessary.

Thirty years old now, age and parenthood—marrying Ida also made him stepfather to her son Jess—spared James from serving during World War I. By then, as his draft board registration card read, he was categorized as "tall," eyes "blue," hair "dark," his profession as "farmer." Two years later, back in the old farmhouse in Luttrell, the census would also report his job as "farmer," something he must have said with resignation. In 1921 Ida birthed their second son, and James's third, Lowell Sylvester Atkins. Three years later, Chester Burton Atkins, named after a sign James Sr. saw on a truck reading C.B. ATKINS MOVING COMPANY, would arrive. His infancy would be complicated by nagging asthma that made him gasp for breath, scaring the family. James and Ida would sit up with him during the night, holding him in their arms until he could fall asleep, which generally happened when

James would sing to him in what Chet remembered as a "beautifully trained Irish tenor voice."

The environment was Steinbeckian. The Atkins children went to a school with no name in a one-room flophouse down the road with no name. One of Chet's regular lines about growing up in a virtual leper colony was that they were so poor, they didn't even know there was a Depression until after it was over. And while unrelieved poverty brought many families in the region closer, the Atkins clan was a bee's nest. They lacked money, and James Sr.'s adultery while on the road always seemed to get back to Ida, and the vibes were seething. James and Ida spent most days bickering into the night, their screaming shaking the house. Chet was too young to make sense of the distance they kept from each other, but it would seem to have a subconscious effect. As he would pointedly recall about life in Luttrell, while he described Ida as "a kind and tolerant woman," by contrast he said, "I never did get to know my father well," adding that when James was away, he missed him only because it meant more work around the farm for him. Worse was that "I knew that he and my mother yelled at each other a lot. I hated the sounds that came from their room and almost wished he would leave again." And, in this recurring melodrama, Ida too seemed to give as much as she took and not spare the rod; Chet recalled how she subjected him to "the switch" every bit as much as James did with "the buckle."

It may be indicative that perhaps the only picture taken of him in the entire decade of the 1920s was not with his fussing parents but with a young woman who was bundling him up. Apparently a midwife or wet nurse, she was named Lula Corum, and Chet was left in her care during absences by his parents. Indeed, if one needs a clue as to why Chet Atkins would grow into a man who kept distant from most people, and never seemed to exhibit any need to show any real emotional feelings, those long days and nights jamming pillows into his ears when the shouting began explain a lot about the man he would be. Shy loner that he was, he didn't mind a bit working in the fields by himself. Nor did he mind taking the only route to school in Corryton—walking a mile down the railroad tracks to Knox County to catch the school bus. Getting there could take two hours, meaning he was out the door by six, in the pitch-black night.

He had a friend his age in Luttrell, Buster DeVault, an overweight kid who would remain on his radar screen long into the future, a picture of him appearing on one of Atkins's albums. But as a shy daydreamer who had fits of coughing and soreness over his body from malnutrition, he was left alone to while away time at the railroad station waiting for the whistle whine that sounded when the train came close, which like clockwork was at 10:00 AM and 6:00 PM. That whine was the sound of the outside world he wouldn't see for years. Sometimes he would hang at the station and watch the trains rumble by, with hobos riding boxcars, just like "The Singing Brakeman" Jimmie Rodgers sang about. He would also wave at the engineer, who'd blow the whistle again for him. He loved that sound so much that he would, in time, be able to re-create it on a guitar.

Being that creative would require a lot of time and practice, and one must give his bounder of a father props for siring two sons to musical distinction. His oldest boy, James Jr., called "Jimmy," had been the first to excel on a guitar, an old steel-string Washburn that James Sr. had bought for him when he was ten. Jimmy would tutor his kid brother on that guitar, which Chester begged him to play in exchange for taking Jimmy's chores. Since Chet had only James Sr.'s old uke and fiddle to play, any time he could get his hands on a guitar, he would, and by the time he was six, he was playing chords on it as well as Jimmy.

Given James Sr.'s regular absences, Chet idolized Jimmy far more than he did his own father. But Jimmy, who at seventeen had enough of James Sr. and Ida's constant scuffling, bid adieu to the farm in 1929 to live in Nebraska with his uncle Charles. When Jimmy left, Chet would recall, both he and his brother were crying. But it would pay off for Jimmy, who was able to latch on with the house band at KAMI, a Nebraska country station a *long* way from the South. He then looked higher, taking his guitar to Chicago, where he got a stupendous break when he was taken into the house band on *National Barn Dance*, which began in April 1924 on the highly rated radio station WLS. It was the first nationally broadcast country music hoedown, carried on the NBC Red Network. The then-novel concept would a year later beget the Grand Ole Opry's competitive Saturday-night broadcasts, originally called the *WSM Barn Dance*. Nashville station WSM—for "We Shield Millions," the slogan for its owner, the National Life and Accident Insurance Company—would be a stepping stone to a splendid career for Jimmy that would be overlooked because of his kid brother, but Jimmy had an edge on Chet in that he had a surprisingly good voice, much like Bing Crosby's *ba-ba-ba-boom* burr.

Jimmy was fortunate not to be around the farm when the '20s ended and the marriage of James Sr. and Ida Atkins fell through the floor. Having mutually agreed to part, they called together the brood. James, wearing his blue serge Sunday suit and straw hat, and carrying his packed suitcase, told them, "Children, I'm leaving." Only six, his youngest son would later try to make sense out of his family breaking apart, mainly blaming James Sr. as a soulless man devoid of any human feeling. "He always whistled when everyone else cried," he said, "and I realized much later he was trying to cover up a broken heart," adding, "he wanted everybody to be perfect [but] he was a man of conflicting ideals, an enigma. . . . I think he believed in God but his was a mechanical belief." Indeed, James's entire life was rife with easily bendable mechanical beliefs. Rather than follow him into a life of fleeting pleasures, his son needed to latch onto something that wouldn't ever break his heart. By the time he turned ten, he had yet to find it. But he soon would, and would never have to look back, and when he did, it was with ambivalence and brambles.

2

SILVERTONE

The spidery James Arlie Atkins soon hit the road as an ersatz evangelist, along with a fellow musician who went under the name Parson Jack. He and Ida got a quickie divorce, with James claiming poverty and leaving his family, not a dime for her or child support, and each wasted no time moving on. Ida wed a man named Willie Strevel, who also lived on a farm in Lutrell where conditions were a little better, though again with no electricity in the house, and even calling the Strevels lower class would be a stretch. Willie, in fact, seemed as unfulfilled on the farm as had James Arlie. Getting away from it all, he too would get in his Model T and drive to Jimtown, a hamlet in the hills east of Knoxville, which during Prohibition was a wink-and-nod depot of moonshine. Willie, recalled Chet, "would get drunk and come in late at night, falling all over everything. Lowell and I would spend half the night getting him sober enough to go to bed."

Four hours farther south, James Sr. soon wound up in Tuscaloosa, Alabama, and at forty-seven he also remarried, to a twenty-two-year-old woman, Addie Elizabeth Bonds, a divorcée whose family owned a farm just across the border in Fortson, Georgia. That farm stretched two hundred acres, which, while roomier than the Luttrell digs and populated by horses and cows out in the field, was just as mired in poverty and without electricity or running water in the pit of what was now a nationwide Depression. Though Fortson today is an upscale place, back then it was just another faceless outpost in a proverbial Dust Bowl, as was Lutrell, where in 1931 Chester, Lowell, and Niona became half-brothers and half-sister when Ida gave birth again, to a daughter named Billie Rose Strevel—and then, at a distance, when down in Fortson, Addie gave birth to Jeanine Atkins. Trying to keep up with all the tentacles of the Atkins family, one seemed to need a scorecard.

The Strevels had no phonograph or radio, so Chester had no way of hearing Jimmy play on the Chicago *Barn Dance* carried on the NBC network. He did build a primitive crystal radio, but it could only barely catch static-filled signals from the local stations. The first records he listened to were played by a teacher at his school, one of which he would recall was the Carter Family's "Wildwood Flower." He also remembered hearing "The House of the Rising Sun," the old English folk tune that was recorded with lyrics about the house of ill repute in New Orleans in 1933 by Appalachian folk singers Clarence "Tom" Ashley and Gwen Foster, and Jimmie Rodgers's "T for Texas," "Waiting for a Train," and "Yodeling My Way Back Home."

Industrious even back then, when the strings of his ukulele broke off, he tried to emulate Jimmy's guitar by plucking strands of steel wire from the screen door and sticking them onto the ukulele. It even worked—that is, until he angered Ida by neglecting a chore, and she tore the uke out of his hands "and broke it over my head." But a uke or banjo wasn't what he really wanted; he wanted his own guitar. And it happened when Willie Strevel, who also played the guitar, bought himself a six-string from a Sears, Roebuck & Co., a store-brand, flattop Silvertone, a guitar sold as a way to bolster sales of the Columbia-backed Silvertone record label (which replaced the Oxford label that distributed artists like Irving Berlin and Black vaudevillian Bert Williams), radios, and amps. When the axe arrived, it was badly damaged. The body was warped, the neck yanked away from the back, and someone had tried keeping it in one piece by sinking a big screw through it. The string setting was a half-inch too high. Four frets were missing, and the bridge was worn out. Subsequently, the initials of Lowell and one of his girlfriends had been scratched into the guitar. It was a mess, but for Chester, it had to be his.

He devised a three-way trade using as barter the one thing that James had left him when he abandoned the family, a deer hunting rifle—a child owning a firearm being just another slice of life in the Tennessee hills—which Chet handed over to Lowell for his one memento from James, a .22 pistol. He then proposed trading the .22 to Willie for the Silvertone. Willie said it was a deal. And so it was Chet's. Stitching it together, he glued a walnut block over the old bridge, but it was crooked and often slipped. Strumming the steel strings was a chore, and though the calluses on his hands were thick and his fingers blistered, he paid it no notice. Years later he would recall the rapture of that acoustic guitar, which he played while he held his ear right up against it; the sound, he said, was "just beautiful." He called the Silvertone "a milestone in my life" and "life itself to me."

It would make it through time, and also into the Country Music Hall of Fame with the Country Gentleman, because Chet would in the mid-1940s give it to his mother, who hung onto it. Chet learned to play it on his own, and in recalling his affixion to it, he spoke of "hammering away" at it, "soaking up every bit of playing technique I could find." Strumming with all his fingers, he thought "it sounded different, more like the way a piano is played, and that was somewhat more satisfying to me. . . . I loved the sound of the strings vibrating and the notes spilling over on each other . . . one at a time in succession rather than struck all at once." And, almost amorously:

> I would lay my ear down on the side of the guitar and practice simple finger rolls over and over, trying to perfect not only the notes, but the spaces between the notes. The full rich sounds you hear when you put your ear right up against the sound box of an acoustic guitar, I think that's the sound I've been looking for all these years.

He would watch anyone who played the guitar when the Strevels would have friends over for a jam. When Willie played, Chester would get right up on him, an inch away, leading Willie to push him away and say, "Get the hell off my shoulders!" He would take the guitar to school, which he now had to walk a mile to, there being no bus rides available in those parts. Shy, introverted, and soft as he was, and belabored by asthma that worsened from exposure to the cold winds and heavy rains of winter, classmates ragged on him as "Fatty" and "Jug Ears." His only relief was to pick up that guitar and play, at home, in school, in church, where the congregation would sit up and listen to him improvising an accompaniment to the Lord's Prayer.

He would look back at those days as if the splintered pile of wood was an all-purpose cure for all ills, almost a human presence in a world of impersonal crudity, Little wonder he would take to identifying his guitars as friends, rare as it was for him to find actual human friends. But when he would tell his mother and stepfather he wanted to follow Jimmy into professional musicianship, they patted him on the head and giggled. Yet by learning how to do the things that would have been easier on a healthier guitar, he would later find it almost too easy to kick it into the gear he wanted. For example, his left hand eventually grew so strong that the neck of a guitar felt featherlike, allowing him to glide up and down as if barely even feeling the strings. While others who picked up his guitar couldn't manage to play a note, when he picked up someone else's, it was so easy for him that it seemed he owned that one too. It would all fit together, forming the "excessive obsession" that stoked his flight from where he hated to the place where he needed to be.

Within his reverie for that Silvertone would come a ravenous desire to adapt its romantic appeal to all musical formats. Unlike the habitual musical offerings on the country radio stations around him, he had an insatiable appetite for learning about the blues that Jimmy had played in the Chicago clubs. But the biggest impulse came, he related decades later, when he went with Ida on a shopping trip to Knoxville when he was around six and they came upon a blind Black man on the street playing a battered guitar and singing for spare change. This may have been the first non-White person he ever encountered, and the effect, he said, was that it "hit me like a bolt of lightning . . . the way he was singing and playing, the way he was projecting his sound . . . it was like he had a P.A. system hidden somewhere. My mother had to drag me away. I think that's when I knew what I wanted to be." He said he even told Ida, "I wish I was blind and had a guitar."

He didn't go further than that in interpreting this fleeting childhood moment on a Knoxville street. But even as young and unfocused as he was, it clued him in to "race music" more than most denizens of country music, who seemed to need assuring it was a White province—never mind that the building blocks of hillbilly music came by way of West Africa and the slave plantations, a dirty little secret that White Southerners may not have even known as they sang folk songs of the 1800s written with blatantly racist lyrics, such as "Jimmy Crack Corn," "Oh! Susanna," "Pick a Bale of Cotton," and Stephen Foster's pernicious mockery of Black dialect, "Camptown Races." The Black country singers who made it through these downgrading transitions and didn't bastardize what had been serious music into horse manure were a hardy bunch; the very first act showcased on the night in 1925 the *WSM Barn Dance* became the *Grand Ole Opry* was a multi-instrumentalist grandson of Tennessee slaves, DeFord Bailey, who recorded in Nashville on the Brunswick label.

On that night, Bailey came on and performed the very earthy railroad song "Pan American Blues," the chugging *wooo-wooo* whistle of his harmonica sounding more like Cab Calloway than the show's regular banjoists and fiddlers. Bailey would make several more appearances on the show—but when the Opry moved to large venues with live audiences, he was fired by WSM and was barely heard from thereafter, making a living shining shoes and renting out rooms in his home, though he did return to the Opry in the 1970s, shortly before his death, and was inducted posthumously into the Country Music Hall of Fame. His cruel denouncement was all too familiar to other Black, blues-based country artists who gave much to this idiom only to be blanched from mainstream sight and mind. Another, Texas bandleader Sonny Clay, had played with New Orleans bluesman Jelly Roll Morton, but when he was booked on a tour of Australia in 1924, rumors of drug use and sexual byplay with White women got him banned from the country, along with all other Black acts for three decades. As with most White music listeners, Chester Atkins didn't hear these names. With the Strevels' crystal radio, which was encased in a big cabinet and like a phonograph was juiced by oversized, expensive batteries that quickly ran down, one could barely tune in to static-shrouded records by the likes of Les Paul and other popular white guitar players like George Barnes and the Sons of the Pioneers' Karl Farr. All that static made him have to improvise specific chords and notes, leading him to develop his own approach to the art of guitarmanship.

The closest he came to hearing hardcore blues on the dial, way down on it, was ironically enough another sightless Black blues guitarist—Blind Lemon Jefferson, another rock forefather called "the father of Texas blues." The portly singer-guitarist had become quite popular in the 1920s recording for Paramount and Okeh, though for peanuts, before he dropped dead in 1929 at thirty-six. He was also a favorite of Willie, who collected Jefferson's albums. When Willie played songs like "Matchbox Blues" and "Longing for Daddy Blues"—something Chester related to—his stepson would run into the room armed with his Silvertone. He recalled that Willie played those songs "using his fingers, trying to copy" Jefferson licks, and that "I was influenced by Jefferson's technique and by the strength he put into blues music." In time, hearing players who "were using the finger of their right hand in some way or other, I would always be drawn to it," and "I liked it because it sounded different, more like the way a piano is played."

As it was, learning technique of any kind propelled him. His life revolved around learning the intricacies of the guitar through that impaired Silvertone. After strumming it during the day, at night it was all but epoxied to him to ease his untreated asthma so he could sleep. Sitting with his back straight in a chair, he would strum until his eyelids sagged, a ritual he would continue through the years, even after his asthma had subsided, the posture he assumed most onstage, being seated always the most comforting. Not wanting to damage the nail on his right thumb—his picking thumb—he wore a glove on that hand wherever he went, marking him for mockery from his classmates. He played sandlot football, but not baseball or basketball, fearing a line drive or blind pass could break a finger. He was surely precocious, his heart hungry, the pieces in there somewhere. He was not quite confident in his talent but teeming with ambition and ingenuity that would lead somewhere over the mountains. Because only over them could Chester Burton Atkins become *Chet Atkins.*

Down in Georgia, meanwhile, James Arlie Atkins may have felt a modicum of guilt that he had ignored his youngest son. With the birth of his latest child, he began to feel part of a new family framework, and thus he began dropping in on his neglected children up in Luttrell. The first time he came, he brought a guitar for Lowell and a mandolin for Niona. He said he had a fiddle for Chester but had never given him one by the time he tired of the visit and headed home. Seeing how dejected Chester was, Willie Strevel went and bought him a fiddle. And when WNOX held an amateur talent show, Willie, Lowell, and Chester got together a fiddling trio and drove to the Strand Theatre in Knoxville. In Chester's first time on a stage, they played "Foggy Mountain Top" and "Cackling Hen" and pulled in third prize. Third prize! They didn't stop there. There was a tourist camp on Highway 11, and they would play uninvited, a hat on the ground for tips. That was likely the first money he ever made, a few cents. It must have felt like hundred-dollar bills.

However, he was also undeniably restless. As a teen, girls were of course on his mind but not on his hands. He recalled the time he and Buster "wanted to score" with two daughters of another resident in the bluff, "but we didn't know how to do it. They chewed gum. You could hear them comin', poppin' it. We'd yell, 'Hey girls! How about a little?' They'd pop their gum and say, 'No thanks.' That's how we thought you scored." In general, boredom was the theme of his life, leading to a frightening incident one day when Willie took him out in the fields. "We were working down field, burning up the shucks and cornstalks," he remembered. "I saw some crabgrass. I thought, I wonder what would happen if I light that dead crabgrass afire. I put a shuck that was burning to it. It went up the side of the mountain like a streak; men fought that fire all night." He added as if by rote, as if it was part of the normal consequences for such roguish behavior, "They probably whipped me."

What's more, his asthma had become so bad, his coughing and wheezing so uncontrollable, that "my health was failing, and Mother had written to Dad and asked him to come home. She thought I was going to die." That had been the fate of too many luckless inhabitants of the hills of Tennessee, where children with compromised immune systems often didn't make it to their teens. Watching him precipitously decline, Ida had all but given up and seemed to be preparing to mourn his death. Chester overheard hushed conversations between her and Willie about it but didn't realize how serious it was until James Arlie pulled up to the farmhouse in his Model A; seeing him there, Chet recalled thinking, "Maybe I *am* dying" and noted that "I was scared."

James put him in the car and drove to Knoxville to see a doctor, who checked him out and said he would "cure" him for a hundred dollars. Not one to easily part with his money, James instead wondered if simply moving his son to a drier, warmer climate would help. The doctor said it couldn't hurt, and so when they returned to the farm, James and Ida agreed to let him take Chester to Georgia, with Niona to go as well to help ease the transition. The plan was for them to stay down there for only one year so as not to disrupt their lives. Chester, who reluctantly packed up his belongings, carrying his Silvertone on the drive, nonetheless grew homesick and several times told James he wanted to go back to Tennessee. James coldly said to forget about it.

James had not changed a bit; if anything, he was more of a lout and impulsively angry. He frequently berated Chester for offenses in his farm work such as milking the cows incorrectly. One time, he erupted and threw him to the ground and stood menacingly over him. Just as in Luttrell, when James was absent for days at a time, it was a relief. However, Addie, whom James for some reason called "Tommie," was a warm, caring stepmother who worked at a cotton mill. Just days after arriving in Georgia, Chet said, Addie "took me to hear blacks in the church. We were in a Model A Ford outside looking in the window. They'd preach, the women would faint, and I'd hear these spirituals. I'd never seen a black person." This, of course, was not true; he had that powerful street-corner experience listening to a Black guitarist in Knoxville. But to the maturing Chester Atkins, such sights and sounds had a value-added effect as he found himself living with Black families not far from his door.

What's more, for all of James's still-loathsome qualities, he was right about the benefits of cleaner Georgia air on his sickly son. He was able to indeed breathe easier, and at the same time live a normal life away from the hopeless acres of Luttrell—which he came to detest even more in his memory bank. As he once told author Nicholas Dawidoff, with some over-dramatics, "In Georgia there wasn't all the killing and moonshine I'd been exposed to in East Tennessee. Somebody was always stabbing somebody in an argument there." Another benefit was that James Sr. began to treat him as a serious music student. When James was around, he would beckon his son to join him in a fiddle-guitar jam. "My dad taught me the rudiments of music when I went to high school," he recalled. "He'd get on my ass"—though he admitted his restless puberty was getting in the way: "I was paying more attention to a fifteen-year-old girl than to what he did on the blackboard."

The most propitious asset he had in Fortson, though, was indeed the school he attended, the Mountain Hill District Consolidated School, a meticulously maintained, two-story building with two things Chester Atkins had never experienced before—electricity and an indoor bathroom with plumbing. Although it only had nine classrooms and a capacity of around four hundred students when built in 1930, Mountain Hill would be the fulcrum of life virtually from the crib through legal adulthood, every grade from kindergarten to twelfth grade, and as it happened, it was also a glen of music appreciation. Assemblies were held in the auditorium where fiddlers and singers would perform, and teachers would go over scales and harmonies.

What's more, those bathrooms had an added bonus, which Chester found when he'd bring his guitar to school and do some strumming while seated peacefully in a stall: no place in the building—and he made the rounds trying rooms and nooks—sounded as good, the acoustics of floor tiles and porcelain fixtures creating deep echoes and crisp separations of notes. In effect, the john at Mountain Hill was Chet Atkins's first studio. He would also find himself in a culture clash of sorts, being in close proximity with Black people, two of whom, known to him only as Gussie and Mamie, lived in a small field house on the farm and worked the fields. Though Fortson was segregated, Georgia having some of the ugliest repercussions of human deprivation and victimhood, Atkins remembered that "there were blacks all around us," though they were called "colored" and lived in Jim Crow separation. But while he recalled that this stratification was "new to me, mainly because I had only seen one or two non-white people in my whole life before I went to Georgia," he didn't keep his distance, and some of the Black neighbors referred to him as "Mister Chester," which he felt was awkward, and he later said, "I should have been calling [the men] 'Mister.'"

For the well off, this sector of western Georgia was actually something of an oasis. Only a few miles east, in Meriwether County, was Warm Springs, the tiny hamlet built around the mineral spa where rich folks vacationed, lolling around in the eighty-eight-degree springs reputed to be rejuvenating for mind and body. It was right around the time that new president Franklin D. Roosevelt, having been diagnosed with polio, conscripted the place as his "Little White House," and where he would die in 1945. And for the inchoate Chet Atkins, the relocation was an eye- and ear-opening phase, when the meaning and feeling of native African American music became clearer and more instructive. James and Tommie permitted him to go hunting with Gussie—a real rarity in the Old Confederacy—and he would ingest some history of the Black experience in the South as the older man related his life while they sat in the snake-infested woods.

James of course knew well of the blues and R&B, and taught Chester the rudiments of eight-bar blues. Tommie was so taken with gospel music that she would take him to a Black neighborhood church to hear the choir belting out songs of pain along with the joyous release of spirituals—which she and Chester would groove to through open windows while standing outside the church. And James now began including his son on his day trips tutoring kids, and at times Chester accompanied his father's lessons, strumming lightly on his guitar. He remembered another trip when a Black man on the street had a soulful ring. The man was selling wares, and when he sang a blues wail called "Get Your Charcoal," as Chet later recalled, "it sounded so wonderful, lonesome. I could tell where the blues came from."

In 1937, at thirteen, Chester was separated from his mother and older brother and still living on a farm with no electricity, with a father who seemed to only tolerate him. However, after five years of Georgia air, his asthma had eased and, missing Ida and Wesley, he cautiously asked James if he could move back to Tennessee and live with Ida and Willie again. This time James was more amenable, perhaps relieved. And so, as beneficial as the Mountain Hill school was, Chester could hear the hills of Tennessee calling him back, or so he thought. James put him and Niona in his Model A and rolled into Luttrell. It was hardly a splendid homecoming for Chester. Once James dropped him and Niona off, totally surprising Ida and Willie, it became evident that she had even less time for him than James did. Chet would almost harshly write in his memoirs that "they treated us like intruders" and that Ida was "busy raising my new half-sister" while Lowell, now fifteen, would drop out of school in the seventh grade and move away from the family himself, straying to Howard, Indiana, to work as a hired hand on a farm owned by a man named Herman Lindley. As Chet lamented years later, "I was a stranger in my own home. . . . I felt out of place. Unwanted."

These remonstrances, which he felt no need to balance with kinder words, explain why Chet Atkins maintained a distance from his parents, speaking of them as biological appendages with no emotional attachment. Though he would be within easy reach in Nashville, James and Ida were virtual no-shows in a life closed to most people and opened only for music and golf. Those whom he called friends, and even his wife and daughter at times, never really felt as one with him, and accordingly gave him his space. If he regretted the loss of an emotional cushion, he didn't show it. For a time, he moved out to live with Niona, who had married a local man, but music was his great escape. He recalled his first real live performance of note was at a talent show at Clear Branch School, when he and a buddy put on a minstrel show—which, as he would painfully acknowledge, meant going on "in blackface, of course."

Even more painful was remembering that he rode home still in blackface, no doubt drawing some memorable stares on the way. But Tennessee seemed a dead-end street now, and after only a few months, Chester was begging to retrace his steps back to Fortson. He wrote to James, who early in 1938 came and got him, but drove a hard bargain. He had leased a thousand-acre tract to raise cattle and his now fifteen-year-old boy would have to work there after school, riding a horse like a cowboy to keep the cattle contained, sometimes splitting rails when the fences needed replacing. James had an old hunting dog who would trap rabbits, and Chester, who packed a revolver, killed a few and took them home for Tommie to cook.

Feeling like a cowpoke, hearing Roy Rogers and Gene Autry on the radio, he made his first real foray into mainstream country music. Slinging his Silvertone over his shoulder, when he climbed down from the horse, he would hunker down in the mud and manure to work on the riffs of "Ridin' Down the Canyon," "Empty Saddles," and "Deep in the Heart of Texas." It would be foundational to his music education, through which he progressed entirely on his own, spending much of his time strumming in the acoustically kind boys' room between classes at the Mountain Hill School, where the other boys could feel as if their time in there was accompanied by soft music. And James, too, found comfort at Mountain Hill, taking a job as a music teacher. Showing no favoritism, when Chester took his class, James worked him hard. And this served Chester well, adding the extra touch of technical knowledge he needed to firm up his gift of improviso.

Nearing the end of the 1930s, his command would prompt listeners to ask him, "How do you do that?" And now he was no kid anymore. He had shot up like a beanpole, over six feet, still bony, and unable to put on weight, but wiry. Matching his oversized hands, his ears shot out like handlebars from his angular face. His grin was the only sign of the self-confidence he had when playing the guitar. With a mind actively curious about many things, he had also become a history buff and rabid reader of Mark Twain, even talking James into buying the complete Twain works sold by Sears, Roebuck & Co. He also discovered another lifelong idée fixe—the opposite sex, though an early girlfriend, one Christine Cook, traded him in for a jock type, whom she would marry. Chet Atkins admitted to being the owner of a broken heart, but that cleaved heart grew some protective coating. "I must have learned a lesson," he once said. "I never got that far from it again."

3

DJANGO ON THE GO

Chester Burton Atkins could sense his life was shifting into a serious and determinative mode. As much as he yearned to become a musician, he was prodding himself to get to where Jimmy was, a challenging thought since his brother had joined with a band put together by Les Paul, the biggest genius modern music has ever known, and the most industrious. A nonstop whirlwind, born in Wisconsin as Lester William Polsfuss, by 1934, a high school dropout and just nineteen, he had moved to Chicago and was playing country music on WBBM by day as Rhubarb Red and Red Hot Red, and jazz as Les Paul by night. An acolyte of Django Reinhardt—whose funeral he would pay for when the never-appreciated jazz guitar pioneer died in 1953—his experimentation on electric guitar all but wrote the manual for playing one, his early amping accomplished by hooking onto it a phonograph needle connected to a radio. He also concurrently played a harmonica he slung around his neck in a wire holder, later made iconic of course by Bob Dylan and Neil Young.

There wasn't a lick he couldn't play on his acoustic guitar, and he began the three-piece Les Paul Trio in 1937, combining with the similarly versatile Jimmy Atkins and bass player Ernie Newton, quickly making it onto WBBM's lineup and onstage with the *National Barn Dance*, and it was on the latter that Chester could not only hear his brother play rhythm and sing sotto voce but also wonder how Paul could harmonize with a vocal with slinky vibratos that sounded human, bending with every inflection. James Sr., who also had one of those bulky battery radios, was duly impressed with Jimmy's work, tapping his foot to the melodies, making Chester wonder what he would need to do to make James groove with his music. And in 1940 there was more wonderment when Paul invented his original solid-body electric guitar, a Gibson L-10 that he called The Log, which only he seemed to be able to play without ruinous feedback.

That working model would propel him to a massive deal with Gibson more than a decade later. The signature line of personally designed Les Paul L-10s is so popular that the guitars are still manufactured as the Gibson SG. Paul would move the trio to New York that year to be the house band on Fred Waring's radio show, and continued his mad-scientist innovating, nearly electrocuting himself in his basement, after which he moved back to Chicago to recuperate. For the young Chet Atkins, however, working with Les Paul-level equipment was still far off in the weeds. Rather than any guitar, especially one like Paul's, with all its doodads, the radio in effect was his guide. Sitting in front of it at night when the many stations went off the air, leaving the dial open to other clear-channel stations like WSM, he could spend his Saturday nights playing guitar to the sounds of the Grand Ole Opry and buffering shows hosted by deejay and Opry host Grant Turner that gave fifteen minutes to individual acts.

Country radio shows were springing up all over the map, including the 500,000-watt powerhouse in Villa Acuña, Mexico, later made famous in *American Graffiti*. Some nights, Chester would fall asleep listening to the radio and wake up with its batteries dead. Not incidentally, what he was hearing in the early 1940s was a new wave of country that bucked the anodyne, chart-topping country hits of 1940: Bob Atcher and Bonnie Blue Eyes' "You Are My Sunshine," Bob Wills and His Texas Playboys' "San Antonio Rose" (which Chet would later record), and Gene Autry's "Goodbye, Little Darlin', Goodbye." And Chet, who looked for more substantial fodder, may have gotten a taste of Hank Williams, who, playing a Silvertone, was tutored by another of those unsung Black street guitar players, Rufus Payne, and had gotten a show on an Alabama station until, in a preview of days to come, he was fired for drunkenness.

While Hank's emotional, self-destructive furnace was still a few years from busting wide open, an underground with a more vulnerable human element was spreading, with Merle Travis's recordings like "Sixteen Tons" and "Dark as a Dungeon," and his duets with Grandpa Jones such as "You'll Be Lonesome, Too," casting a deeper, larger prism, with Travis's label, King Records, building a stable of country acts that included the harmony-rich Delmore Brothers. These influences were there for the taking, and Chester Atkins liberally did, his most immediate influence of course being the affable Travis. On a good night, Atkins recalled, he could also pick up WLW out of Cincinnati, where Travis played as a regular attraction. Chester had already taken to thumbpicking by habit, and the breadth of Travis's application of it was stunning for its gateway to notes more intense, full, and complete than any other fingerpicker could muster.

But he could only imagine what Merle was doing with his fingers, which in Travis's Kentucky folk style had him use only his thumb and index finger and is sanctified as "Travis picking," the method taught him by someone Atkins referred to in his memoir only as "a Negro in Kentucky"—whose name was Arnold Shultz. In his time, Shultz played in white hillbilly bands in the 1920s, and stories were told about young White guitarists who would find their way to Schultz's Black neighborhood and hide under his porch so that they could hear him play (Shultz himself had been taught the style by a white guitarist, Mose Rager). Ensuing pickers would adhere closely to the finger patterns of the style. Even blindness couldn't prevent Doc Watson from mastering the intricacies of flat-picking with a *boom-chucka* beat not unlike the later blues patina of Muddy Waters and Bo Diddley. Arnold Shultz, meanwhile, was left in obscurity and died in 1931 at forty-five, with rumors that he was poisoned by a jealous White musician.

Chester, too, could play only what he heard but not what he saw. Not following any pattern, he recalled that he "invented my own way, using my thumb and three fingers." He would much later record a Grammy-winning duet album with Merle, which many believed confirmed how identical they were—the sort of assumption that made Chet's neck get red. Even a year before he died, he was still a little hot under the collar, stressing that

> I never tried to play like Merle. . . . He didn't play alternate bass [strings] like I play. He played two bass strings at once [and] when you listen to me . . . I'm playing alternate basses all the time. You know, back then when I was learning to play, my influences were George Barnes and Les Paul and Merle Travis, and I'd play something and one of the other musicians would say, "Yeah, Merle Travis," or "Les Paul," and it would make me just furious. I was determined to play my own way. I never listened to Merle after I was about 18 or 19 years old. I never knew what he was doing and, fortunately, I never saw him play. I always tried to get my own thing going.

He also broke into playing the electric guitar by juicing up his Silvertone according to an article about pickups he read in *Popular Mechanics*. After taking a summer job with FDR's National Youth Administration, helping to build a new gymnasium at Mountain Hill School, he had the dough to order an amp and magnet-and-coil pickup that conducted electricity from source to guitar from the Amperite catalog. Yet, with no electricity on the farm, he could only plug in at the school, and did so often when his senior term began. Still, this sort of debilitation was just one of many debits being chained to an environment that he feared would leave him a talented nobody forever.

Taking stock of himself at seventeen, he had a guitar, a method, and a means of playing acoustic and electric. People were knocked out when he got to cranking out songs he had memorized from the radio, and his sense of the emerging musical topography was wise. "I was beginning to find my own licks," he remembered. "I had finally realized that there was a strong link between hillbilly music and jazz. . . . The freedom and spontaneity of it appealed to me." As such, his instincts figured out how to "bend" notes and chords in blues style. Les Paul he wasn't—yet. Nor was he Jimmy Atkins, who in 1940 could be heard on record for the first time, when the Les Paul Trio's cover of the Smith Ballew Orchestra's 1931 "Out of Nowhere," with the notation "Vocal chorus by Jimmy Atkins," was released on the Vocalion label. Advanced as Chester Atkins was, he was still a rather naive kid with unfocused aims and a stifling home life he couldn't shake from. Seemingly worse, the next phase of his life would have to succeed while the nation was living under the veil of war.

Early in 1941, James Arlie Atkins was once again an unwitting beneficiary for his restless son. James had latched onto another smooth-talking, foot-stomping evangelist to perform with, a Baptist tent-show evangelist who called himself Preacher Jack, whose real name was Ezra Johnston. He had come from Alabama that year and founded the Baptist Tabernacle Church in Columbus, from where he preached on Sunday mornings, wedged between hillbilly music. He was good, and his shows were diverting—but he had a dark underside. A rabid Klansman, he ran with a Georgia lynch mob known as the Columbians, founded a hate group named Christian Crusaders League, hosted a radio show on WRBL in Columbus, and published a notorious newspaper, the *Trumpet*, until his death in 1961.

The remarkable thing was that he was convincing enough to tailor his sermons to his audiences—some of which were actually made up of hard-working Black people, for whom he would come and preach in the sticks, tempering his racism with fervid appeals and singing to the Lord. What's more, James had no problem with whatever angle Pastor Jack was playing, as long as Jack paid him for each show, and Chester seemed not to know of Johnston's viral side; looking back years later, he praised him as "a good and sincere man" and "a funny man" who would stop by the farm after he had "preached to the black folks nearby." Pastor Jack even helped get rid of the mice and rats on the farm. And, like his old man, Chester saw the "tabernacle" as a good showbiz venue, and thought that "the religion business was flourishing." On one visit by

"Ol' Jack," as James affectionately dubbed him, he got to hear Chester play, and over dinner asked him if he wanted to be on his radio show.

That broke the seal for him. Chester got himself to Columbus and had a ball in what seemed like the big time from his limited perspective, quietly strumming standards like "Amazing Grace" on his Silvertone when Jack took five between sermonizing. He even started getting fan mail at the station, where he spent much time getting to know other radio hosts, including Johnny Barfield, the hawk-faced Georgian who had played with the Skillet Lickers and Georgia Wildcats, and who in 1939 recorded the jukebox favorite "Boogie Woogie" for Bluebird Records, bridging crazy-leg boogie with traditional country. Johnny took a liking to him and offered him a spot on his show, and Chester arranged for him to put on a show at Mountain Hill School. He also had a crush on Johnny's niece and singing partner, Becky Barfield—"I got a little sweet on Becky," he recalled of the girl who would later sing at the Grand Ole Opry. But when James forbade him from joining Johnny's Saturday barn dances, it shut down any chance of late-night canoodling, a real bummer.

It was still a step up, and seemed to set in motion the path Chester Atkins could follow once he could work himself free of James's clutches and hit the road like Jimmy and Lowell had. Like them, he dropped out of school in the fall of 1941, not bothering to show up at Mountain Hill for his senior year, not that the school wouldn't in time proudly note on a plaque outside the auditorium where "Chet Atkins perfected his distinct guitar style." Apparently, James didn't care enough to order him to attend class, and Chester continued doing the Preacher Jack radio show and a few local dances. And he was ready to put that distinct guitar style to good use. But then, with the suddenness of a thunderstrike, everything seemed to stop dead when bombs rained from the sky thousands of miles away in the Pacific.

The morning of Sunday, December 7, the date that would live in infamy,

Chester was trying to tune in music stations on his radio when the bulletin came about Pearl Harbor being sneak-attacked by Japanese bomber planes and the Navy's ships being sunk or destroyed. When the shock wore off, everyone across America was in fear that their families and way of life would be affected as their men and boys would go into battle against superior enemies. Turning eighteen six and a half months after Franklin Roosevelt declared war on Germany and Japan, he was prepared to be called into the service. Because Jimmy was in his thirties and had a family now, he got a pass, but Lowell immediately enlisted in the Navy, to serve with distinction in the Pacific. Now his turn, Chester marched down to his draft board, prepared to be inducted. However, after his physical, he was spared by the ailment that had caused him so much misery and was still extant and sometimes debilitating—his asthma, which led to his classification as 4-F. But safe as he was from combat or even the rigors of basic training on his thin anatomy, he felt much guilt as young men his age vanished, some never to come back home alive. Moreover, he felt stranded. On his registration card, filed in 1942, under "Employer's Name and Address," he had printed, starkly, "Unemployed."

James Sr. hardly seemed to care whether Chester was military bound or gainfully employed. He was too busy making his own plans for life during wartime. Swept up in a patriotic fervor, he altered his life. Learning that there was a B&O Railroad supply line in Cincinnati that needed workers to supply trains with metal and other materials to be unloaded at defense factories, he made arrangements with relatives out there to move in, leaving Tommie and their daughter on the farm and virtually ensuring the end of the marriage. He then told Chester that because he would be leaving, he had no choice but to send him to his mother in Luttrell, where Chester had promised himself he'd never go again. With barely enough time to pack his things, he was in James's car on the way to the Columbus Greyhound station. There, James paid for a one-way ticket to Knoxville, where he assumed Chester's mother and Willie Strevel would be waiting for him. Still reeling from this latest uprooting, Chester got on the bus with his suitcases and his guitar and fiddle in his lap, feeling so disoriented that, as he would say, "I felt numb . . . like a man without a country."

He had to change buses in Atlanta, and when he got to Knoxville, Ida and Willie weren't there. And so he waited, eating the ham and cheese sandwich Tommie had sent him away with. The Strevels had no phone, and when night came, he spread himself out on a hard wooden bench in the waiting room and fell asleep. In the morning, he washed his face and then spent the twenty-five cents it cost to catch a local bus to the station in Luttrell, where he had to repeat the routine he'd had as a child, walking down the railroad tracks, with his luggage and instruments, all the way to the Strevel farm. When he neared the house, Ida, who was standing outside, saw him down the road and called out, "Chester, is that you?"

Her mystified look made it clear that the incorrigible James hadn't even bothered to inform his ex that their boy was headed there. Chester, though, had decided on the journey that he would indeed not call Luttrell home again. Rather, he planned on making something of himself in Knoxville, where music thrived in honky-tonks and on the country radio stations. After spending a few days doing some spare chores—though he couldn't milk the cows because of the long fingernails he'd grown, the better to pick the guitar—smoking cigarettes, and listening to what was being played on WNOX, an old friend told him about a songwriter he knew in Knoxville, whose address he knew. Though Chester had never written a song, he believed he could offer himself as a cowriter, and he promptly walked back up the railroad tracks with his fiddle and Silvertone, and took the bus to Knoxville.

Arriving, he found his way to the address and knocked on the man's door. As fate would have it, inside were two Knoxville music brokers. One, songwriter and promoter Mel Foree, was a key middleman for Roy Acuff's new music publishing firm in Nashville, Acuff-Rose, which owned the publishing rights to country singers such as Hank Williams and, down the road, Don Gibson, whom Foree would manage. He also had connections to WNOX, appearing on country songwriter Arthur Q. Smith's popular roundup show *The Midday Merry-Go-Round*, as well as with Lowell Blanchard, the station manager, who also had a show cohosted by the other house guest, songwriter and steel guitarist Tommy Covington.

Running across these top dogs by pure chance had to seem heaven sent. After Chester shook hands with them and cockily said he was a musician and songwriter, one told him, "Well, go ahead and play, boy." He took his fiddle out of its case and played. Then, asked to look at some sheet music for songs that had not yet been completed, despite never having written a song and just barely knowing how to read sheet music, he made a few suggestions. The clutch, which included Lowell Blanchard, must have been impressed with him because after Chet made his way back to Luttrell, the friend who had given him the tip came by the farm and said that Mel Foree had a job for him at WNOX playing fiddle.

After being driven to the bus station, later in the day Chester was met at the Knoxville station by Archie Campbell, a pop-eyed, mustachioed absurdist from Bulls Gap, Tennessee, who had cohosted the *Merry-Go-Round* show for a decade, originally with Roy Acuff before Acuff went to Nashville, and now did so with Blanchard and another future Country Music Hall of Famer named Bill Carlisle, a lightning-fast guitar picker who inserted his own comedy shtick under the alter ego "Hot Shot Elmer." Because Chester was a new kid in town, he said he was Jimmy Atkins's brother, which made them pay attention to him. After a quick audition fiddling "Sally Goodin," Blanchard's instant reaction would seal his destiny: "Hire him."

4

HIRE HIM . . . FIRE HIM

For three dollars a show, Chet began fiddling for live audiences that had filed into the studio trying not to step on loose cables strewn around the room. Soon the hosts were asking him what songs he would like to play, and he was even asked for his autograph by spectators. When Campbell and Carlisle played outside bookings, they included Chester in their backing troupe, earning him some extra cash. Then came more when, during an outside gig Campbell and his troupe played, Chester, in the back of Archie's car, picked up Carlisle's Martin guitar and began strumming. Blanchard, in the front seat, was struck by how fluidly he played it and gave him another job at the station, as staff guitarist, appearing on a show hosted by bassist Johnnie Wright, who had been in a primordial country band called Johnny and Jack until his partner, Jack Anglin, went into the service.

Wright's bubbly wife, vocalist Kitty Wells, was in the station's lineup as well, one of the few female country singers, backed by guitarists Eddie Hill and Henry Haynes and mandolinist Kenneth Burns—the latter two of whom had enjoyed some success as the semisatirical act Homer and Jethro—and Kenneth's brother, bassist Aytchie Burns. Naturally, Chester needed a worthy guitar for all this work. Using Carlisle's Martin for publicity pictures for the station, but with too little dough in his pocket, he was saddled with his old Silvertone until, while speaking on the phone with his older brother Lowell out in Ohio, Lowell said he would lend Chester a Martin acoustic archtop that he had bought. Chester would make refinements to it, adding a removable DeArmond pickup that could morph it into an electric. He wouldn't stop searching for the guitar that was perfect for him—a search that would never end as long as he lived—but he was moving up every day. When Ida came in one day and told him how proud she was of him, he remembered that he felt on top of the world. When he had enough in his pocket, he was eating at restaurants, which led him to give his wartime food-rationing coupons to Ida and Niona. James, on the other hand, withheld similar praise.

Now part of the "in crowd" of Knoxville's music scene, Chester accompanied the boys who before and after shows gathered at a dive bar called Three Feathers Tavern on Gay Street and Jackson Avenue, drank watered-down Manhattans by government decree limiting alcohol consumption, and told tall tales. The owner's wife, Helen Shersky, was herself a country songwriter, and shop talk was heard over the clinking of beer bottles and glasses of Scotch and gin. Not a big drinker, Chester was there mainly for the company and the stories he inhaled about the business from a tableau of characters.

The best part for Chester was feeling free now that he was no longer caught in the tangled web of his splintered parents. What's more, as he was finding his way in Knoxville, he would feel no pain from the war. In fact, he would recall those years as a *benefit*—not only to him but to country music as well. During the duration, the idiom was spread countrywide and worldwide by Southern boys in uniform, introducing the idiom to many Northern men who had ignored it as folderol before but now heard the Grand Ole Opry on Armed Forces Radio. In that time frame, Roy Acuff's Nashville-recorded songs were selling more than Frank Sinatra, and the rise of Hank Williams made that city the unofficial citadel of country music. Within this font, *Billboard*, the entertainment industry spreadsheet written in the shorthand of geeky industry types, expanded its awareness of the idiom. Having already recognized R&B music by running its first R&B chart, "Harlem Hit Parade," and then under the most shameful slur of all—"Race Records"—it did the same for country, which it had covered previously with a chart called "Hillbilly Recordings," ruled by Jimmie Rodgers and the Carter Family.

Big changes were in the air. That same year, *Billboard*, noting that "operators of music machines [are] finding a more generous flow of coins coming in for the hillbilly and cowboy tunes," began a "Most Played Juke Box Folk Records" chart, albeit refraining from using the word "country." The first number-one song on it, "Pistol Packin' Mama," a favorite of GIs abroad, was listed as a compendium of four versions, one by Bing Crosby and another by the Andrews Sisters, hardly country names. But a new column, "American Folk Tunes and Tunesters," subtitled "Cowboy Songs, Hillbilly Tunes, Spirituals, Etc.," carried news about even niche acts like "Cowboy Jake" Watts and Mary Low and Her Rambling Hillbillies. Soon, tunes like Bob Wills's "Smoke on the Water" and Eddy Arnold's "I'll Hold You in My Heart (Till I Can Hold You in My Arms)" would have a wide fan base, and in a decade there would be three charts that said "country" out loud—a future that would be waiting for Chet Atkins.

With his borrowed Martin, he played some mighty licks on WNOX shows as he belted out country songs like "Bye Bye Blues" and "Maggie" when Archie took five. As importantly, behind the scenes, when Lowell Blanchard gave him a key to the station's door, after hours he would sit in the storage room where the records were kept and flip on a turntable and listen to, as he recalled, "all the people I liked . . . learning songs and stealing licks [from] pop and jazz songs as well as country." People at the station, he said, "thought I had gone off the deep end."

But he had actually found a slice of heaven.

> This was when I first heard the playing of Django Reinhardt and Segovia. I was impressed with Segovia's command of those complicated classical pieces, and I had never heard anyone

> play with the energy and fire that Django put into his music . . . and I would come up with my own way of doing it. . . . Actually, I was more influenced by piano players than guitar players. I was trying to get that two-handed piano sound on the guitar. Frankie Carle was my favorite. He played with such great taste and control.

Now, even James Sr., out in Cincinnati, was finally paying attention. The biggest skeptic of his son's potential had bent to the wind, writing Chester a letter reading, "Everybody listens to it," meaning country music. "And maybe there's some future in it." As Chet Atkins would look back at that letter, "Although he never would have said it directly, it was his way of saying that maybe I wasn't as dumb as he thought I had been for following a country music career instead of playing the 'legitimate' music he wanted me to play." It certainly massaged his ego, though it was still clear that Jimmy's "legitimate" career was James's pride and joy—and still Chester's beau ideal. Which is why he was thrilled when Jimmy checked in from New York, where he and the Les Paul Trio were still performing on the Fred Waring radio show.

In late October 1943 Jimmy called him and said he would pay for Chester to come up and visit him. Excited to no end, he took some time off and boarded for the long train ride to New York. The night he got in, Jimmy met him at Grand Central Station between the two segments the Les Paul Trio played on the Waring show at the nearby Vanderbilt Theatre, where he took Chester to see the second show and introduced him to Waring and Les Paul. With stars in his eyes, Chester could hear and see greats like Paul play for the first time. He hung around town for three days, based in Jimmy's apartment in Jackson Heights, getting to know Jimmy's wife and two infant kids, Gale and Gary, but mainly cruising with Jimmy, who took him to see the Statue of Liberty, ride the Staten Island Ferry, and watch the Rockettes at Radio City Music Hall. They camped at the Three Deuces jazz club in Times Square, digging the great blind piano legend Art Tatum. Buddy Rich was also in the crowd and stopped by to greet Jimmy, as Chester sucked up the ultrahip drummer's lingo about the "beautiful cats" in the band. Jimmy seemed to be something of a PR man for his brother. Whenever he ran into a musician who would hail his playing, he would pull Chester closer and say, "You ought to hear my little brother!"

In New York, though country music was an afterthought, Chester could feel the transformative effect of music during wartime. People were out on the streets, which seemed to have an impatient, jazzy rhythm of their own in the honking horns, reckless cabs, and endless nights at the clubs where one might spy Duke or Louis or Ella as well as big-time newspaper columnists in the room, adhering to the booze restrictions but partying hearty. But Jimmy was saving the best for last. On Chester's last night in, he showed him a gorgeous sunburst, sixteen-inch Gibson L-10 acoustic, which Les Paul had given him some years before. Now, handing it to Chester, he told him, "Here, it's yours." Naturally, he was blown away by the gift, which had been tailored by Les, with six supplemental frets on the B and E strings that resonated in the F key, a workaround Paul had copied from Django Reinhardt's guitar. On the train ride back, he kept opening the case of the Gibson and staring at it, thinking it was the most beautiful thing he'd ever seen, loving even how the splintered wood smelled. Clearly, as Jimmy knew, his kid brother's attachment to guitars was something beyond normal.

He would visit Jimmy several more times during the war, loving the vibes, but he was born to see life through more native vibes. And while Knoxville was no Big Apple, having a steady job at WNOX allowed him to continue making upward strides. Back home, Kitty Wells asked him to join a concert sponsored by a junior high school at the Roby Fitzgerald Auditorium. The Three Deuces it wasn't, and the temporary band he was in, the Tennessee Hillbillies, not quite the Art Tatum band, with the ticket prices being twenty cents. But there he was, with Kitty Wells, "Smiling Eddie" Hill, the teenage guitar-playing Johnson Brothers, and comic Cousin Nimrod. However, as secure as he was in the city, Chester's relationship with Archie Campbell began to wear thin. Chester had become a drudge for the cornball comic, doing things like hauling his comedic props in a heavy bag when the troupe hit the road. Once, he recalled, Lowell Blanchard's wife sidled over to him. "Don't carry that damn thing," she said. "He's not the show any more than you are." But he didn't feel like he was, admitting later that "they were kind words . . . but I still was afraid to cross Archie." And he didn't, even as other people around town were pumping up his ego, marveling at his fiddle and guitar work and how many songs he seemed to know by rote.

After Archie had gone into the war with the Navy, Bill Carlisle handled the midday show and moved Chester up to be the opening act, stepping out front to sing and play three songs. He was often out on the road as well, not just with the Campbell-Carlisle troupe but with other acts that starred Kentucky Slim, a human freak show standing nearly seven feet and weighing around 275 pounds, yet so light footed that he had initiated a fad by creating the Pork Chop Dance, doing it while nearly screwing himself into the ground. One of Roy Acuff's first bands, the Crazy Tennesseans, starred Slim and other musicians who wore blackface, an all-too-common habit that Slim himself often indulged in. Chester, who would have sooner worn a blindfold than blackface, had to tolerate being onstage with men who did, and even though being a vital *Midday Merry-Go-Round* contributor was a buffer, he knew he was underselling himself and his guitar, hamming it up with stereotypical country fodder, another part of which involved a comedian called Hot Shot Elmer, a pig named after Mussolini called "Mussoloomis," and a three-tailed chicken, which Chester reluctantly carried to and from the car trunk.

Thinking far more long term, he seemed to be laying the groundwork by collecting guitars for the long run, each with subtle tonal differences only a savant like him could decipher. Wanting to return his brother Lowell's Martin archtop, in 1944, when Lowell returned from his hitch in the Navy and James moved back to Columbus, Georgia, Chester bought himself his first new axe, a spanking Gibson L-7 acoustic that he was able to afford when Aytchie Burns signed a promissory note for him at the music store. He also bought a Gibson P-90 pickup for three bucks that he permanently affixed to it, and a Rickenbacker Vibrola vibrato control that Merle Travis put on his guitar to elicit the swaying effect that fascinated Chester. As a footnote, Lowell electrified the Martin but gave up on a music career and would send it back to Chet, who made it part of the collection; the primitive Silvertone survived too, when Ida asked if she could keep it, which she did for the rest of her life, right next to his old Mark Twain books.

So now he had two fashionable guitars and a good thing going. Sometimes very good things. A side benefit was that, suddenly, pretty young things drew closer and more willing—that aspect of success, with the girls hiking up their hoop skirts in the front row and more so after shows, "blew my mind." Country bumpkin that he was, Chet had limited success wooing girls, though hanging with more worldwide musicians had added value, both on and off a stage, and he was a quick learner on both fronts. The music, of course, was his main priority. Taking cues from another station hand, accordion player Tony Cianciola, who used after-hours time to sneak women into the darkened studio, one result was that, as Blanchard noted to him, Chester was suddenly "hitting a lot of clunkers" on the guitar. When Blanchard suggested he practice more, Chester agreed, puckishly admitting, "I don't think I'm practicing the right thing."

Still, to some around the station, the shy kid on the surface had always been an independent sort, a wise guy, not that much removed from the kid who had damn near burned down his stepfather's farm on a self-dare. Now on his own, he tied up a napping Cianciola from head to toe one day with a guitar string for the hell of it, and had to run for his life when Cianciola worked his way free. Nor was he down with the Grand Ole Opry-style template of country clownishness, and it served him well that the Knoxville players he hung with wore no Old West-style raiments, dressing in sometimes tattered flannel shirts, wrinkled blazers, slacks, and loafers. When booze began to flow again after the war, he was spending as much time at the bars as the station, drinking whiskey and rye with Arthur Q. Smith—until he was so drunk one night that he provoked the shambling, also-besotted Smith to knock him flat on his ass. Chester picked himself up and, forgetting where he lived, booked himself into a cheap motel to sleep it off, an experience he claimed made him dry from then on.

Meanwhile, his ambivalence about his family always played havoc with his head, and his thorny feelings about James Sr. were heavy on his mind. Things could ease when James would come to see him play and tell him how proud he was of him, moments that could put tears in his eyes. But those moments were fleeting. Even when death in the family came, the man's coldness knocked their relationship back down again. One of the most tragic times arose early in 1944. After Chester got back from New York, he found a letter from Ida in his mailbox that carried the sad news that his sister Niona had been diagnosed with tuberculosis and confined to a sanatorium in Michigan. He was floored by it, and when her husband had to go back to Tennessee to work so her medical bills could be paid, Chester took a bus to Michigan to be with her. Niona knew she was dying and broke his heart when she told him, "I want to live so much." He sent her whatever money he could, then she returned to Luttrell to live out her life.

Unable to live with her husband because of her TB, Niona moved into a small house built by Willie Strevel behind his and Ida's home, with her meals left on the doorstep. Like the Strevels and Niona's siblings, Chester could only speak with her by raising his voice while looking into her closed bedroom window. On April 23, 1944, Nancy Niona Atkins Nisely died at just twenty-six. A few days later, most of the family came in for her burial at the Luttrell Cemetery. James Sr. was there, as were Chester, Jimmy, and Lowell, but while everyone on that sad day was grief stricken, James would leave Chester with enduring contempt. As he wrote in his 1974 memoir, "I will never forget the scene at the graveside. Everybody cried as they lowered her casket into the ground. As the tears poured down my face, I turned to look at Dad. He was standing with his head bowed [but] he was quietly whistling, just as he had done when he first left us."

It was, his son believed, one more signpost of a man who never seemed to be able to deal with reality beyond self-entertainment. There would be some fleeting incursions of apparent human bonding from James. Once, he showed up in the audience at the *Merry-Go-Round*, and Chet would remember him having dewy eyes after watching him perform. "I actually think he was proud of me," hc wrote, "but he never said a word about it." Chester would take what he could from these respites, but what he felt most from existing with James Arlie Atkins was, until the day James died, a gulf of emptiness and estrangement.

With no shortage of work as a WNOX attaché, Chester's idle thoughts about going out with a band of his own were held in abeyance. However, it was Archie Campbell who forced the issue by leaving WNOX, a titanic event in Knoxville, when he got back from the war in 1945 and was lured to rival station WROL; he would go on to host the first country music TV show when the station branched out into the television age in 1952. That launched him onto the stage at the Grand Ole Opry and to a record deal with RCA, and later on he was one of the self-mockingly dimwitted comedians on the *Hee Haw* TV series. And Campbell was hardly the only restless soul at WNOX. When Henry Haynes, who also served in the Pacific, came home, he and Kenneth Burns reunited as Homer and Jethro, took an offer to host the *Midwestern Hayride* show in Cincinnati, and signed with King Records. Losing Campbell as a lifeline would have a shriveling effect on the station, though for a time Chester still could be slotted into one show or another, such as with the Dixieland Swingsters, who were more big-band jazz than country, each member of the band sitting behind a little stand with the sheet music on it, just like Benny Goodman's band.

It was during one Swingsters show that he looked up and saw James Atkins Sr. in the audience. After the show, James once again came backstage and, as in the past, "he had tears in his eyes when he told me how proud he was of me." As special as these drive-by reunions were, however, those irregular attempts at warmth soon abated, replaced by continued callous indifference. It surprised Chet not a bit when James junked another no-longer-useful wife to take up with and marry his fourth wife, Vera Jewell Harris, leaving another child in his junk heap of abandoned souls as he and Vera moved back to his native grounds, the Appalachians, in Corryton, Tennessee.

Rather than a new lifeline, the Swingsters were a false start for Chester. The band didn't know much about him and showed him scant respect, caustically calling him a "hillbilly," which must have burned him good, given his eclectic tastes. And though Blanchard would find new, fresh country acts and over the next two decades put on lunchtime shows before large audiences at an auditorium from which the *Merry-Go-Round* would be broadcast, Lowell, perhaps as a way of sparing his him from a firing, told Chester it was time for him to spread his wings and move up to a bigger market, where he belonged. But when he left, all that did was put him out of work and leave him wondering if he had already hit his peak at twenty-one. Yet what he learned was that country music was a remarkably tight-knit community, even a family. A family that needed him as much as he needed it.

5

"THE REAL, FRESH-SQUEEZED THING"

Chet Atkins recounted all his life that he felt on top of the world when he would visit Jimmy in New York and how his brother boasted about him. But self-effacing as he was, all that was a lot to lay on him. He would tell Jimmy to cool all that talk, and Jimmy would smirk, tell him to get used to it and that he was indeed going to be famous one day. However, over the summer of 1945, when the war would mercifully end following two terrifying nuclear bombs dropped on Japan, it did Chet little good to be an über-talented musician who had no job or discernible future at a time when the country was awash in a new working class with disposable income. As it was, others like him at WNOX were moving on to what they assumed would be bigger and better stages. One of the most talented, Arthur Q. Smith, tried to branch out but was his own worst enemy. Often stoned drunk, he rigidly steered clear of publishing companies to sell his own songs for whatever he could get, even if just five dollars. Chet would himself later buy one of his songs, "Once Upon a Time." When he did, he asked Smith if he ever thought about all the money he lost by selling his own stuff. "Yeah, Chet," he said, grinning, "but you don't know how many times I've sold them!"

Smith would sign with King Records in Cincinnati in 1946, writing for country acts but losing a fortune when Hank Williams in 1949 recorded his song "Wedding Bells," which Smith had sold to country singer Claude Boone for that mere twenty-five bucks. Smith then bounced around with Hank, seeing who could drink himself into a stupor first, and had other songs ripped off by predatory writers and performers, including Don Gibson, who took credit for writing "I Can't Stop Loving You." After getting into trouble for beating his wife in 1963, Smith returned to Knoxville and drank himself to death in a flophouse down the street from the Three Feathers pub. This was just one object lesson of the every-man-for-himself nature of country music and the sort of private profiteering that usually backfired, leaving writers stiffed of any writing or publishing royalties—it was part of the alley-cat nature of the business that Chester was learning about in Knoxville, and why a hard-eyed but mainly whistle-clean company like Acuff-Rose was so imperative in protecting artists' rights, not that it wouldn't also engage in rip-off policies.

The terrain out there was clearly more than a bit scary. In surveying his own life, Chester was, as he would recall, not only scared but "damned depressed," and he noted, "I didn't want to see anybody I knew." Mainly, he added, "I just walked the streets," four dollars in his pocket and chain-smoking cigarettes, an addiction that took him years to quit and would take a serious toll. He knew he could still comb through the talent at WNOX to scrape up a travel band. A year before V-J Day, as bottom barrel as it was, he put together one with Tony Cianciola and guitarist Tommy Trent. Bowing to the need for an obligatory comedian for the rubes, he also convinced the ectomorphic Kentucky Slim to come aboard. Chester was no virgin when it came to hitting the road, having made do even when gas was being rationed and bands had to beg audiences for their gas stamps or a spare tire that would hold for a few miles. Good news in war was hardly a ticket to fame, since it would be some time before a postwar economy kicked in. The South was still in many ways a reiteration of *The Grapes of Wrath*, but Chester's new band, called the Cumberland Mountain Ramblers, was up and running through the mud.

Blanchard lent a hand at the start, having promoted and emceed some early Atkins shows as far back as May 1944 at "the Junior Order hall over Penney's store," as a blurb read in the Morristown, Tennessee, *Gazette and Mail* headlined Cumberland Mountain Ramblers Coming, the main attractions being "Kentucky Slim, the black face comedian . . . the Cope Brothers, Dynamite Dan [and] Chester Atkins, the guitar wizard." Another, in the *Rogersville Review*, was pitched as "plenty of good old mountain music, singing, dancing and black-face comedy." Mostly, though, they had to arrange their own gigs on the fly, unpacking themselves and their instruments from an old Chevy, sometimes getting out and appealing to passersby to come see them perform. At a dive bar in Williamsburg, Kentucky, when they stepped on a stage, it came crashing down, which the sudsy audience guffawed at, believing it was part of the act. On a good night, such as a gig in Crossville, Tennessee, the band earned $132, $33 each.

Usually, it was catch-as-catch-can in areas much like Luttrell, still without electricity or indoor plumbing. For some shows, they would need to remove the battery from the car and use it to fire up a makeshift public address system to amp their music. Overnights were spent at flophouses, meals were usually a candy bar. That is, if they could get into a town. Often, the car got stuck in the hills, especially in winter when the engine refused to turn over in fifteen-degree cold, and they all slept huddled in the car waiting for the sun to come up. When the bloodcurdling *Deliverance* would hit movie screens decades later, Chet Atkins might have thought it looked very familiar. All of them got through it alive, but it was hardly enough to stay on it for long seeking deliverance. The Cumberland band disbanded only weeks into the adventure and drove back to Nashville—sans Chester, who by his choice was dropped off at a train station and, his guitar case and carry bag over his shoulders, proceeded alone, a scary proposition at best. With tongue in cheek, he wrote in his memoir of the dimensions of his life on the roadshow circuit—"a fifteen-cent room with the bums and winos. Otherwise I slept at the train station." Sarcasm flowing, he added, "I had made it big in show business."

Still, he was adjacent to others making inroads. Tommy Trent, for example, would settle into the rockabilly arc during the rock 'n' roll era. Kentucky Slim would grow even bigger, no small feat for a seven-footer. In the 1950s, he was doing his Pork Chop Dance with Flatt and Scruggs and Hylo Brown at the Grand Ole Opry, still doing his thing (not in blackface) in his eighties before he died in 1996. And for Chet Atkins, the moon was waiting. The next step for him was to jettison Knoxville after the WNOX job was gone. His value proven, he fantasized about Nashville and the Grand Ole Opry but had not yet scaled the wall high enough. But he could follow the route taken by Arthur Q. Smith to the next-highest country music step-notch—Cincinnati.

That route had also been taken by Henry Haynes and Kenneth Burns, aka Homer and Jethro, when they signed with Cincinnati's big, clear-channel country station WLW. That outlet was a logical target for Chester, particularly considering that Merle Travis himself had recently hosted a show on WLW. Moreover, the station itself was a big draw. Built in 1928, it was the fourth in the country to broadcast at 50,000 watts—and the first, in 1934, to go up to 500,000 watts, booming seemingly to the ends of the earth after President Roosevelt ceremoniously pressed a key from the White House to put it on the air (though it interfered with so many smaller stations that it was forced to cut back to 50,000 again). By the early forties, the station, located in a converted Elks Lodge downtown in the high-tone Crosley Square, was arguably ground zero for country music, though it would lose its place to Nashville. Having founded the Mutual Radio Network, WLW beamed its signal across the country as well, more clearly than even the NBC network that carried the Grand Ole Opry or Chicago's WLS.

Dubbing itself "The Nation's Station," its franchise offering was its own branded dance show, *Midwestern Hayride*, which expanded in 1948 when it was simulcast on the WLW television station. The company had a tie-in with King Records, but virtually *everybody* in country music seemed to parade through the *Hayride*, including Red Foley (who would record a song in tribute to the city called "Cincinnati Dancing Pig"), Tex Ritter, Grandpa Jones, and the Delmore Brothers—who in 1946 recorded what some regard as the first rock 'n' roll record, "Freight Train Boogie," along with other recordings that would be liberally covered by both early rockabilly singers like Gene Vincent and country rockers like the Everly Brothers. The station intermingled mainstream pop, its on-air personalities including no less than Doris Day and Rosemary Clooney.

In Chester Atkins's mind, he was a technical heir of Travis, and getting a job at the station would mean he would be living close to his brother Lowell; fortunately, James Sr. had moved away from the city. Thus, it was somewhat symmetrical that Jimmy once more came to his aid. Because Jimmy knew all manner of industry bigwigs all across the country, he was able to call and set up an audition for his kid brother at WLW with someone Chet recalled only as a "Mr. Chamberlain," though this may have been Joseph A. Chambers, who had designed the studio into a state-of-the-art shop. As it happened, the bus ride to Cincinnati made a stop in Mount Vernon, Kentucky, a mile or so from Renfro Valley, a hamlet like seemingly dozens of places that have claimed to be the birthplace of country music, and where the Kentucky Music Hall of Fame is. The Valley's signature attraction, the *Renfro Valley Barn Dance*, was the first "barn dance" show in the country, but those Saturday-night hoedowns were carried by WLW before host Red Foley brought the show to the actual Valley in 1939, to be broadcast over WHAS in Louisville and simulcast nationally on NBC and then CBS radio. (It still runs today as a syndicated classic bluegrass and gospel show called *Renfro Valley Gatherin'*, making the franchise the second-longest-running country program in America).

Hank Williams and Homer and Jethro were among the horde who had performed on the Renfro dance show, and as a side trip, Chester dropped by the show's offices to gauge his hiring value. After playing a few chords, he was offered a job by the *Barn Dance*'s host, John Lair, for fifty dollars a week—a bundle. But, figuring the job would still be there, Chester politely turned it down and headed back to the bus station to make it to the hub, WLW. When he arrived, he played on the guitar and captivated "Mr. Chamberlain," who hired him on the spot at the same salary of fifty dollars to be a regular performer on the station's morning show. Inserted into a cowboy-style band called the Trailblazers, his high-energy guitar licks pepped up sleepy Cincinnatians. And although he was obviously ill fitted as a cowboy, "trailblazer" even back then seemed perfectly fitting.

Just having turned twenty-one when the war ended and still needing to fill in his tall, splintery frame, he seemed uncommonly mature. When requests came in from women for a headshot of him, a publicity headshot was taken of him, unsmiling, eyes burning. Truthfully, he was still nowhere near insouciant. That Bogart-like pose came about to avoid showing his goofy-toothed smile. He could still only afford living out of a room at the YMCA and hardly felt like a star walking to work early each morning on streets he recalled as being occupied by "winos, weirdos, and rats." He was also fan-like himself. He heard that Merle Travis, who had left the station to freelance around the country, was returning on a visit, and Kenneth Burns and Henry Haynes, who had known Travis for years but only met Chester when he came to Cincinnati, invited him to have dinner with them. Chester reacted like a kid about to meet Joe DiMaggio. He made sure to bring along his guitar and breathlessly told Travis of playing it the Merle Travis way. Merle, who in 1946 had a two-sided hit record of "Cincinnati Lou" and "No Vacancy," asked Chester to play something. The guitar came out like a quick-draw, and when he was done, Merle, a most generous man, said, "I can't play like you can, Chester," which damn near made him faint.

It was no mere table talk. As Chet Atkins would relate decades later, "Whenever anyone has asked [Merle] who the greatest guitar player in the country is, he says, 'Chester Atkins.' I can't understand why because my playing is so much like his. [He would say] that 'most guitar players are like imitation orange juice, but Chester Atkins is the real, fresh-squeezed thing.'" And meeting Travis wasn't his only brush with greatness in 1946. That was the year he had a face-to-face with Django Reinhardt. It happened in Chicago, during a road trip by a group of

WLW stars through the Midwest, when Chester saw the cool hepcat who smoked cigarettes as he played onstage. Years later, he remembered it like it was yesterday:

> [Django] played the Civic Center up there with Duke Ellington and I saw the show. He played great—I remember he knocked out all the musicians in the band. And so I went backstage—which took a lot of courage. I got the only autograph I've ever got in my life. I didn't know until I read his biography that he was illiterate. That's all he ever learned to write. And I still got it. The only one. He couldn't speak English and I couldn't speak French. Just stood and grinned at him and he grinned back and he knew I was a real fan because he patted me on the back.

That interlude would be even more frozen in his mind since, as he noted, "that tour was a fiasco for Django," as American music writers "chopped him up, made fun of him, and he was just brokenhearted because he really did teach the country how to play guitar. He got on a boat and went back to France," where he died six years later after a gig in Paris at only forty-five. But in his time, Django, as Chet said, "had an awful lot of drive. Hell of a beat. I heard everything he ever did and I never heard him slow down." Neither would Chester, who glided along the circuit, landing on the *Renfro Valley Barn Dance*, the *Old Dominion Barn Dance* in Richmond, Virginia, and the WWVA's *Wheeling Jamboree* in Wheeling, West Virginia, home base of the honkytonk star Hawkshaw Hawkins. On the circuit, tidbits and ads appeared in Southern and Midwestern papers about him as a headliner, one of which actually marked the moment when, at least in one dispatch, he eclipsed his famous family tie. In the "Radio" column of the Greenfield, Indiana, *Daily Reporter* on August 1, 1945, an entry read: "Did you know that Chester Atkins, star guitarist of the Trail Blazers . . . has a brother, Jimmy Atkins, now a baritone soloist with Fred Waring?"

Moreover, while Chester judged himself a nerd from the mountains, he had no trouble turning the heads of women, though he was smitten with one who also made the circuit. This was Leona Johnson, a sprightly, smiling brunette who was a trouper herself, half of a singing act from Clermont, Ohio, called the Johnson Sisters, who were also heard on WLW shows. The twin sisters, Leona and her sister Lois, born on September 12, 1924, part of an enormous brood of ten children, went under the stage names Fern and Laverne, singing tight harmonies in matching *Rebecca of Sunnybrook Farm* outfits with white carnations in their hair. It took a while before Chester summoned the nerve to hit on Leona, and he had one of his bandmates, Louie Ennis, do it for him.

It worked. She came to him and invited her to drink a Coke with him. From then on, only when he was onstage were they not together. When Chester came down with the mumps and was hospitalized, he told the nurses the only person to let through to see him was Leona, who would spend nights sitting by his bedside, holding his hand and reading to him. The love story got even more radiant when "Jethro" Burns began courting Lois, whom he called "Gussie." He and Chester had a good time when asked how they could tell the twins apart. "We don't ask," was their one-liner. After only a few weeks, both couples declared their engagements, though Chester and Leona agreed to wait to wed until they had more financial security. But the manic-depressive cycle he seemed to be born with rose again. His chronic asthma kicked up, keeping him off the air while he recovered. Then came the mumps. His physical frailty, which seemed rather sickly to begin with, caused him to brood about losing ground in a cut-throat environment. Then, out of nowhere, he was fired, putatively for the same reason as his more sympathetic release from WNOX—the habitual tendency of country stations to overspend and change personnel, and the quickly ebbing popularity of even star hosts, which is why even a superstar country figure like Red Foley worked at so many stations in his life.

Chester had likewise done himself no favors as a dour kid who never kicked up his heels, a product of his shyness and aversion to long-winded self-adulation and cheesy comedic turns that interfered with his serious musicianship. Nor did he put much effort into honing his infrequent singing. It seems the fans cared enough to find other stations in the morning. And so, within only weeks of starting, the bosses who had been taken with him pulled the rug out, telling him he was no longer employed at WLW—on Christmas Eve, no less. Growing depressed again, he called Johnnie Wright, who with Kitty Wells and Jack Anglin had landed in Raleigh, North Carolina, doing a Johnnie and Jack stint on WPTF, another 50,000-watt station affiliated with the NBC national network. He asked Johnnie if he had room for him, and when he said yes, Chester was on the air again, gaining more traction with his continual experimentation. As he recalled, "I was using the Vibrola combined with fingerstyle licks to get some guitar sounds that were considered unique at the time, so they billed me as 'Chester Atkins and His Talking Guitar.'"

The gig didn't elevate him any, though, and when he read in the trade papers that Foley had taken over Roy Acuff's show on WLS in Chicago, he quit WPTF and, like a rolling stone, boarded the train for the Windy City, in his head a plan to hook on at WLS—no doubt playing the Jimmy Atkins–Les Paul card, to sidle up to Red and ride the country tide with him. He was so confident about it that he made a stop in Cincinnati to tell Leona to sit tight, he was about to break wide open in Chicago. She wondered if this bravado was a cover, and if she might have seen the last of him. Some of her friends figured that she already had.

Cocky as he could pretend to be, when in Chicago he marched into WLS, asked for a job, and was promptly turned down by station honchos. The only recourse was to go to the less legendary but viable country station WBBM, a CBS affiliate. Chester thought he was set but learned how different it was to be a professional musician in a place like the Second City, a union town with membership rules; in order to play a note on the radio, he needed to join the union, a process that took time, during which he would only be able to play his guitar at the jazz clubs. That didn't seem like the worst thing in the world. He got a quick job at a place he called a "dive" on Madison Street, and the $150 he pulled in for a week's work sustained him. But the club was a pit, rife with drunks fighting in the aisles. One night, a chair thrown by a barfly almost hit him in the head. Getting back to another YMCA room, he recalled it as "the only time I ever considered quitting music."

Instead, he tried a last-ditch stab, taking his case straight to Red Foley. Walking into the downtown office of the city's main country talent booker, Bill Ellsworth, he introduced himself, swallowed hard, and said he had come to Chicago to team up with Red. Ellsworth chuckled. Red, he said, happened to be somewhere inside the office—a coincidence that must have made Chet Atkins believe in destiny. Liking the kid's nerve, Ellsworth went to find Foley, who came out, shook his hand, and said, as so many others had and would, "Play something for me." In a touch of fate, Red was about to switch horses again in his twisty career. He told Chester that he was leaving WLS and the *National Barn Dance* stage to become master of ceremonies of the Grand Ole Opry's subfranchise *The Prince Albert Show*, the hour-long segment of the usual six-hour Opry presentation on Saturday nights carried on NBC radio, sponsored by the tobacco company.

Being the host of the Opry broadcast was the height of country privilege. For Roy Acuff, it led to the formation of the first homegrown country music publishing agency, when he teamed with Fred Rose, a songwriter who'd had a hit with "Back in the Saddle Again." With Acuff as the headline talent, Acuff-Rose Music burgeoned quickly, its ten-strike coming in 1947, when it signed Hank Williams, whom Rose managed, produced, and ushered onto the Opry stage. The fact that Acuff-Rose requisitioned most of the publishing royalties was acceptable as the price for having songs recorded and sold to big record labels, and Acuff was so entrenched that he had the leverage to quit the Opry when he had a run-in with its corporate sponsors. That left the door open for Red, who would start the job in April, with a band of sidemen called the Cumberland Boys—apparently not the same unit as Chet's former posse, the Cumberland Mountain Ramblers. On a whim, he asked Chester the magic question—"Ches, how would you like to go to Nashville with me?" Before Red got the question out, "Ches" was saying, "I sure would."

What he didn't know was that he was about to enter music's answer to three-card monte. The biggest little secret in Nashville is that it was never an actual country market, its pride being the blues. Although its Black population has historically remained under 30 percent, former slaves found a home here and Black universities like Fisk and Tennessee State led sit-ins demonstrations during the 1950s. Even as the capital of a blood-red state that likes to wave the American flag and bow to the Grand Ole Opry "heritage," the biggest fallback word in the Southern dialect, Nashville has through the years chronically elected Democratic mayors and Black legislators. The people who dutifully filed into the Opry were mainly not natives but tourists who heard country music on WSM, a clear-channel radio station that beamed country through the night. The Opry played out its mythology at the Ryman Auditorium at 116 Fifth Avenue North, a drab brown brick building to which the tourists genuflected as a house of God, its tabernacle-like trimming in contrast to the lowbrow entertainment on the stage.

Built in 1892 as a music hall for aging Confederate army veterans by a businessman and saloon owner named Thomas Ryman, the premises were bought in 1943 by the Opry's board of directors. It could hold thirty-two hundred people squeezed into hard oak, wooden pews. There were two levels, the ground floor and the balcony, known as the Confederate Gallery. And it has refused to die even as the neighborhood morphed from a pleasant, brownstone-lined urban haven to a skid row of porno shops and massage parlors, basking in its own "heritage" fifty years after the last Opry show there, a creaky national landmark and tourist trap, dipped in the fable of the "Mother Church of Country

Music," owned by WSM, which bought the property for $200,000 in the 1970s and still puts on low-level concerts there.

Yet there are some fairly cosmic things about the place. The most remarkable is that the acoustics were almost preternaturally perfect, with no dead spots anywhere, for reasons no one could quite figure out. No microphones were even needed for every note to be heard clearly by anyone in the place. Having learned to cope with cramped radio station studios, where Chester would sometimes need to stand on a chair to get close to a single, ceiling-mounted microphone, the Ryman was like Valhalla. There was also a kind of egalitarianism among performers; all of them were paid the same lousy ten dollars a show, the theory being that anyone lucky enough to play at the Opry would gladly take anything the board would give them, and for most, that theory proved correct—though the pooh-bahs were digging themselves into a hole. Indeed, Roy Acuff quit the Opry when the board refused to pay him more than fifteen dollars a show. (There were actually two Prince Albert shows on Saturday night, the second one featuring lesser talent, and the stars of the first show were given nothing for the follow-up show, though the other shows the Opry staged during the week, without radio coverage, upped the tab to around fifty a week.) Acuff's departure would lead to lower ratings and foment a higher pay scale when the board begged Roy to return in 1947 as a regular performer.

With all this heritage all around him, the still-precocious Chester Atkins began earning his keep at the Opry when Foley made his debut there on April 13, 1946. Chester was still using the Gibson L-7 acoustic with the DeArmond pickup, and he was not yet satisfied he had done all he could with it, the third string refusing to be electrified, causing a severe lack of balance in the sound. Accordingly, he only played acoustically at the Opry, but while playing the Opry was, he would say, "a big thrill," the downside was "terribly tough," for reasons other than the acoustics.

> The audience was noisy with rowdy kids running up and down the aisles, people milling around and talking, and vendors

> hawking songbooks and popcorn. I was a quiet-type musician, and playing my acoustic in front of a microphone, even though it sounded good on the radio, just didn't cut it for the live audience. All the time I would be playing my tune, everybody would be looking at the ceiling like they were wondering when the next big star was going to appear.

It seemed more cattle call than showcase—two cattle calls on Saturday nights. For each show, only a handwritten set list on a single sheet of paper taped to the wall of the stage told the acts when they would be called on, and they had better be ready or forfeit the spot. Red Foley always had his boys ready, but the Opry's cluttered lineup of country acts large and small left only around five minutes for each before the host would step in, shoo them off the stage, and spend ten minutes on a Prince Albert commercial, usually involving a headliner and a comedian doing a badly written skit that still left the audience in stitches. Often there was open chaos onstage, which the crowds believed was part of the show.

The Ryman had no air conditioning and in the summer, the smell of sweat and beer were worse than at an August baseball doubleheader. What's more, as honorable as it was to play there, with no backstage area or dressing rooms and only a tiny room for the brass and VIPs, there was no place to do any rehearsing. Foley was so taken with Chester that he would give him a solo spot on the first show he hosted, moving him to the front of the stage to play the 1920s bluegrass song "Maggie," and Chester worried that a key or chord might go awry. He did fine. After the show, one of the main Opry stars, comedian Minnie Pearl, whose trademark was a hat with a dangling price tag and shrieks of "how-dee!" hastened to tell him, "You're just what we've been needing around here."

In subsequent solos, Chester grew confident enough to branch off into some Django accents, which made the Opry's advertising company in New York, the William Estes Agency, apparently omniscient merely from handling the Prince Albert account, very nervous about him. Ironically, all these people were based in New York and likely detested

Southerners as redneck morons, yet they were so myopic that, trying to put themselves into Southerners' mindsets, they judged Red Foley, from Berea, Kentucky, as too "northern" himself, for having worked in Chicago. Foley, of course, was a star, yet he too suffered years of contempt at the Opry. Right away, it was decided that Red would be the conduit for the flak about Chester. Word was soon passed down to Red to have Chester stick only with country fodder. Red dutifully told him but probably didn't lean on him, so Chester went on playing what he felt, continuing to expand country corners. Indeed, neither Red nor those Southerners in the noisy, sweltering hall had any problem with it, or him, but the flak from New York became angrier, no doubt stoked by the fact that a relative amateur had the nerve to ignore the Opry chieftains.

Worse, the "country" consumer model wasn't exclusionary only toward Black performers but toward anything that was even remotely pop, jazz, or blues; that used drums, horns, or hand-held bass guitars; or that had female backing singers—all this was banned as too "uncountry." (There were only two exceptions: when Pee Wee King played an impromptu performance *outside* the Ryman including a drum and trumpet after President Roosevelt died, and Bob Wills and His Texas Playboys a year later; both had to take heat from the Opry brahmins by doing so.) To gain Opry membership, a singer or musician was required to make twenty-six appearances a year there, which put a crimp in their ability to accept higher-paying work elsewhere. And while Opry musicians would dress themselves in spangly cowboy suits—a mode that began when Pee Wee performed in a custom outfit by designer Nudie Cohn, who ran the Nudie's of Hollywood clothing shop—Chester regularly wore his usual casual sport jacket and string tie.

Clearly, he was the square peg. Easygoing, measured, and mannered as he seemed, he was never adept at making friends, buttering up, or pandering—by his own assessment, he was "aloof"—and sensitive as he was, he felt like he was being picked on as an outsider. Even as he played on a stage meant not only to entertain audiences but to intimidate performers, his mind was weighing how long he should put up with all the aggravation. It seemed that it would not be long.

Chet Atkins noted in his autobiography that he married Leona in Cincinnati in October 1946. However, the actual date was three months prior, on July 3, when she was a month pregnant. The wedding took place during one of Chester's periodic trips back to Cincinnati to see her. Kenny Burns was his best man and her sister and singing partner, Lois Johnson, her matron of honor. Burns liked to say that it was in Cincinnati where the two men corralled the sisters "and that's where we married 'em." And Leona continued to live there while Chester was in Nashville, sparing her the indignities he was suffering even as he began to fall in with a new circle of country stars who became great fans of his, including icons like Eddy Arnold and Ernest Tubb, who, like Minnie Pearl, stood in the wings during Opry shows listening to him mesmerize people on guitar. He also got to record for the first time. When Foley recorded with the Cumberland Valley Boys in New York for the Decca label, he specifically wanted Chester to perform guitar solos. He did so on Foley's country hits "That's How Much I Love You," "New Jolie Blonde (New Pretty Blonde)," "Freight Train Boogie," and "Never Trust a Woman."

Chet took Leona with him on the trip to New York, introducing his half-brother Jimmy to his new sister-in-law, and the newlyweds enjoyed the vibe of the big city like the tourists they were. But when they returned to Nashville, the hammer fell. The Estes Agency hounded the Opry board to yank Chester's solo turns at the Ryman. He did remain in Red's band, but believing this demotion to be step one in his eventual firing from the Opry, he would not play along, or grovel. As he recalled, "I didn't take [it] very well. It hurt my feelings, and rather than stay on as a sideman, I quit."

To be sure, that very word—*sideman*—got under his saddle. Never tolerant of other people determining how and what he played, even in his formative years he envisioned himself as a leader, on his own. But after spurning apparently more sensible advice to stick it out at the Opry for his own good, he could only look for work in Nashville backing already established bands, which ironically might get him back to the Opry in the very role he had rejected. He hooked on quickly with a band called Men of the West, and the group's leader, Jim Boyd, was so knocked out by his guitarmanship that, by chance, he led him to more work in the growing arena of recording. He had done some back in Knoxville, cutting two cheeky demos written by others in the WNOX studio, "Why Don't You Leave Me Alone" and "Empty Slippers," the first about a married guy being stalked by a woman and weighing the consequences—"If my wife should take the call, well brother that is all"—the latter about losing a woman who bailed and left only her slippers behind. But the demos were never released, not even on the 2007 compilation *Chet Atkins—The Early Years 1946–1957*, and appear only as the last two tracks on the extensive Bear Family 2004 CD package as badly scratched curios.

Boyd put in a few good words about him to Nashville producer Jim Bulleit, the co-owner of a small independent Nashville label, Bullet Records, a repository of blues, jazz, and gospel created by Bulleit and fellow producer C. V. Hitchcock just that year. They had assembled an eclectic roster since debuting with the Cecil Gant Trio's "Train Time Blues," including the York Brothers' "I'm Not Fooling," the Texas Troubadours' "That's All She Wrote," Wynonie Harris's "My Baby's Barrel House," Sheb Wooley's "Oklahoma Honky Tonk Gal," and "The Call of a Broken Heart" by Owen Bradley and His Tennesseans, the first by Bradley, a thirty-year-old bandleader and radio host on WSM, the Opry's home station, who would soon be arranging songs at Decca Records for Foley, Ernest Tubb, and Kitty Wells.

Bullet Records surely wasn't in the same league as big labels with country music divisions such as Decca and the biggest, Columbia, which yielded the most played country song of 1946, Bill Monroe and the Bluegrass Boys' bluegrass waltz hit "Blue Moon of Kentucky," recorded in Chicago as the first of many versions of the song, including Elvis Presley's rockabilly cover. Still, Bullet was a lifeline, and Chester signed a standard deal with the label (though in his memoir he also mistakenly wrote that he signed with Boyd) for two sides, at a royalty rate of two cents per record sold and the publishing rights on any songs written by Chester to be the property of Bulleit and Hitchcock—the sort of routine extortion that low-level artists accepted as part of the price to pay for getting on a record.

With a studio date in late summer, he made some calls to Cincinnati and brought to Nashville two old bandmates, rhythm guitarists Louis Innis and Roy Lanham, and added three others associated with Owen Bradley, guitarist/vocalist Jack Shook, bassist Ernie Newton, and, as a curveball, jazz clarinetist Dutch McMillin. They gathered in the in-house studio of WSM to lay down a real marker, the first song Atkins wrote, "Guitar Blues (Pickin' the Blues)"—which on later releases would add Jimmy Atkins as cowriter—and "Brown Eyes A' Cryin' in the Rain," cowritten by Wally Fowler and Curley Kinsey, the former being the leader of the Oak Ridge Quartet gospel group, a regular act at the Opry, and someone Chester had known when they both worked at WNOX. The song, not the same as "Blue Eyes Crying in the Rain," written by Fred Rose and recorded by Elton Britt that year, and later by and covered by a profusion of singers, including Roy Acuff, Hank Williams, Elvis, and Willie Nelson, was basic country fodder, but with the touch of swing blues inherent in Atkins's nimble fingerpicking.

"Guitar Blues" was a finger-snapping instrumental with McMillin's horn solos; the second was a mid-tempo story song that, not by coincidence, featured a nippy vocal by Shook that sounded a lot like Jimmy Atkins's baritone, merrily telling of leaving a series of "fickle from the start" brown-eyed gals crying in the rain. It was cleverly piquant, with Owen Bradley called upon to play the piano—the first conflation of a long, productive relationship with Atkins. "Guitar Blues," the A-side, seemed to have a good chance of taking off, but if it did, Chester wouldn't be in Nashville to see it. By the time it would be released in November, his summer of discontent had led to an autumn of exploration.

He could have stuck around, perhaps made more records, but he knew the money would run low, and besides, he had a black mark against him in Nashville as a foil at the Opry. While he felt like damaged goods, he rationalized his failure as a reason to spend more time with the pregnant Leona back in Cincinnati. Yet he would have precious little time to do that before he was on the run again.

6

PAGING CHET ATKINS

The country grapevine was so gossipy that everybody seemed to know when somebody either made good or failed. And while the Opry pitfall and recording swing and miss stung Chester like a hornet swarm, simply cultivating an audience there led other potential employers to broach him. At first, looking for a paycheck, he was about to call Lowell Blanchard at WNOX and ask about having his old job back, if again as a backup player on the Homer and Jethro show. But then a call came from Mary Workman, known as "Sunshine Sue," a country singer who had a show called *Sunshine Sue & Her Rangers* in Richmond, Virginia, on WRVA, and was emcee for the station's drawing card, the *Old Dominion Barn Dance*, for which she was given credit as the first female host of a music program.

The *Dominion*, staged in Richmond's Lyric Theatre, was not small potatoes; it attracted sellout audiences and star power like Gene Autry, Tex Ritter, and the Carter Sisters, who had a show of their own on WRVA. Workman and her husband, John, practically ran the station and the barn dance show, and she could sign anyone she wanted. She offered Chester the industry norm of fifty dollars a week to host a show and play on the *Dominion*, and would introduce him on the air as "the world's greatest guitar player." He could hardly say no, and only a couple weeks after the Nashville exile, he and Leona got in her 1941 Ford and made the drive to Richmond. Again, his guitar captivated the radio audience, and he backed Sunshine Sue at the Barn Dance, as well as on road shows such as the one on September 27 at Hopewell High School, sponsored by American War Mothers and featuring WRVA regulars Pappy Ridgeway, Cousin Elmer, "king of the harmonica players," Curley Bradshaw, the Tobacco Tags, and Daffy Dan.

For sixty or thirty cents a ticket, the audience would get to see, according to a newspaper ad, "Chester Atkins [the] champion guitar player" and "the finest and funniest stage show to Ever Appear in This Section." But Workman could tell that, as Cheser related later, "my heart wasn't in it." And after only two weeks, "before I could quit, she fired me." If this massaged his pride, it could not hide that if there was one other thing he was good at, it was getting fired. And now, feeling the pressure of impending fatherhood, he seemed to fall back into physical weakness. His asthma roared back and his mood was dark. The strain was also getting to Leona, whom he had brought to Richmond but who would need to progress toward childbirth without him being at her side. In the fall of 1946 he dropped Leona off at her parents' home in Williamsburg, Ohio, and took off for the next stop, back to Chicago, hoping his Red Foley connection would dig up some work.

Instead, perhaps because of the Opry stigma, nothing was cooking for him at WLS, and even the jazz clubs were well stocked. He could only get a break when one of his old friends in the city, country songwriter-singer Karl Davis, who wrote the standards "Kentucky" and "I'm Here to Get My Baby Out of Jail," and worked on a WLS show hosted by Karl & Harty and the Cumberland Ridge Runners, let him stay in his South Side flat while he looked for a break. He was this close to either taking work in a shoe store or giving it all up and going to Ohio to be with Leona when another confrere, Louis Innis, who'd played on his two recordings in Nashville, found out where he was while speaking on the phone with Leona. Innis rang him up and told him there was an opening for a guitar player at KWTO in Springfield, Missouri, another branch of the loosely knit country radio tree—a conglomerate that Atkins dubbed "almost like a big employment agency."

The station, the call letters an initialism for "Keep Watching the

Ozarks," had some outstanding talent under its roof, with shows hosted by the veteran Missouri singer Slim Wilson. He had played guitar in bands like Flash and Whistle and Slim and Shorty, and was the fulcrum of KWTO as host of the morning show sponsored by Goodwill Family Flour, a product created for Slim, who fronted the Goodwill Trio as "Uncle Slim" on that show and the noontime show *Lumberjacks.* Driving down through the Ozarks, Chet Atkins would recall that, tuning in to KWTO, "I had never heard as many hillbillies in my life" and worried he would again face problems as a country pop performer. The station owner, Ralph Foster, hired him as soon as he walked through the door. He joined Slim's on-air band, the Tall Timber Trio, which was modeled on the Sons of the Pioneers, and soon was given his own fifteen-minute show at 7:00 PM, between *Sports Spotlight* and the nighttime edition of Wilson's *Goodwill Family* show.

Chester was at the station day and night, relied on to juice up any given show, such as *The Haden Family*; *Boots and Bobby*, hosted by Boots Faye; and the cornball primetime hoedown show *Korn's a Crackin'*. The Wilson show and *Korn's a Crackin'* were syndicated on the Mutual Network as well, giving Chester more exposure. Early in the 1950s, the station would premiere arguably the first of many TV barn-dance versions, *Ozark Jubilee*, carried by ABC-TV, with Slim plying his many talents; the show was hosted—small world that it was—by Red Foley, who would introduce his son-in-law, vanilla pop singer Pat Boone; new country icons like Porter Wagoner; Carl Perkins, who would write and record the rockabilly revelation "Blue Suede Shoes"—and a guitar wizard going under the name of Chet Atkins. However, in 1946 he was still Chester Atkins, desperately trying to get a leg up somewhere in the industry without thinking he was prostituting himself too much. Still, he felt secure enough in Springfield and fetched Leona to the city. They moved into a rented two-room cottage on Route 66 near Joplin, which had a tendency to flood when it rained hard. But they were together and made do. He had enough work, and only weeks after he had made it to Springfield, he even had a pair of records on the market.

In early November, word came from Jim Bulleit that "Guitar Blues" was against all odds doing well in the Nashville market. Released on the then-standard ten-inch, 78 rpm record format, it was billed to "Chester Atkins and the All-Star Hillbillies"—a word Atkins hated but had no say in choosing—on Bullet Records' bright yellow inner-groove label reading "BULLET—Always a Smash Hit," with the catalog number 617-A for "Guitar Blues" and 617-B for "Brown Eyes A' Cryin' in the Rain." Unusual for its day, the label carried the names of the other musicians, exempting Bradley, who had his own band. The disk got onto the desks of disk jockeys at WSM, and ads ran in newspapers pushing the latest Bullet releases, which also included Bradley and the Tennesseans' "The Call of a Broken Heart," Johnny Barfield's "Doin' the Boogie Woogie," and Peter Pyle's "Love Turned to Hate." But otherwise not a lot of money was put behind the record, and few jockeys spun it.

As with the two WNOX rejects, one can find the songs on the *Mister Guitar: The Complete Recordings* CD, yet enough original copies survived the years following the label's demise in 1952 that they are available for around seventy-five dollars. (As a footnote, Bullet would in 1949 release the first single recorded by a then-fairly-obscure electric guitar wiz, B. B. King, whose two sides, "Miss Martha King" and "When Your Baby Packs Up and Goes," were similarly ignored and left un-rereleased for decades until included on King compilation box sets.) Even so, Chester had gained a new identity—"Chet Atkins"—which was what a KWTO executive with the rhythmic name Si Siman, whose real name was Ely E. Siman Jr., took to calling him when they formed a friendship.

Siman produced the show hosted by Shorty Thompson, not the fictional U.S. marshal of the Old West novels but leader of the Saddle Rockin' Rhythm band, and was also vice president of Ralph Foster's RadiOzark Enterprises, which produced syndicated radio shows for Tennessee Ernie Ford, Smiley Burnette, and Shorty and his singing wife, Sue. A former batboy for the "Gashouse Gang" St. Louis Cardinals, Siman would until the late 1980s be a kind of Babe Ruth of country music, a manager and producer for Porter Wagoner and co-executive producer of the *Ozark Jubilee*, for which he hired Red Foley and booked most of the guests. (He also ran the song publishing company Earl Barton Music, later delivering major songs like the Box Tops' "The Letter" and Willie Nelson's "Always on My Mind.") Among the horde of industry types who would later claim to have discovered Chet Atkins, Siman did have a clearly positive effect. Focusing on his name, he urged Chester to permanently rechristen himself, telling him, "Chester Atkins wouldn't make it in country music. Chet Atkins will." Chester took that to heart, believing it had a cool ring and "seemed to be a natural and it stuck," quickly being applied to all his shows and appearances. Foster would brag to people that he had the greatest guitar player in the world, right there in Springfield. Even a glass-half-empty type like Chester conceded things were going pretty well there, a feeling only bolstered on March 1, 1947, when Leona gave birth to a daughter, Merle Niona Atkins—named jointly for Merle Travis and Leona's mother, who by coincidence was named Merle Hancock Johnson.

Although it had been four months since the records first hit the shelves, they were still being peddled by music shops in Nashville, Roanoke, and other key markets, and pitched in ads that also trumpeted what were called "hillbilly" songs like Roy Acuff's "Tennessee Control," Cowboy Copas's "Kentucky Waltz," and Homer and Jethro's "Rye Whiskey" and "Five Minutes More." They were also touted in "Take Home Some New Records" ads by Sears, Roebuck & Co. that also included records by Perry Como, Frank Sinatra, Dinah Shore, and the Woody Herman band. This proved that, even if his first songs were not chart hits, there was something about Chet Atkins that made a lasting impression. What he also had, though, was a habit of being fired, for reasons sometimes never made clear. And when Siman took a vacation, someone in Ralph Foster's office, whose name Atkins never divulged, used Si's absence to peremptorily fire his fair-haired boy. This sudden termination jarred him and Leona. Chet wanted to ask Siman what was going on, but he was unreachable, and Foster didn't take his calls.

Yet, with his usual yin-yang existence, around the same time an opportunity arose when Shorty Thompson was also fired. Rather than stick around Springfield, Shorty and Sue made plans to take their Saddle Rockin' Rhythm band on the road. Their first gig would be in Denver, and Shorty was happy to let Chet join his troupe. In July they headed west, which would be Chet's first time in real country-western territory, though he would miss key time in Merle's early childhood development, something left in Leona's hands back in Springfield. Thus began what Chet would refer to as his "cowboy period," spent in the airy, snow-capped Rockies melding into a genuine cowboy culture. In fact, he would go against his own sartorial rules and even don a cowboy hat and a fancy, spangly shirt at performances. He recalled playing at private parties, dances, and rodeos, and taking "breathtaking" drives through non-smoky hills as well as ghost towns, past abandoned railroad yards. The clean mountain air did wonders for his asthma, and he could understand what people meant when they spoke of the "high and lonesome" patina of country music that people sang about but never knew what it meant.

Not knowing if he'd ever go back east, he rented a little house on Yarrow Street in Lakewood, looking down from a perch in the mountains. But his future would be redirected to territory more familiar and able to earn him some handsome money. As it was, even in his absence, people who could make that happen were looking to reach him but had no idea where the heck he was.

One of those people had sent Si Siman a letter that sat on his desk during Si's own absence. It was from Steve Sholes, a man whose letters needed to be read. Sholes, a native of Washington, D.C., had lived most of his thirty-six years in and around RCA Records. His father had worked for the company in its early years, working his way up from a messenger boy to selling records, radios, and the equipment to build the latter with, then helped develop the Victor Talking Machine division that birthed the phonograph. The resulting boom refashioned RCA into RCA Victor Inc. in 1920. Now thirty-six, Sholes after the war was promoted to president of the fledgling country division, which while based in New York made a connection to Dixie, establishing RCA Records Nashville, which the haughty company, headed by the imperious Robert Sarnoff, planned to make into a vital hub.

Even so, few industry types, even Sholes, a well-fed, Falstaff-looking man, believed that country could be equal to pop and big-band music—but a hint of what Nashville could accomplish was to be found in the most popular overall song of 1947, which was released by none other than Bullet Records. Called "Near You" and played by the Francis Craig Orchestra, it was a pop song that would be covered by country artists and even, eons later, by the Black Eyed Peas. RCA, thus, pictured Nashville as an overall seeder of pop, with country given a chance to shine on its own, which it was already doing elsewhere. The postwar, post-Jimmie Rodgers era was favorably inclined to edgier country pickers like Merle Travis, whose fabulously leering "So Round, So Firm, So Fully Packed" topped the nascent *Billboard* country chart for nineteen weeks in 1946. Records by Red Foley, Tex Williams, and Eddy Arnold were cracking the pop chart as well.

Sholes in fact was playing catch-up with Decca Records (which had Foley, Ernest Tubb, and the Carlisle Brothers); Columbia Records (Gene Autry, Bill Monroe, Bob Wills); and Capitol (Travis, Tex Williams, Pee Wee King, Hank Thompson), and MGM had caught lightning with Hank Williams. But Sholes made inroads with Eddy Arnold, who had signed with RCA in 1944 and would have five songs on the country chart simultaneously in 1948, and thirteen of the twenty top country songs over 1947 and 1948. Arnold would be with RCA for nearly forty years and Hank Snow for forty-five, and Sholes also had a long-term arrangement with Johnnie and Jack, which led to Porter Wagoner and Jim Reeves coming aboard down the road.

Sholes's letter to Siman came after transcriptions of Atkins's radio shows had been diverted to him by Al Hindle, a Chicago-based RCA executive, to whom Siman had sent the primordial examples of tape recordings. Sholes liked what he heard and wrote to Siman requesting more, saying he was impressed and would sign Atkins to RCA Victor. But when Siman returned and learned about Chet being fired, "he hit the ceiling," as Chet wrote in his memoir. Siman may have wanted to rehire him, but when he read Sholes's letter, he knew it was the break Chet had been waiting for and made it his business to contact him, wherever he was. It took days of tracing him—even Leona had no current phone number for him—until a sharp-eyed music publisher in New York, Jean Aberbach, who with his brother Julian ran the New York music firm Hill & Range, and whom Sholes asked for help locating Atkins, saw a tiny blurb in a Rocky Mountain newspaper that Shorty's band was playing gigs and included a guitar player named Chet Atkins. Jean put a call through to a motel in the area of the gig, somehow got through to Chet, and told him some very important people were trying to find him and to call Siman in Springfield. Not losing the chance to gain something for himself, Aberbach offered him a deal with Hill & Range to write music. When Siman got the call from Chet, he told him of Steve Sholes and RCA. The next call was to Sholes's private number.

"I tried to cover all the bases," Sholes recalled years later, "so I asked Chet if he sang too; and Chet said he did. . . . He was afraid to say he didn't."

Sholes told Atkins to be in Chicago within a week, that being where Sholes would be milking talent for RCA. They would meet there, and Sholes would produce his first recordings in the city where, along with the bluesmen and blueswomen, many country acts came to lay down tracks. Chester tried to be blasé about it, leading Leona to tell him he was acting as if "you just found out your laundry was ready," but Chet would admit that, inside, his gut was "doing cartwheels." Still, this brought about a complication. When he went to Thompson to tell him he would be gone for a while, Shorty suggested that he should come along with him, saying, "Everybody knows you can't sing." Chet told him no thanks. The next day, Shorty informed him he was out of his band and that "there's no use for you even to come back from Chicago."

That put more pressure on Chet to impress Sholes. As it was, he had no security, only an audition he needed to pass. When he got to Chicago, Karl Davis again made room for him, and Chet went to meet Sholes and Aberbach at the plush Knickerbocker Hotel, where he signed a standard recording contract. Sholes, whom he described as "a fat, jovial man whose eyes squinted when he smiled," had made sure to surround him at the recording session at RCA's studio on Lake Shore Drive on August 11. Chet was blown away when Sholes told him he had brought in George Barnes, the jazz guitar great and one of Chet's heroes, as well as bassist Harold Siegel, fiddler Charles Hurta, and accordionist Augie Klein. Chet was so nervous that he was unable to play with confidence at first but eventually became comfortable, and Sholes produced six songs, two written by Chet, "Canned Heat" and "Bug Dance" (not the jump blues song by the Treniers from 1953). Another was "(I Know My Baby Loves Me) in Her Own Peculiar Way," written by Philadelphia's *Hayloft Hoedown* figures Riley Shepard and Don Canton, which had been originally recorded by Red Murrell and His Ozark Playboys and later covered by Ernest Tubb.

It was one of four tracks Chet reluctantly sang on, his baritone a bit ragged but melodic and cheeky enough to carry tunes in conjunction with his acoustic Gibson L-10 riffs. The B-side, "Canned Heat," was a semi-yodel, Chet lifting its name from Black Memphis blues man Tommy Johnson's 1928 "Canned Heat Blues," a country wail about an alcoholic who guzzles Sterno, the flame-starting fluid that skid row types called "canned heat." The songs were lost in a wash of releases by unknown country artists, but Sholes saw great potential in the way Chet elevated the backwoods blues beat into a semi-jazz roll, his fingerpicking chemistry with Barnes's quick and flavorful notes a requital of Sholes's first taste of Atkins's art and style. RCA would release a single of "I Know My Baby Loves Me" and "Canned Heat" in mid-September. It missed by a year being released on the seven-inch, 45 rpm format that was introduced by RCA in response to Columbia bringing out ten- and twelve-inch, 33⅓ rpm records suitable for albums; instead, Atkins's first round of RCA recordings appeared in the old ten-inch, 78 rpm format, with the catalog number 20-2472 and the helpful notation "Best Used with RCA Needles."

Both sides, as with all the Atkins vocal compositions to come, read "Vocal Refrain by Chet Atkins." Settling on a name for the act, Sholes chose Chet Atkins and the Colorado Mountain Boys, a nod to the environment and market he had left behind. The disk would show up in newspaper record roundups, and both sides were played on country radio. The November 1 *Billboard* highlighted both songs in a review praising Atkins as a "Western maestro piping with a flair for rhythm blues" who sang with "ease and intimacy," though this verdict wasn't unanimous. One newspaper reviewer slighted the Atkins fare as "corn right out of the West" but added that "some people speak highly of it." Like the Bullet offerings, neither "My Baby" nor "Heat" would make the country chart, yet Sholes was satisfied he held a winning hand with Atkins and would soon release all six sides—"Standing Room Only" by Cy Coben and Charles Grean, "Ain'tcha Tired of Makin' Me Blue" by Jenny Lou Carson, "My Guitar Is My Sweetheart" by David Rhodes—about a guitar that the singer holds in as high esteem as any woman, because it "doesn't drink, doesn't smoke, she doesn't flirt, she doesn't crack a corny joke"—and "Bug Dance."

The records were solid, albeit in a simple, even crude context, with "Makin' Me Blue" a precursor to the rock 'n' roll beat out there on the blues horizon, Chet's high-range guitar licks dominating a remarkable instrumental that funkily teams with a swinging piano riff. None would find a place on the charts, but they marked a notable progression. "Blue" would be reviewed as a "lively and spirited instrumental with the strings riding and picking their way torridly around a *Tiger Rag* lick fashioned in sagebrush."

As well, "Bug Dance" shined a light on Chet's Django Reinhardt side, which he seamlessly integrated into a more hip, urban country swing than Bob Wills and his Texas Cowboys did. Every song seemed to find a sweet spot when Chet would do his solos. And Sholes could barely wait to get him back inside a studio, a mission that would never abate for as long as he lived.

As the summer of 1947 ebbed with no further recording arranged for him, Chet decided to return to Springfield to get to know his wife and daughter again, then went back to Denver, where he had left some belongings. If in the lull between his studio work he had any notion about rejoining Shorty's band, who had since gotten a radio gig on KOA radio in Denver, the latter's cold shoulder meant the firing stood. This could have caused another panic attack for Chet, but Sholes followed up and paged him again to meet up in Chicago in early November, this time not to record there but to accompany Sholes to New York for more recording sessions in RCA's famed studio on East 24th Street, where Benny Goodman's "King Porter Stomp," Artie Shaw's "Begin the Beguine," Glenn Miller's "Moonlight Serenade," Tommy Dorsey's "I'm Getting Sentimental Over You," and Duke Ellington's "Harlem Air Shaft" had taken on life. The Atkins sessions weren't to record his own stuff but rather to play as a side man for other, more pressing RCA acts, which Sholes knew would have to tide the label during an impending nationwide strike by the musicians' union in 1948. Needing to build up inventory, he scheduled about every major RCA act he could to record, and Chet quickly acquired a union card and sat in, though few of the veteran studio cats knew who he was. But they soon would. As Atkins recalled, he came in strutting.

> I would get in the studio with [Sholes] and start telling everybody what to do . . . what to play and work up the arrangements on the spot. It wasn't easy working with those New York musicians because most of them were jazz or swing players, not country, but I managed to get the job done. After that, Mr. Sholes seemed to have confidence in me and began to give

> me more responsibility [to] conduct sessions for him in places like Chicago and Atlanta.

The down side was that his shyness and directness congealed into what seemed like a curtness that turned off more than a few musicians. Neither did it help that he found little common ground with the New York musicians. But never let it be said about Chet Atkins that he didn't learn from hearing skilled musicians of any kind. In the studio, he related, "The fiddle players sounded like Jascha Heifetz, and I found myself just listening to them." When he summoned up the nerve to shoot the breeze with the studio players, they in return came to see his smart, quick, and subtly humorous side.

He was obviously on track for advancement, and an important flash point came during his two-week stay in New York. It was clear he was moving up on Jimmy, with whom he again stayed in Queens. Jimmy, who himself was taking some big steps, had left Les Paul when Les left his wife for Mary Ford. After recovering from a car crash that nearly cost him his arm, Les married her, and they would record as a twosome with revolving side men. Jimmy then hooked on with a New York jazz band, which in the summer of 1947 released "I Think I'm Gonna Cry Again," billed to "Jimmy Atkins with the Billy Mure Trio," Mure being a popular guitarist and host of a New York radio show. Jimmy also played in the crew when Sholes arranged two sessions to record more Chet Atkins material—and while this was another historic union of the two brothers, having authority over his big brother was another transition for Chet from wide-eyed kid wiz to hard-eyed music man.

Those sessions, a week apart in mid-November, were produced by Charles Grean, a former copyist for Glenn Miller and Artie Shaw's big bands who arranged Nat King Cole's "The Christmas Song." One of Sholes's nabobs, Grean became RCA's head of A&R, and in the 1950s he produced and managed Eddy Arnold, which would again bring him into Chet's world. His conventional approach was apparent on the first song from the session to go out, Chet's "(I May Be Color Blind but)

I Know When I'm Blue," on which Sholes again went with Chet as a guitar-playing vocalist, though he sounded something like a lowercase Gene Autry, or Jimmy Atkins, making it obvious that his singing voice wasn't why he was moving on up. This was proven by the B-side, an instrumental of the hoary 1884 campfire folk tune "I've Been Working on the Railroad," the title changed to "I've Been Working on the Guitar," which sounds absolutely nothing like the old evergreen. Chet had played his version out in Denver with Shorty Thompson's band and took control of the arrangement. His new wrinkle was to go electric, which he had held back on in deference to the top-notch guitarists in his recording sessions. Now he hit magical bebop chords on his Gibson L-7, his solo riffs couched by some swinging fiddle and accordion runs sounding like a railroad train chugging along, a sound he knew all too well from childhood.

Even so, it was going to take a lot more to get people to hear what Chet Atkins could do. Released in May, the record hit the same skids as the ones preceding them. This precipitated the same chain of succession as before: RCA sticking to its guns with Atkins and every few months going with the next songs in line. In May 1948 came "I'm Gonna Get Tight," written by the acerbic Texas bandleader Jerry Irby, who had previously written the 1946 country hit "Drivin' Nails in My Coffin" (covered by Floyd Tillman and Ernest Tubb), and "Dizzy Strings," an Atkins-composed instrumental. "Get Tight" was chosen to give Chet a harder edge, the phrase a metaphor for getting mean and disagreeable. "Dizzy Strings" also hit the spot and would endure as his most memorable early song, arpeggios flitting up and down the board in quick-trigger modes, the rapid tremolo tones indeed dizzyingly intense yet overall soothing.

The sore spot for him was that he simply could not get any better as a singer. Chet would in the years ahead poke fun at himself about his attempt to croon, saying that among the fan letters he got, he may have gotten just one making any reference to his voice. Overall, though, he tried "using vibrato and all that to make [my voice] a pretty sound, but that didn't hack it," he told Johnny Carson when he guested on the *Tonight Show* in 1973, "so I'm pickin' my guitar and makin' myself happy." Back in 1948, however, it was getting in the way of his real function, evolving—or perhaps *de*volving—hillbilly music into a brand-new animal. As Sholes would tell him, he was looking for a New York–style country music, which Chet couldn't assimilate right away. To Carson, he explained that when he had appeared on hillbilly shows, the rule was to "go out and sell it, boy. Smile at the people. Well, I can't do that. I can't concentrate on playing." Carson joshed him, "You don't exactly beam at the audience, do you?" And that was after decades of playing before live audiences who loved him. At twenty-four, with a mere fraction of an audience, however, his crustiness seemed to be frustrating to the RCA in-crowd.

Still, he had a following, small as it was, and Sholes's staff could detect that, even if there was no great Chet Atkins wave, he was making incremental progress in sales and appeal. And before Sholes would have to give up trying to make him a singing guitarist, Chet would refuse to believe he couldn't propel himself to that level. But he was really only comfortable when composing instrumentals. All he could do, he would say, was to write music with one guideline—you just had to play to your touch, meaning the touch he was given at birth, in his fingers and in the coordination between them and a guitar. He would either float or sink on it. The trouble was, with a few recording sessions and a glitch in Nashville on his résumé, he still had a lot of water to tread before Sholes could be sure his new find wouldn't drown.

7

GALLOPING GUITAR

In October 1948 RCA released Atkins's "I'm Pickin' the Blues," backed with "Barnyard Shuffle," the A-side crediting Chet and Jimmy Atkins as cowriters, the B-side credited solely to Chet, though it was yet another version of an oldie, the 1884 ragtime piano song that had been combined with "Turkey in the Straw" in the 1900s and used for honky-tonk line dances. (The reworked tune would be covered by Red "Shorty" Shedd and His Hoot Owls in 1950, with Shedd cadging the writing credit.) Chet recorded "Pickin'," a nifty two-guitar, two-step run with a middle eight an octave higher and a beat faster, with Chet's usual, underplayed vocal. It didn't ruin it, and future performances of the song would usually be abbreviated to "Pickin' the Blues."

The record, like the ones before it, was prominent in RCA's ads, one of which had it paired with Eddy Arnold's "I'll Hold You in My Heart" and the Sons of the Pioneers' "You'll Be Sorry When I'm Gone." Yet it did not make the charts, and with no other recording sessions on tap due to the musicians' strike, Chet called Lowell Blanchard at WNOX and begged him for his old job back at the station, though he admitted years later that "it was the last thing I wanted to do." Blanchard took him back, inserting him into his former early-morning spot, and Chet, who had spent too much time away from his family, drove them to Knoxville and found a small house to rent. When he returned to the station, he saw some familiar faces, the most welcoming being Kenneth

Burns and Henry Haynes, whose Homer and Jethro hillbilly satire act had also taken some hard turns; after being fired as well from WNOX, they had a brief run in Cincinnati on WLW's *Midwestern Hayride*, cut some songs for King Records, did session work for blues pianist Moon Mullican, and were fired by WLW and like Chet retreated back to WNOX. This intercession reunited Leona with her sister Lois, and with Burns and Haynes, Chet put together a new incarnation of the act that in reality didn't exist, the Colorado Mountain Boys, to perform with him on the *Midday Merry-Go-Round* show and at the regular Saturday-night *Tennessee Barn Dance*. What's more, Leona began singing again with Lois Burns as the Johnson Sisters on a competing station, WKGN.

For all the work, however, Chet recalled that the two clans were "depressed about our careers" and that, having stalled as a recording artist, "I was disgusted with myself and very close to giving up" after all the twists and turns he'd endured. He was closer still when Burns, Haynes, and Lois cleared out of town and, as if on a leash, jumped back to KWTO in Springfield. Following them there would have likely meant another radio job, but Chet figured it would represent a bigger step backward. As he recalled, the old insecurities still vivid years later,

> I felt everybody hated me because I was ugly and retarded. There was no question in my mind that my bosses didn't like me because I was just plain stupid. . . . I had gone through a long period of thinking that I was the only one who ever had it that hard, and I hated the world for it.

Aytchie Burns virtually played shrink for him, listening to Chet sink into a shell of self-loathing, and could hardly believe he was hearing this well of self-pity from someone so exceptional. He urged him to stop holding his gripes against the world and pitch himself, with bravado, to all but demand a rewarding opportunity, never mind the RCA inroad still playing out. It sounded like good advice, but whenever Chet would take such an initiative, he would sound shrill and confrontational. To be sure, he was hardly alone believing he was stuck on a too-low rung in the business. Others were just as self-tortured, and because of his supernal talent and RCA contract, they would be asking *him* to help deal with their own problems. Within this slow-moving dervish, he made the rounds, as patiently as he could as he shared stages with lesser musicians and slapstick comedians like Ray Mears, not the great basketball coach at Tennessee but a steel guitarist who had no arms and played it with his feet, and could put a dime in a pay phone with his foot. Others included one-armed banjo player Emory Martin and Little Moses, who weighed just ninety pounds but was so strong he would offer anyone in the audience $500 to lift him, which no one ever could.

Chet years later called these sideshow acts "freaks," and he was about to jump ship again, to rejoin Burns and Haynes in Springfield, when out of nowhere the biggest break he ever had found him, to the eternal debt of music everywhere.

The Carter Family, one of the longest-surviving country acts in history, had been performing since 1927. Founded by A.P. Carter and his wife, Sara, in Virginia, the group included Sara, their three children, and her sister Maybelle, whose husband Ezra, A.P.'s brother, managed them, and they became immensely popular weaving gospel, bluegrass, and pop. They went through lineup revisions, but their act was remarkably consistent. Recording for RCA in Bristol, Tennessee, for the near-mythical producer Ralph Peer, they not only recorded with Jimmie Rodgers but were provided songs by Lesley Riddle, a one-legged Black thumbpicker who wrote for them country standards such as "Cannonball Blues," "I Know What It Means to Be Lonesome," and "Bear Creek Blues." They were led by stone-faced "Mother Maybelle," who like Sister Rosetta Tharpe played electric guitar like the rock 'n' rollers would decades later.

In 1949, as Chet was stewing about his future, at one point even contemplating quitting showbiz and working with James Arlie Atkins as a music tutor, the Carter Family—Maybelle and her daughters Anita,

June, and Helen, who sometimes did gigs as the Carter Sisters—played the *Tennessee Barn Dance* and, on the *Midday Merry-Go-Round*, were backed by Chet. Both appearances drew hundreds of people who lined the streets outside, hoping to get in. The Carter clan was so blown away by Chet's wide range on acoustic guitar that Ezra Carter took him to a restaurant across the street from the station and said the family wanted him to join the act and travel with them. He would be paid one-sixth of their box office proceeds. And, not incidentally, Chet would recall that working with four lovely young ladies was quite a step up from freak shows.

Though it would again mean separation from Leona and Merle, the pathway was ideal for him. All the women were accomplished musicians, and Mother Maybelle could sense in Atkins's playing the pulse of the Delta. This versatility was the payoff for his years of apprenticing, having seen country from all sides, one of them being honky-tonk bars that were called "black and tan" clubs in the Black parts of town, which had a regular clientele of hip White blues fans. It was in such places that he could take serious notice of the ongoing legacy of country blues he would hear on the radio stations on the far end of the dial, playing guitar masters like Robert Johnson and Elmore James, as well as the twelve-string acoustic of Huddie "Lead Belly" Ledbetter, the blues harp of Sonny Boy Williamson, and music from two future avatars of rock 'n' roll, Arthur "Big Boy" Crudup and Big Bill Broonzy. Crudup would have three songs recorded by the young Elvis Presley, who called him "a music man like nobody ever saw," and Broonzy's fingerpicking and laid-back blues vocals made Chicago a blues junction.

Immersing himself in this wide world of blues guitar that he had first experienced on that Knoxville street corner as a child, Chet had become proficient at integrating it into his country style, especially Lead Belly's "walking" bass line, which itself had stemmed from the Mexican-rooted *bajo sexto* guitar. In replicating it, Chet's long fingers could perform his version of Merle Travis's bass notes, two strings with one finger, not two, leaving the other free to contour the melody. It subtly etched a fuller emotional portrait in his chords, forefending the modern pentatonic "bend," which he would further achieve by keeping his long pinkie simply anchoring his strumming hand as if it were a vise. Accordingly, he could play notes that almost wanted to weep, aping the sound of a countrified pedal steel guitar as an adjunct—which would, also far off in time, be a fixture in the late 1960s, when the idea was modeled by the ex-Byrd Gene Parsons and bluegrass guitarist Clarence White into a handle—the "B-bender"—that easily bent a weepy B-string without causing the finger pain Atkins learned to live with his entire life.

The Carters became the beneficiaries of Chet's playing and banked so much on him that he not only played but was the straight man for June Carter's ditzy comic asides, a perfect use of his deadpan persona. The Carters and Chet Atkins—which is how the act was billed—were soon the brightest lights at KWTO, and Si Siman, who was thrilled to have Chet back, benefited as well. Signing the Carters to the station, he renamed the morning show *The Carter Family and Chet Atkins*, which was syndicated to other country stations across the country. Siman also invested in a proto-magnetic tape system, recording the show on acetate disks. Sometimes, if the act was late getting back from a gig, Siman would be able to play an acetate of a previous show. He would release some of the material to the public, and other country acts would routinely cover Carter records that had Chet on guitar, one example being Red Foley's "Someone Else, Not Me."

For Chet, it was a renascence that he called some of the happiest days of his life. With Maybelle personally collecting the proceeds of any given show—and no promoter would dare hold out on her—Chet pulled in not only fifty dollars a week for the radio show but fifty more for each outside gig, and such gigs were plentiful, though at times their travels were perilous. They got around in an old Frazer, driven by Chet, loaded down with instruments, amps, and speakers. On one winter trip, it broke down in the Ozarks, and with the howling wind and snow crashing down, Maybelle and the sisters were praying to Jesus to save them. Only because a trucker hauling pigs to market happened to drive by and tow them did they make it to the next town. Chet may have even believed that it wasn't the Lord but the Carters who kept him safe.

Moving ahead, publicity photos of him with the homespun matron and her prim daughters made the still-pubescent Chet look like a delivery boy. But his solidified place ushered him to more work, including his next recording sessions as the Carters' rhythm guitarist.

Those sessions dovetailed with Steve Sholes's plans to record again, the strike now being settled. His first new country act was Slim Whitman, a Floridian yodeler who worked in a post office until his manager—a strange fellow who went by the name "Colonel" Tom Parker—signed him to RCA, whereupon he would sell around seventy million records. Sholes recorded Whitman at first when he was playing at the Fox Theatre in Atlanta, and Sholes had a portable recording system placed on the stage for him to record in an empty hall between his concerts. Sholes dispatched Chet to get himself down to Atlanta with a couple of other Nashville musicians, and with them backing him, Slim recorded eight sides. Sholes also had not forgotten Chet's recordings from New York and, after the turn of the year, would release the last of the Chet Atkins and His Colorado Mountain Boys songs: "Don't Hand Me That Line," by "Boogie Woogie Pony" writer Maurice Kregal, a trifle sung tentatively by Chet, backed with "The Nashville Jump."

Though the records stalled, "The Nashville Jump" was a harbinger of things to come, a jumpin'-jive instrumental that had Chet's electric Gibson blending with a tootful fiddle and harmonica. Then, on February 3, Sholes and Charles Grean came from New York to coproduce a new Atkins record, on which Grean would play bass along with Homer and Jethro on rhythm guitar and mandolin. Chet also invited his stepsister Billie Rose Strevel, who fancied a singing career, to come as well, adding vocal backgrounds and sharing the leads with Chet. The first four releases of these songs had Chet singing lead, then Sholes produced four more as instrumentals. In late February, RCA began to get the new songs on the market, now under the name of Chet Atkins and His Guitar Pickers.

The first was "Money, Marbles, and Chalk" / "Galloping on the Guitar." The former, written by Kentucky bandleader Garner "Pop" Eckler, was recorded by Eckler for King Records just before the new year, and Sholes tried to get the jump on it by having Chet do it better. The record, another shot by Sholes to situate Atkins in the country guitarist-singer mold, was again standard pop-country fodder. But by the time RCA could get it out, the Eckler original had come out, sapping the Atkins cover. Yet the B-side seemed more tuned to Chet's visions. As musicologist Mark S. Reinhart (no relation to Django Reinhardt) notes, Atkins "does some nimble banjo-style rolls consisting of multiple hammer-ons and pull-offs that are built around notes in the key of B. . . . [He] put a capo on the second fret" and played the break "in the key of C but the capo makes it sound as if he's playing in the key of D"—though it only matters that Atkins did these wonderful things by rote, smoothly and confidently, and drew the ears to a sweet but kicky melody, in obedient detail, bar by bar, beat by beat. There was no great rush by record buyers to buy the records yet, but Sholes knew he could wait as long as it took for Chet to break into a niche. Time was on his side, and would be on Chet's, for around five more decades.

Chet went back to his alternating day jobs with the Carter Sisters and Homer and Jethro, and as the months passed, three more of the RCA records were released—"Guitar Waltz" / "Barber Shop Rag" in June (the first Chet Atkins record to be released on the seven-inch, 45 rpm format); "Telling My Troubles to My Old Guitar" / "Dance of the Goldenrod" in August; and "Wednesday Night Waltz" / "Centipede Boogie" in November 1949. The best was arguably the last, the A-side being a cover of a tune by Spencer Williams, one more Black bluesman many had already forgotten but not Chet, who knew that Williams had written unforgettable songs like "Basin Street Blues" and "Wednesday Night Waltz," a fiddle-heavy lullaby that Chet covered with muted, comforting dual lead vocals by him and Billie.

Sholes had gotten him back in the studio as well, having him come to Chicago to lay down tracks at RCA's Studio A there on October 13. This time, he took with him not only Homer and Jethro but also the three Carter sisters, who knew by instinct when to play or sing and when to recede and allow Chet's L-10 to eat the scenery; Anita Carter would also play the bass. Indeed, the second Chicago recordings are historic as a soldering of three of the mightiest country acts of all time. The first release, "The Old Buck Dance" / "One More Chance" in January all but gleams. "Buck Dance," written by Chet, the first Atkins instrumental issued as an A-side—and often misidentified in the newspaper record roundups as "Bug Dance"—is synergistically tight, with Homer and Jethro feeding off Chet's lead in a glorious shuffle that gets the toe to tapping. The flip, cowritten by western swing singer Smokey Rogers, who also cowrote "Spanish Fandango" with Bob Wills, is notable for a duet with Helen Carter and the infectious, intricate guitar duel between Chet and Haynes on the bridge.

The record hit the market in January 1950, and two more from the session followed within the year, both rising entirely from the pens of the "family" team—"Main Street Breakdown" / "Under the Hickory Nut Tree," the A-side written by Chet and the flip by him and the three Carter sisters, who sang harmony on a cheeky, woe-is-me mandolin-guitar singalong about a cheating woman who "pounced on me" and had the singer's ten children. Then came "Boogie Man Boogie" / "I Was Bitten by the Same Bug Twice," the A written by Chet, the B by Helen Carter. "Boogie" was also the last time Chet sang on a record with Homer and Jethro, and one can sense the ease and fun they all had doing it. The common thread between these songs is the ingenuity of each, the air of freshness around them sunk into record grooves by the essential primordial "funk" that Chet put into the country bloodstream without losing the old-time taste buds. But the new decade would not find Chet Atkins in Chicago or New York. Neither would it find much country music in any big Yankee towns. Country was now in a geographic transition as the Delta blues migration settled firmly in the urban centers.

Sweet Home Chicago was becoming the preeminent blues colony now, the studios pouring out songs by Joe "King" Oliver, Big Bill Broonzy, and Sonny Boy Williamson, presaging the soon-prominent rock 'n' roll wave stoked by the soul-soaked chugging hambone beats of Muddy Waters and Ellas McDaniel, aka Bo Diddley. By 1952 the *National Barn Dance* would be canceled by its radio network, and WLS would by decade's end be a rock 'n' roll station. And yet this transition opened the portals to home rule in Dixie. And Steve Sholes could read the tea leaves. His intended country kingdom, Nashville, was now more than a mere talent tap for RCA. Not that the label had any inclination to invest in expensive office space for RCA Nashville, but it could get a jump on signing the talent that came to town with the objective of playing at the Grand Ole Opry, always a potential gold mine. Because Sholes would still be spending nearly all his time in New York, he needed boots on the ground embossing a characteristic native sound and process. And, as it happened, it seemed that fate's hand was leaning on Sholes's biggest Nashville discovery.

8

DOWN ON MUSIC ROW

This fortuitous turn of fate would not have happened without the imprimatur of the Carter clan. That tie-in had a power all its own in the country galaxy, and when Nashville came back into the picture, the Grand Ole Opry, despite the mutual dislike between them and Atkins, had to face up to the reality that the most popular of all country acts would steer clear of the Ryman stage unless Chet was backing them. Yet the thaw didn't happen right away. Instead, it took until country crooner George Morgan, a Grand Ole Opry habitue, whose song "Candy Kisses" topped the country chart for three weeks in 1948 (and whose daughter Lorrie Morgan is a longtime country star), acted as a conduit. Morgan had a gig in Springfield at the Shrine Mosque Auditorium headlined by the Carter Family with Chet Atkins and was so incensed that the Opry was sitting on their hands that he acted on his own to make it happen.

George had a promotion deal with the Opry sponsor Martha White Flour and urged them to sign a deal with Chet. They did, and it meant that Atkins was now technically a part of the Opry substructure, like it or not. And Martha White could schedule anyone they wanted to appear at the Opry. For Chet, this was no big deal, and it certainly wasn't for the Carters, who had so many gigs that the Opry was an unnecessary stop. But they and Chet agreed to play there, one of the results of their well-received performance being that they were given a show on WSM three times a week as well as a regular spot on the Opry roster. Thus, going to Nashville wasn't, as the Carters had intended, a temporary visit. In order to take the WSM job, the Carters had to quit the radio show they had at KWTO—a particularly touchy subject with Chet, who felt he owed Si Siman a lot. When Si refused to let the Carters out of their contract, Chet took no stand, letting Ezra Carter handle it rather than cross Si, who tried to leverage Chet against the Carters, saying he would let them go but offered Chet a new deal of his own: to take over the morning radio show and receive double his salary.

Suddenly, Chet Atkins found he had *power*. Able to bargain on his own, he concluded after much thought to take Siman's offer and part with the Carters, who he knew would be moving on from Nashville anyway before too long and meandering out on the road, which Chet dreaded. But he was so in demand now that he received a call from Fred Rose promising to use him on Nashville recording sessions if he stayed in town. Still, the complications of this contentious industry still had a roadblock—Jack Stapp, the WSM program director, nixed him, saying the station's offer to the Carters didn't apply to Chet. This was clearly a grudge lingering from the bad vibes Chet had left the Opry with, something the Estes agency reminded Stapp about. Jack thought he could freeze him out of Nashville, noting that Chet had no union card as a Nashville musician and rationalizing that, as Chet recalled, "there wasn't enough work to go around for the guitarists who were already [in Nashville]."

It was a genuinely ludicrous dodge. But Ezra, tired of the games people were playing, again entered. As Chet remembered, Ezra "put on his serious business suit, as he called it, and went to Nashville to meet with the WSM people" and made clear that Chet Atkins was part of his family and that the Carters wouldn't take the offer without him. No decision was made and Chet, not wanting to be a fly in the country ointment, told Ezra the family should go without him. But Ezra and the mighty women held firm. Once, speaking with someone at the station, Ezra began screaming into the phone that the Carters "come with Chet Atkins or they don't come, period!" It took six weeks before the station caved—arguably the wisest decision anyone in Nashville ever made—and in early June, Chet told Leona she could pack up again and come with Merle to their newest home, Nashville.

Sholes certified the decision by quickly extending Chet's RCA contract and—contrary to the dire observation from WSM that the musicians' union wasn't giving out membership cards to any more guitarists—Steve made it easy for him to obtain a card. Chet could now rent a small house on Granada Avenue in East Nashville, though it had no cooling and got so hot during the daytime that the family had to spend afternoons outdoors. He also had the freedom to go off somewhere with the Carter Sisters and Homer and Jethro, their day beginning at 6:00 AM for the Carters' WSM show and extending to nighttime appearances wherever they arose. The Opry gigs were almost an afterthought, and at those, Chet could almost hide behind Maybelle, June, Anita, and Helen's embroidered hoop skirts. Each of the women did their own thing, reflecting each one's personality, but Maybelle would stay right next to Chet as she played her Gibson L-5, alternating guitar lines with him while June danced and mugged comically, Anita seeming to be devoured by her big bass, and Helen standing off to the side working her accordion. They were the top Opry act from the start, normally drawing other acts and musicians to take seats behind them, getting into the groove.

Chet would come on the stage carrying not one but two portable Fender amps that almost blocked him from sight. He also bought himself, for $350, a brown D'Angelico Excel 1838 electric guitar from the Brooklyn guitar shop owned by John D'Angelico, who worked with Chet to mold it with a wide neck that muffled the buzzing noises of his thin-necked Gibsons, and Chet would continually season it with add-ons like his P-90 pickup, a Vibrola, and a Bigsby bar for extended dips and peaks, a thingamajig that would in time be standard on guitars. All this would turn the D'Angelico, and future guitars Chet used, into what he would call "Rolls Royce" guitars, yet looking back, he admitted to guitar writer Tony Bacon that he was just throwing Jell-O at a wall to see what would stick, while he went on framing what he had already heard from his guitar heroes like George Barnes, whom he called a "damn machine," Django Reinhardt, and Merle Travis, none of whom he ever believed he could equal.

In fact, Chet's own maturation had fed off the most shared trait within the music fraternity—respectful larceny. "Les Paul and Django Reinhardt, they're the two I copied," he said. "And, of course, Les copied Django, so I got some of it second-hand. Third-hand."

Whatever the line of succession was, it had put him in Nashville to stay, the checks from the Opry, Fred Rose, and Steve Sholes well spent. And down the line there would be another source of benefaction that could literally be measured by how many thousands of times Chet's name would be carved into a certain brand of guitar.

Barely a year into his Nashville cocoon, by December 1950 he was already a new addition at sessions by Hank Williams, one more stepping stone for Chet Atkins, who said that "when I first came down here, I was anxious to meet Hank because of 'Lovesick Blues,' which is the best damn country record ever made." Fatefully, Hank was managed by Fred Rose, who also produced and published his songs. And Fred, keeping his word to get Chet into the studio, had him play guitar on Hank's sessions at a shop created by three WSM engineers in 1946 called Castle Studio, in the Tulane Hotel on Church Street. It had an eight-input mono mixing board but couldn't be used to record until WSM left the air for the day. Thus, sessions were held long after dark, which was fine by Hank, who drank all day anyway. Still, he was always good for a strong take before crumbling to the floor.

He had readily agreed to record with Chet, having been a fan of "Guitar Blues," and Chet played his electric D-Angelico, joining two of Hank's Drifting Cowboys side men, fiddler Jerry Rivers and steel guitarist Don Helms, as well as other Nashville cats, including bassist Ernie Newton, rhythm guitarist Sammy Pruett, and Owen Bradley on piano. For Chet, the styling of a Hank Williams song was easy to perform, requiring that he play what he called a "dead-string guitar," meaning "dead string rhythm," turning up the guitar volume very high and creating a plucking sound while playing the four rhythm strings and muting the overall sound with a hand held over the bridge. Combined with the yowl of the steel guitar, it produced an almost physical sense of heartbeat and weepiness.

Two singles would arise from the session. The up-tempo "Dear John" would be released only days after the session, though it was the B-side, the blistering "Cold, Cold Heart"—one of country's most twisted songs by one of its most twisted performers—that broke big, setting to chillingly sincere lyrics Hank's story of how he and his wife Audrey regularly cheated on each other, the full story being that Audrey had been hospitalized after a complication from an abortion, and when Hank visited her there she hissed at him, "You sorry son of a bitch . . . you caused me to suffer like this."

His retort about her cold, cold heart bled so openly that after Hank played it on his WSM radio spots and Kate Smith's national TV show, it soared to number one on the country chart and high on the pop. And Chet surely had something to do with Hank's bluesy burr cutting soul deep, his chords turning dark and sinister while he and the other session guys riffed off Hank's semi-yodels and long-held notes. Indeed, Rose tried to persuade Hank to shorten some lines, telling him he was singing "two meters too long." Not having a clue what that meant, Hank told him to do nothing else in the booth but "just watch me." Chet quickly struck up a friendship with Hank, although it was never easy being around him. "Hank had an awfully big ego," he said. "Tried to write a song every time he picked up a guitar." For another, "He wasn't in shape a lot . . . he was so skinny his ass rattled like a sack of carpenter nails when he walked." He recalled when Hank tried to set up a writing session with Chet early on.

> Hank said let's go to the house and try to write one. I was awe-struck being around him. But we finally knocked out a couple—I've forgotten 'em. But he'd come up real close to

> you and say, listen to this hoss, and he'd sing "Jambalaya" or "Hey Good Lookin'," and that bourbon breath would knock you down and say, how you like that? Great, Hank. He'd say, you damn right it is.

When Hank played at the Opry, he had Chet double up his duties. The first time he backed Williams there was on October 13, 1951. Chet came onto the stage that night as a solo, following Cowboy Copas and Little Jimmy Dickens. He would then remain onstage to play rhythm lines for both Hank and then the Carters. For the second Opry show of the night, Chet played with Ernest Tubb, George Morgan, Hank Snow, his old benefactor Red Foley, Bill Monroe, and Roy Acuff, not to mention the redoubtable Duke of Paducah, aka singer Whitey Ford (not the New York Yankees lefty). To do all this, Chet had to vamp, change chords, or those meters on the fly. It was a metaphor for the always wild and crazy happenings at the Opry, and Chet was expected to pump up the stage presence of already glittery performers who wore their finest Opryware—the best being the rhinestone-covered, four-foot-ten guitar dynamo Little Jimmy. There were of course a slew of other musicians who worked behind the stars, guys like bassist Floyd "Lightnin'" Chance and guitarist Vito Pellitteri, and all the players lived for the moment when an Opry host like Foley, Bill Monroe, or longtime Opry announcer and comic Rod Brasfield would call one of them to the front for an impromptu solo bit. But Chet Atkins was the only one who knew it was coming.

He was so solidly entrenched that, up in New York, Jimmy Atkins, who had moved on to performing with organist Don Baker and Jerry Packer and the Rainbow Orchestra, was thrilled when his little brother asked him to write a song for him. It turned out to be "Columbus, G-A," which was released by RCA in February 1951 as the B-side of the Carter Sisters' "I've Got My Share of Trouble." By then, Chet had become the prize possession of Fred Rose and Steve Sholes. In fact, Sholes and Rose struck an agreement to share Chet's services for their mutual benefit—the genesis of Chet's highly unique arrangement to work with basically anyone, from any label, as long as it made money for Acuff-Rose, with a little something off the top for Chet and Steve.

Under the complex agreement, RCA would share publishing rights on songs Chet would be recording under his name—and such royalties were already being shared on the Carters' songs for RCA, split between RCA's publishing arm and Acuff-Rose, which also sold songbook folios of the act. Thus, without even really understanding the ins and outs of publishing, Chet would himself become a conduit for Acuff-Rose, pushing other acts under his wing to sign with the imperious firm but also having something for himself by skimming some of the publishing as a reward for his bird-dogging work. He learned the rules and loopholes of the game early, leveraging his growing influence in Nashville and easing the way for his permanent stamp on the town. That was how fast he had come, just when things looked so bleak. The problem was, for the first years of this system, despite a growing number of men with wondrous talent and judgment, Nashville's studios were bottom-of-the-barrel facilities. Sholes once recalled, "We used to record in a garage; we shared space with a house painter and we had a little booth there. It was in this garage that we cut the Davis Sisters in 'I Forgot More Than You'll Ever Know,' as well as aides by Hank Snow and many others."

Actually, this is only half-true. RCA did most of its early Nashville recordings in a cramped studio, Brown Brothers Transcription Services, on 4th Avenue North. It had a few microphones and scant space for musicians, which was why a separate studio called Thomas Productions—which was indeed a garage space on 13th Avenue North—was used as a backup alternative, to stash the portable equipment that Sholes brought in from New York and to be, with a single desk and phone, where RCA Nashville basically hung its hat. Sholes also cut records at a studio known as the Castle. Yet even under these low-rent conditions, Snow, aka "The Singing Ranger," whom Sholes had signed to RCA and brought to Nashville after popularizing country music in his native

Canada, rolled out hit after hit, all tailored in some way by Atkins's magic-fingered accents and low-key suggestions that stuck. As Sholes said, "His ideas were great, and the musicians always listened to him. So I realized that here was a man who, in addition to being a great guitarist, had a fine talent for head arrangements. I also realized that he enjoyed the respect of the musicians. Because of these qualities, I began using Chet as a leader on dates."

The effect was dramatic. On the Snow sessions, the cool, reserved Canadian's Perry Como-like style was given a quick charge by Chet's smooth but tangy accents, helping push three consecutive Snow songs in 1949 and 1950—"I'm Moving On," "The Golden Rocket," and "The Rhumba Boogie"—to the top of the country chart, the first three of Snow's seven number-one country hits; he also recorded a duet with Anita Carter in '51 that went to number two, "Down the Trail of Achin' Hearts," and would remain on Atkins's dance card down the road. Given time to fit in sessions for his own recordings, in August 1950 Chet went into the Brown Brothers studio with Sholes, who produced four songs that adhered to Sholes's previous formula for Atkins—two with vocals, two instrumentals—and any song releases would still go out under the name of "Chet Atkins and His Guitar Pickers," though the only other studio musicians, chosen by Chet from the Opry house players, were Jack Shook and Ernie Newton, who had been one of Jimmy Atkins's mates back in the Les Paul Trio before moving to Nashville.

The single that would go out was Chet's instrumental take on "Indian Love Call," the hammy 1924 Oscar Hammerstein show tune made famous by Nelson Eddy and Jeannette MacDonald in 1936. Chet cast it as a dreamy sleepwalk and had a nifty chord change mid-song, though he was not overly happy with it and would redo the song in 1956 as a guitar duet with Snow, enhanced by high strings, a far more nuanced, easy-on-the-ears float down a lazy river. Released in February 1951, it didn't dent the charts and receded altogether a year later when Slim Whitman's yodeling cover became a monster crossover hit, aided by Slim's then-cool, now-comical shrewling. Indeed, the real gem of that record was the B-side, "Music in My Heart," written by Helen

Carter; its inclusion being Chet's thank-you for the Carters' loyalty to him. With a vocal duet by Chet and his sister Billie Rose, it was a pleasant love avowal very different from other examples of Helen's impressive and underrated writing, which would surface in some quite daring themes for the country set, such as "Unfit Mother," "Heart Full of Shame," "Satan's Child," and "The Pickup" (about a suicide), all of which made "Under the Hickory Nut Tree" seem as harmless as "The Wheels on the Bus."

Even before the record was released, to little attention, Sholes anchored another Atkins session at Brown, producing four more sides aided by Shook and Newton. The single that came out of it, "You're Always Brand New," written by Los Angeles radio "singing cowboy" Stuart Hamblen, who would write Rosemary Clooney's "Our House" in 1954, was another harmless country rag but with a new wrinkle: the vocal was supplied by Opry crooner Danny Dill, giving it a higher-toned feel. But Sholes must have recognized that the Atkins tunes that registered the most were the instrumentals that fully displayed his fingerpicking dexterity. This was the case with the B-side, "Mountain Melody," which Chet cowrote with Mel Foree, the man who had given him his first radio job back in Knoxville. "Melody" upped Chet's profile with its slick and saucy licks, played for the first time on record on his D'Angelico Excel, which he played in a proto-"tapping" style popularized much later by Eddie Van Halen, his open hand tip-tapping up and down on multistring chords on the fretboard, switching tones and tempos with lightning speed.

There was another benefit in such innovation—being able to keep the backbeat without drums, which not incidentally saved Sholes and the union from paying for a drummer. Almost none of Chet's studio turns in the early 1950s made use of one, yet long before condensers, compressors, and low-pass filters were invented, many of his songs seemed as if a snare was keeping a distinctive *chuka-chuka* backbeat. He had done this at the Opry by appropriating one of Merle Travis's methods, playing a down-up, up-down repetition of his forefinger, setting off a brushy percussive effect many country bands utilized, most famously Hank Williams—who only used drums on two songs, "Moanin' the Blues" and "Take These Chains from My Heart"—and then Johnny Cash, who also used a less-deft technique: inserting a playing card under the strings of his guitar that his fingers scraped. At other times, Chet would have his rhythm guitarist scrape the body of his axe with the palm of his hand for a sandpapery cadence.

These methods became endemic within Atkins's primal Nashville sound, and even later, when drums were deemed acceptable to the Opry barons and a harder edge needed in late '50s, real drummers on his sessions played with finesse, not crashing snares but massaging them. Over in Memphis, Sam Phillips got the clue; he had opened Sun Records in the late 1940s as the "Black" answer to Nashville, with R&B acts that soon cross-fit White rockabilly. Songs like Carl Perkins's "Blue Suede Shoes" had a hiccupy, Atkins-style, guitar-rooted drumbeat. Not that the general population knew it yet, but the "Atkins sound" was already a thing in the early '50s, when people were prone to ask, "Who was that guitar guy I heard on the radio?" One music writer, Verlin Mays, for a Bristol, Virginia, paper wrote, "Since hearing 'Galloping on the Guitar' by Chet Atkins, people here have been wanting to know a little about this guitar wizard [who is] recognized as one of the greatest guitar players in the country," and who had "released 13 songs, and has been with the Carter Sisters." He was, the writer added, "a country minstrel [who] proves he digs boogie as well as bucolic ballads."

Despite his bookish veneer, Sholes was one hip dude, and he fed Atkins the most propitious big-band and show tunes to cover in his countryish manner so amenable to other idioms. The latest was the November 1950 recording of "The Birth of the Blues," the famous instrumental from the movie of the same name—written by Buddy G. DeSylva, Lew Brown, and Ray Henderson—backed by Chet's instrumental "Confusin'," requiring not only experimentation but sonic upgrading. Accordingly, in April 1951 Sholes took Chet and Danny

Dill to New York to utilize RCA's new multitrack system, allowing Sholes to mix different elements into the finished product, whereas in Nashville he had to make do with just two tracks with no means of any adjustment. The first session, backed again by Jimmy Atkins on rhythm guitar along with bassist Frank Carroll, laid down a cover of Fats Waller's undulating three-quarter-time jazz classic "The Jitterbug Waltz," Chet's guitar taking the place of Fats's piano tinkling with creative slip-sliding (which he would later redo with a font of strings). The B-side was a tune he had penned with Helen Carter called "My Crazy Heart," and the record came out in May 1951 on both the 78 and new 45 rpm formats, though it didn't land on many Victrolas.

His work was still divided between his own songs and those by others, including the individual Carter Sisters and Mother Maybelle RCA releases, taking him back to traditional country-folk and gospel. Normally, when Sholes left to go back to New York after tending to work in Nashville, it meant that Chet would be going with him, as if they ran as an entry. Steve always wanted to test Chet's output in the top-line RCA studio up north, where Sholes produced big records, and he had Chet cover the 1928 show tune "Crazy Rhythm," sung in a recent movie by Doris Day, the vocals handled by yet another RCA act, the Beaver Valley Sweethearts; it would go out as a single, the B-side being Chet's instrumental of the traditional square dance number "Hybrid Corn." But the significance of this record was that it was the last one under the purview of Chet Atkins and His Guitar Pickers. For the foreseeable future, his solo act would be all him, billed as Chet Atkins and His Galloping Guitar, on some releases spelled Gallopin' Guitar, which seemed to be a human life form in itself.

The effortless variety of his songs kept broadening, and he covered the swinging Glenn Miller evergreen "In the Mood" in a breezy, minimalist style with two cheeky false endings; its B-side was the Atkins-cowritten "Sweet Bunch of Daisies," coupling his overheated guitar picking with overweening lyrics by the Beasley Singers, including lines such as "Kiss me, my darling, daisies won't tell." This pattern was that each record would have one instrumental side and one with a vocal. His next record's instrumental was a cover of Alfred Bryan and Percy Wenrich's 1908 "Rainbow," backed by a cover of the 1939 Mills Brothers' big-band classic "Goodbye Blues," on which Chet goes toe to toe with the original's four-string electric bop played by the Brothers' guitarist Bernard Addison, with the Beasleys re-creating the famous four-part harmony.

Notably, among the releases in 1952 and into 1953, few were conventional "country." Other examples were his lullaby-like arrangement of the eighteenth-century flamenco folk tune "Spanish Fandango," released in April 1952, the B-side of which united him with Boudleaux Bryant, who with his wife Felice had been brought to Nashville by Fred Rose to write songs for Acuff-Rose and had penned songs for Red Foley, Carl Smith, and Little Jimmy Dickens. Boudleaux's "You Mean Little Thing," with the vocal by the Beasleys, was tailor made for Chet, with its plucky chords and swirling vibratos—the anatomy of a "new" country that would be played in a wondrous fingerpicking duet by Chet and Doc Watson on a 1980 episode of *The Tonight Show* (when they also sang an ambrosial version of the Carter Family's "I'm on My Way to Canaan's Land" using country stars' names sprinkled through the lyrics).

One can glean where each Atkins song was recorded, the thicker echoes earmarked to the New York-produced entries, through which Chet could gain expertise with multitracking—including doubling *himself*, adding a second guitar track that made it seem like there were two guitarists at work. He would also tinker with his D'Angelico to delay passages already bent into infinite shapes by his tremolo bar. Song reviews marveled at Atkins's "flying fingers," as a Johnson City, Tennessee, scribe wrote, and noted that "Mean Little Thing" "exhibits his many styles and some real improvisation."

These recordings appeared with clockwork regularity, the next in line being two instrumentals, covers of Les Paul and Mary Ford's "Meet Mister Callaghan" backed with the Mills Brothers' "Chinatown, My Chinatown," then Chet's collaboration with Bryant, "Midnight" (which

Red Foley covered that year and took to the top of the country chart), with vocals again by the Beasley Singers, the flip being the traditional folk tune "Rustic Dance." The presence of Boudleaux, who was writing songs both alone and with Felice, took Chet from Sholes's ambit of show and jazz tunes into country pop just as the musical tide in America was leaving room for creative sampling of the blues. In the South, the first great breakout of new country was the rockabilly that was making waves at Sam Phillips's studio in Memphis. In New Orleans, Fats Domino was contouring the blues to melodic piano pop, as soon would Little Richard. Up in Chicago, Muddy Waters, Bo Diddley, and John Lee Hooker had strong White crossover. Chuck Berry would come with a comforting assurance that a guitar could be played just like ringin' a bell.

Chet Atkins fell into his own niche. When time came to record his first album in mid-May 1952, rather than go in with a full crew, he went in with Homer and Jethro as well as Charlie Grean on bass, but sometimes the only crew was Chet himself. This was perfectly reasonable, since he was the best musician he knew, and he had come far enough to be able to implement a primitive multitracking system even in the primitive Brown studio on a single track, piecing together separate tracks by manually splicing them together with a stapler-like device—though he never completely let go of live recording, little mistakes and all, for a live feel. For the album, titled *Chet Atkins' Gallopin' Guitar*, his D'Angelico galloped over not two tracks but two recorders, separately, playing the melody as usual on one, then with slightly different chords on the other, something still considered too technically complicated without a built-in two- or four-track system. Chet knew that Les Paul had done stuff like this, and so he, Sholes, and an engineer put it all together. Even more radically, Chet rigged his guitar to be able to play separate notes as if he was playing two guitars at once. When he played at a concert before ten thousand people in Nashville's Centennial Park a year later, the *Tennessean* reported that Chet "brought gasps from the crowd by playing 'Dixie' and 'Yankee Doodle' at once, one with his thumb, the other with his forefinger."

Even so, he was not overly happy with the album, which was released in early 1953 on both 78 and 45 formats, its eight instrumentals crackly and the "double"-track songs a tad muffled. Worse, there were only three songs from Atkins's pen on it, one a redo of "Gallopin' Guitar" as "Galloping on the Guitar" and, with Bryant, "Hangover Blues," done as a medley with Chet's "Imagination." The shank of the album were his ingenious covers of evergreens like "The Third Man Theme," "St. Louis Blues," "Lover, Come Back to Me," "Nobody's Sweetheart," and a Stephen Foster medley. It was as if Sholes was loath to waste Atkins on an album performing mainly original material on a platform most record labels saw as chaff, and he didn't see fit to release any as singles, though the irony is that modern-day music writers' retro-reviews of Atkins's catalog save their highest praise for his '50s albums. One such review of *Gallopin' Guitar* ventures that "every song here is played as if written just for Chet. Truly masterful handling of each song. Chet fans will wrap up a warm fuzzy of familiar yet unexpected treatments."

In real time, his debut album and many thereafter were in fact keepers for Atkins's emerging followers. And Sholes hardly felt any need to cut back on Atkins's work, nor would Chet discard songs that didn't become hits; instead, he would rerecord many of them on later albums, with improved equipment, sometimes making home recordings on equipment he developed experimentally. Moreover, if RCA was slow to enter the hard-driving realm of rock, one reason was Sholes's conviction that he already had a hold on country music's matriculation into crossover territory without crossing into screaming noise. He had a right to see things through a sedate lens. Among the top pop hits of the early '50s were Les Paul and Mary Ford's "How High the Moon," Patti Page's trusty "Tennessee Waltz," and "Because of You" by Tony Bennett, the Italian kid from Queens, New York, who had an early hit covering Hank Williams's "Cold, Cold Heart" when Columbia Records A&R head Mitch Miller, a country buff, convinced him to sing country with a jazz feel. Hank Snow's "I'm Moving On" would be covered by both country and pop singers, including no less than Ray Charles and, in time, the Rolling Stones. Not insignificantly, when Pat Boone broke in, he came to Nashville to appear in an all-White outdoor concert at which Atkins was headlining with Louis Innis and Bob Moore. Boone would make his bones covering Little Richard and Fats Domino songs as the worst excuse for soul ever heard, but it made him rich and famous in an America that would settle for race-neutral ersatz.

Chet was where Sholes wanted him. And Steve would let him have greater authority to record what he wanted, and always be on standby for acts that needed him to tap into Nashville's broadening market. This was what had drawn Hank Williams to town and where he did some of his best work. The down side to that subplot, however, was that Chet could sense the smell of death surrounding Hank. Indeed, country music's ultimate loss was waiting just around the corner, and unfolding right before Chet's eyes.

9

"THE BOURBON WOULD ALMOST KNOCK YOU DOWN"

In some ways, Hank Williams reminded Chet Atkins of himself when he was stuck in the backwoods, a loner in a hostile world with only his guitar for relief. Like Hank, if someone didn't fancy him, he shrugged and kept a distance from them. But while Chet never brooded himself out of his potential—and it was close at times—he had watched Hank sink into a booze-soaked dead end, the mutually destructive marriage to Audrey deadening his mood and singing, which he could barely do by 1952, his wheezing body sinking to the floor of the studio and needing to be revived by the addled Fred Rose. His inability to record a single song stretched on for over six months into early '52, and after Audrey filed for a merciful divorce for a second time, he was physically ravaged by a congenital back condition that he eased only with addictive drugs and booze, writing self-diagnosing songs about being psychologically crippled by jealousy and revenge against his "cold-hearted" wife. And Chet, who never thought this would be part of the bargain of teaming with Hank Williams, was an eyewitness to some of these horrific scenes.

As the hours ticked away into early morning at the Castle studio, Chet would later recall, Hank would take five and "call his wife at two o'clock in the morning and she would be out catting around. And that drove him to drink, of course. He never stopped loving Audrey." Then, with the surety of a pseudo-shrink, he posited, "Men tend to fall in love with women they can't control." After Audrey ordered Hank Sr. to move out of their house, he moved in with Ray Price, a young Opry singer who had recently come to Nashville to record for Bullet Records. Hank's life was a haze of hootch, morphine, and potent chloral hydrate prescribed by a sham doctor. In the studio, Chet recalled, when Hank came close to him, "the bourbon would almost knock you down." Still obsessed with Audrey, who had sung with Hank on his radio shows and even now filled in when he missed concerts, Hank stuck his pistol in his waistband one day and fired shots at Audrey and her friends, fortunately missing.

Chet, who believed Hank was the greatest performer he ever saw, kept hoping he could get himself straight. By late 1952 Hank had moved for a while to California, then lived with his mother back in Alabama, impregnating another woman. When he returned to Nashville, Price recalled, Hank "went off the deep end. Don Helms and I wound up taking him to a sanitarium up in Madison. Then he started raising hell again." He seemed to know his time was short, telling a newspaper reporter, "God comin' down the road after me." Even so, Fred Rose got him to record again in mid-June. Working with Chet, Helms, Jerry Rivers, and bassist Charles "Indian" Wright, he cut four amazing songs, the first to go out from the session being "Jambalaya (On the Bayou)," cowritten with Moon Mullican, which had Hank pining for gumbo and crawfish pie, yodeling out, "Me oh my oh, son of a gun we'll have big fun on the bayou." Released in May, it hit number one on the country chart and was his first top-twenty pop hit.

However, if one took this as Hank moving beyond his depression, that was disabused by another new song, "I'll Never Get Out of This World Alive," cowritten with Rose, which was the ultimate Hank predicate. The last song of his to be released while he was alive, it too went to number one country and would be covered by, among many others, Jerry Lee Lewis and both Hank's singing son and grandson. It also damn near killed him right then and there. As Atkins would recall, "after each take, he'd sit down in a chair. I remember thinking, 'Hoss, you're not jivin',' because he was so weak that all he could do was just sing a few lines, and then just fall in the chair." Hank was so weak, Chet said, that "I thought that song was prophetic."

He somehow cut two more—"Window Shopping," the B-side of "Jambalaya," and "Settin' the Woods on Fire," which would be released in September, ushering Hank into rockabilly territory, a new horizon that Chet had suggested he broach, and he did, the song hitting number two on the country chart. A month later, Hank managed to do another session, laying down "You Win Again," another jeremiad about Audrey that he had originally titled "I Lose Again," but even this flippant bring-down was engaging in a smirky way and would be the B-side of "Settin' the Woods on Fire," getting to number ten. Hank also insisted that Chet back him up at the Opry on April 4. A photo taken that night is worth more than a thousand words. Almost giddily, Chet is seen gazing at Hank midstage in wonder. Hank's wan face was almost devoured by his ten-gallon hat, but he sang and strummed with an engaging smile while dominating the stage, going through Prince Albert spots and introducing Little Jimmy Dickens, Rod Brasfield, and Minnie Pearl.

Chet, standing to his back left during the songs in his usual non-cowboy attire, wearing an open-necked shirt and casual sport jacket, was clearly amazed at how Hank could raise himself almost literally from the dead and capture an audience. But three months later, when he was scheduled to appear again in July, he didn't show up, and the Opry manager, Jim Denny, went to his house and fired him—a ban that ludicrously stands to this day. It was ludicrous back then too, as Hank gave as much of a hang about the Opry as did Chet. As Atkins put it years later, "Normal things didn't excite Hank, he drove himself past other people's limits." And rather than protest his canning, Hank left town for Shreveport to play on *The Louisiana Hayride*. While there, he married nineteen-year-old Billie Jean Jones—who was dating Faron Young until Hank threatened to shoot Faron to death in a honky-tonk bathroom. Hank got back to Nashville to record in September, taking Chet into Castle with Jack Shook on rhythm guitar, Floyd Chase on bass, and Tommy Jackson on fiddle to lay down four songs, three of which came right from his tortured soul—"Your Cheatin' Heart," "Take These Chains from My Heart," and "I Could Never Be Ashamed of You." "Cheatin'" was really "Cold, Cold Heart," part two, and "Ashamed" a self-serving nod to his new wife, whom he had married before his divorce from Audrey was final.

Despite the sourness of his life, these were some of the greatest country songs ever recorded. And the fourth of the session, "Kaw-Liga," a whimsical fable based on an old legend about falling for a wooden Indian maiden, was only the second song recorded by Hank for which Fred Rose employed a drummer. Hank then went out on a fall and winter tour, just as "Cheatin' Heart" hit number one on the country chart. He was being ferried in his Cadillac en route to a New Year's Day show in Canton, Ohio, when the driver stopped for gas in Oak Hill, West Virginia. He checked Hank in the back of the Cadillac and found him dead, empty bottles of liquor and pills strewn across the backseat and floor. Like the rest of the country arc, Chet was hit hard by the news while not being one bit surprised by it. All in all, the bizarre saga of Hank Williams was messy, complicated, and ugly, but also useful, as the posthumous number-one rankings and million-plus sales of "Cheatin' Heart," "Kaw-Liga," and "Chains" only added to Chet's status as a hit-making factor. To be sure, the songs he had helped conduct for Hank are some of the most affecting and addictive songs ever made, in any genre. Yet his regret was that he never really could penetrate Hank's loneliness, which bridged Chet's own. Indeed, it made him ponder if people like Hank and himself lived on the edge of a curse that fame only made worse.

Positioned as he was along the watchtower, he would have similar feelings each time he was asked to attend numerous funerals of other compatriots who were too young to go. Two years before Hank's death,

Red Foley's second wife, Judy Martin, had taken her own life, sending Red into years of alcoholism that Chet also tried in vain to stem. Red was able to straighten up and host the TV run of *Ozark Jubilee* and would make it to 1967, the year he went into the Country Music Hall of Fame, before dying moments after singing his last song, "Peace in the Valley." Another grim milestone was Faron Young's suicide after his life of mental torture. Guitarist Hank Garland sustained a brain injury in a car crash; he was nursed back to health by his wife, Evelyn, who four years after died in another car crash. But here was Chet Atkins, Red's now-wizened discovery, seemingly forever young as he approached thirty and immune to the self-induced tragedy he saw all around him.

He would have his health scares that seemed ready to do him in. In 1953, not having tended to his teeth through the years, he developed a tumor on his jawbone that needed surgery. He worried it was malignant, and Fred Rose was so worried he gave Chet a book in the hospital that concluded, "If the Lord is for you, who can be against you?" It turned out not to be malignant, but he never believed religion was the panacea, given that for all the trips to church he made with Leona, his future bouts with cancer made him more skeptical that, as he put it, "any religion has an answer." The scare over, he went on guiding country music to his own instincts while keeping its flavor. As it was, his meticulous fingerprints were being left all over Nashville, including on a jazz album he recorded with musicians who played on his WSM radio show, Homer and Jethro, Jerry Byrd, bassist Ernie Newton, and fiddler Dale Potter. The album, *String Dustin'*, is still a wonder as a technically country work, its eight tracks tripping lightly from nuggets like "Sweet Georgia Brown," "The Lady in Red," "Stompin' at the Savoy," and "Midnight Train," not stopping to wonder how country fits in, needlessly, as it does so, by rote—and Chet so favored it that its CD rerelease in 1994 as *Jazz from the Hills* would have thirteen additional tracks recorded from 1953 to 1956, including one with George Barnes; two Potter tracks, "Fiddle Patch" and "Fiddle Sticks"; and Chet's 'Tennessee Rag."

Still a marquee name at the Grand Ole Opry, Chet could signal to the crowd with just a few notes from his guitar that he was next up.

On January 3, 1953, Rod Brasfield brought him on by cooing, "Right now he's a boy that's made a lot of records by himself, by crack. When it comes to pickin' up on a standard guitar you'd have to go a long ways to beat this young fella. I'm talkin' about Chet Atkins. Here he is to pick out 'Five Foot Two, Eyes of Blue.'" The hoots and hollers from the musicians onstage set him off on his melodic thumb-plucking that made it seem as if he were strumming on two different guitars at once, getting the folks in the old hall stompin' until the end of the song prompted Brasfield to shriek, "Yeah!" He was always ready as well to handle formalities, such as in 1959 when he would present Jim Reeves with a gold record for "He'll Have to Go," But the love affair with Chet Atkins was still being met with gritted teeth by the William Estes Agency, notwithstanding Chet's cushion of the Martha White company. As Chet would look back, the Mad Men up north would press the Opry to fire "that guitar player." While the static from above annoyed him, and portended that his regular gigs at the Opry would only persist until the Opry executives decided his popularity was bad for business—a logic only understood by music promoters who feared losing sponsors more than losing customers—he had the strut of a man with a following. As it was, he even had himself a formal ring of adherents, with the *Nashville Banner* reporting that "The Chet Atkins Fan Club plans a big deal [from] July 23–25, prexy Margaret Fields of Louisville tells us. She says members of the club from 30 states are expected [to] elect new members and meet Chet personally."

He also knew he was Steve Sholes's boy and a fixture with the Carter family—no small honors. Either of which alone seemingly would have kept him on the Opry stage indefinitely, but for him nothing was permanent. Early in 1953 the Carters figured their work in Nashville was done and inevitably moved on, this time without him, as Ezra Carter knew Chet now had his own agenda to tend to.

Mother Maybelle and her daughters thanked him for helping to give them stability, which ensured that the three daughters would branch out on their own, bringing them back periodically to the Opry, June as a major act, combining singing and ditzy comedy, as well as writing "Ring of Fire" for Johnny Cash, whom she wed in 1968 and with whom she became part of a profitable team act. The Carters' exit provided Chet with more opportunity, WSM giving him the Carters' Sunday, Monday, Wednesday, and Friday midafternoon shows. He was undeniably fattening his wallet, also writing songs for Acuff-Rose with Boudleaux Bryant, whom he called "Boodle O'Bryant" until he learned it was pronounced "Boodlow." One of the songs, "How's the World Treating You?" became the B-side of Eddy Arnold's number-four country hit "Free Home Demonstration" in 1953, which would be covered by thirty-seven other acts, and was performed by Chet himself on the 1964 Elvis Presley TV special. Though most of the royalty spoils went to Acuff-Rose, the spare cash helped Chet buy a new home for the family on Caldwell Avenue, just south of Music Row.

That term came into the general parlance in 1950, when WSM announcer David Cobb coined it along with Nashville as "Music City, USA," although some in the country intelligentsia had their own lofty nickname: the "Athens of the South." And, as beneficiaries, Chet and Leona had enough to send Merle to the private Peabody Demonstration School, an all-grade institution much like the Georgia school Chet dropped out of, Mountain Hill. He was now so coveted at WSM that it kept him in the building all day, plugging himself in to any show as a guest musician, and the bosses scheduled him on promotional gigs. The station also enforced its own rules that he admitted in his memoir "bothered me," noting that these duties came before all else, crimping his prime yen, making his records. As well, the Opry kept sticking little pins into him, mainly by its manager, Jim Denny, who was constantly badgered by the Estes Agency to use Chet only sparingly. Sick of the rumors he was about to be fired again at the Opry, Chet went to Jack Stapp, who as the head man at WSM could either cause problems or make them go away—even though Stapp had already tried in vain to keep him out of the Carter Sisters act. As Chet remembered it, he had to "plead for my job," and Stapp saw it his way, keeping the Opry job safe, and safer when Denny left the Opry to open his own song publishing company, cashing in on the action that drove Nashville's new prosperity.

Chet became surprised that his name was known outside of Music City too. Newspaper reporters came looking for interviews. In 1954 the *Knoxville Journal*'s "Home Folks" columnist Vic Weals spent time with him and called him "a serious, restless young man," noting that "he hasn't made any fortune like some of the big names have," which could only have come straight from Chet, who could never quite figure out why he was making money but not anything like the people he was recording with. He would through the years self-effacingly joke about it, then get more strident. He latched on to the theory that it was because he was progressively stopped from singing on his records, and Weals assumed that "asthmatic trouble has made his [voice] uncertain and has kept him out of the big money bracket." The writer then reached deeper:

> He's not a crier nor a premature complainer, but he does ponder a lot on the short working life which nature allots to most musicians. Many suddenly lose their public appeal when they get middle-aged and middle spread. [Chet] can reasonably expect another decade or so of make-a-living years. Or maybe he'll be that one in a few whose popularity will continue [for] many, many years. I asked him if he'd ever thought of getting into something with more security. He grinned and said, "If I ever get real hungry, I might think about it."

Much of this, like many of his complaints and self-criticism, amounts to famous last words. He would go on all right, his records growing more confident and experimental, not making the charts but making waves. His newest releases included "High Rockin' Swing" (backed by an Atkins-Bryant version of Scott Joplin's "Fig Leaf Rag") and a cover of "The Bells of St. Mary's" that would be famous more for its B-side, another signal co-project with Bryant, "Country Gentleman," the title that would define him in perpetuity, the simple arrangement a one-man stomp with a neat intro vibrato that met up with his brush-guitar backbeat in a snap-finger beat. In December 1953, Sholes put songs written solely by Chet on the front and back sides: "Barber Shop Rag" and "Centipede Boogie." As well, the second Atkins instrumental album, *Stringin' Along with Chet Atkins*, also released that year, employed only Homer and Jethro and the now freelancing Anita Carter on bass, maintaining the intimate acoustic mien.

The album was marginally more ambitious, the track list again channeling the old-time crowd, with W. C. Handy's "Memphis Blues" and Tin Pan Alley offerings such as "Hello! Ma Baby," "Oh By Jingo!," and "Alice Blue Gown," and it tacked on Hank's past covers of "Boogie Man Boogie" and "Indian Love Call." The keepers were the Atkins-Bryant "Blue Gypsy" and Chet's "Main Street Breakdown," but Chet would undervalue the work as "a lot of notes and fast runs." Yet it kept the pace, feeding his fans' appetite, which would lead to it being rereleased in 1956 on the new twelve-inch, 33⅓ rpm vinyl format and, long into the future, as a posthumous two-CD package with bonus tracks "Country Gentleman" and his fourth ragtime piece, a cover of "The Third Street Rag." However, it was the next Atkins works that stand as his breakthroughs.

In mid-November 1954, even on his way to bigger things, he never would shed the fear that he was being held back from exercising his own vision. He was often assured by Fred Rose, who needed to keep him happy enough, and who even bought him an expensive movie camera so he could capture Merle's childhood on film. But Fred couldn't deny that the name of the game was profit, a game that in the end was almost always unwinnable.

Until then, the profit that Fred enjoyed had only tangentially come from Chet's records, though more than a few of the records he had produced or been a major part of as a sideman were bona fide hits that enriched Acuff-Rose. That equation continued after Sholes signed an unknown "sister" act out of Kentucky, Skeeter and Betty Jack Davis, who were actually not sisters but sang in perfect sisterly tandem. Their first release, in May 1953, was "I Forgot More Than You'll Ever Know," a song of heavy sorrow and loss on which Chet played lead guitar, with Velma Smith—the first female to be given a solo spot at the Grand Ole Opry—on rhythm guitar. It hit a raw nerve, about a woman turning the tables on a cheating fool, ringing in what was called gut-punching "hard country," taking the song to number one on the country chart for eight weeks, and it crossed over as a top-twenty pop hit, later covered by Johnny Cash, Jerry Lee Lewis, Kitty Wells, and even Bob Dylan on his *Self Portrait* album and later as a duet with Tom Petty. And yet Sholes and country took a major blow when, just after "Forgot" was released, Betty Jack and Skeeter were driving through Ohio on tour and their car was hit head on by another car, killing Betty Jack and badly injuring Skeeter.

After her recovery, Skeeter (née Mary Frances Penick) would continue singing with Betty Jack's sister Georgia and then go solo and become a towering country-pop star under the production stewardship of Chet, who encouraged her to continue performing, subtly dipping her recordings in pathos, one technique being to end songs on a down, or "doom" chord. He called this a "modern ending," the sadness emulated by an arpeggio lingering a half tone above the key before almost safely returning to the original key. Pretty as all his songs were, this drop-off in tone was subtle, but one night at the Opry, when Chet played a modern ending, announcer John McDonald, who thought he knew better, told him, "You hit a sour note, Chet, didn't you?" But Sholes got it. It was why he dropped the need to pair a vocal song with an instrumental per each release, which Chet had his misgivings about, though he had already proven that instrumentals—to be accurate, *his* way with instrumentals—could have extraordinary power.

Pop music had owned this franchise—RCA's own easy-listening maestro Hugo Winterhalter not only arranged cottony songs for Perry Como, Harry Belafonte, and Eddie Fisher but had a string of somnolent, string-and-horn-laden instrumental cover hits, and he would reach number one pop with the dreamy "Canadian Sunset" in 1956. The last time Chet sang a lead vocal was late in 1953 on a ballad called "Get

Up and Go," which remained unreleased until the *Early Years* set forty years later. In 1974 he would tell the *New York Times* that he hadn't sung since 1947, which may have been a memory lapse but was also part of his long habit of making light of his singing despite never really reconciling having been eased out of it by Sholes. Another example was him saying, grudgingly, "They said then that they wanted some vocals. I decided I could do it as well as anyone—which proved to be wrong." He was so self-conscious about it that he told the *New York Times* that he had actually destroyed the masters of all those vocal songs, a fallacy given the numerous remastered rereleases of them. Still, given all the freedom he needed making instrumentals, that would be his signature, and a franchise he all but owned.

There were more releases made at the Thomas studio as the pivotal year of 1953 closed out—the 1919 Tin Pan Alley waltz "Three O'Clock in the Morning" backed by Chet's "City Slicker," and in December a combined rerelease of his 1949 records "Barber Shop Rag" and "Centipede Boogie." In early '54 came "Wildwood Flower," an 1800s folk tune that had been sung by the Carter Family in 1928, which he played with elegant simplicity in tribute to the brood that took him back to Nashville, backed by Chet's "Simple Simon," riffed from the children's game. Then in April came the novelty "Kentucky Derby" backed with Chet's raucous "Downhill Drag," the latter of which he had recorded on a quickie side trip with Sholes to Chicago, taking Homer and Jethro as sidemen—the last time they would record together for three years, as Haynes and Burns would also hit the road as "The Thinking Man's Hillbillies," singing self-effacing parodies of country hits for RCA on such records as *Homer and Jethro Fracture Frank Loesser* and on numerous country music TV shows, winning a Grammy in 1959.

Chet was truly getting funkier now, egged on by the bearded, egocentric Boudleaux Bryant, who had little affection for the old-time fossils, not seeing how they applied to country, pop, or rock. Since Chet was producing his own nascent albums, he had the leeway to get out of the play-it-safe box, as he had with "Hangover Blues" by bending notes into the mewling sound of a hangover, and on "Derby" with runs of *clippety-cloppety* horseshoe steps on his guitar. Some of his funk didn't fly, such as his and Boudleaux's "Peeping Tom," when he added sound-effect reels of a woman screaming and a police siren screaming. It was a good idea, but Sholes turned thumbs down and it too went unreleased until the *Early Years* anthology in 1993. Sholes nonetheless knew Chet's restless progressions needed a better studio. The chronic hangup was that RCA refused to build it, preferring to make do with the existing ones, none of which were satisfactory. But Sholes came around to openly fantasizing about a place he could have at least built to Chet's specifications that RCA could hang a shingle on. And, typically, it would fall to Chet to make it happen.

Fortunately, he had a model he would be able to draw upon—Owen Bradley, who had come a long way himself in Nashville since playing piano on Chet's Bullet sessions. The native Tennessean had been WSM's musical director, leader of a country jazz band, and writer of Roy Acuff's "Night Train to Memphis," and he had joined Decca as a producer and arranger, working with the likes of Ernest Tubb, Kitty Wells, and Red Foley. His career, in fact, almost exactly mirrored Chet's, and Owen got the jump on him when, also in 1954, he recognized the need for an uppercase studio and teamed up with his younger brother Harold, who had played guitar in Tubb's band at the Grand Ole Opry and recorded with Tubb, Eddy Arnold, and Pee Wee King (and later, when president of the local musicians' union, he would record three albums for Columbia and be on Nashville sessions for Bob Dylan and Joan Baez).

Pooling their finances, the Bradley brothers bought a condemned building at 804 16th Avenue South, gutted it, and oversaw the construction of the Bradley Film and Recording Studios, soon to be known as the Quonset Hut Studio, which was up and running early in 1955, the first studio specifically located on Music Row. The Bradleys hired top-notch engineers and fitted the place with state-of-the-art equipment. Like Chet, Owen would personally pick which "A Team" musicians would be the house session men and opened his doors to any label that rented time, progressively becoming the home base of Columbia Records. A testament to how vital Quonset was is that two of the most popular Christmas songs ever were recorded there for Decca: Bobby Helms's "Jingle Bell Rock," produced by Nashville veteran Paul Cohen, and thirteen-year-old Brenda Lee's "Rockin' Around the Christmas Tree," produced by Owen himself.

Conceivably, Quonset Hut could have been the studio base for RCA as well. But Sholes's ego needed a place that he could claim he had built. Regardless, Chet turned to Owen for guidance and connections once Sholes would give him the go-ahead. In the interim, Chet went on recording at either Brown or Thomas, recording in August his swinging cover of "San Antonio Rose," backed by the B-side "Mister Misery" on the ensuing single release. "Misery" was cowritten with Louis Innis as a sad, sad song about "a "broken love affair," sung lugubriously by carrot-top steel guitarist and singer Red Kirk, whom Chet had met back in Knoxville as a member of Archie Campbell's troupe. In retrospect, one can project the song as something broader, something Chet Atkins saw when he sometimes looked in the mirror; if so, his guitar didn't gallop, it weeped, his almost baleful solo chords on the bridge making self-pity utterly convincing. And now, that beyond-wide range would have a new means of release, through a glorious instrument that would bear his name.

10

A GRETSCH IN TIME

Chet recalled that he first heard from the Gretsch guitar company in 1954, when the company was in an expansion phase. It began in 1883 as a small music store in Brooklyn but had not actually manufactured guitars until the 1930s. Yet those axes were basically chaff after Gibson cleaned the playing field and in 1954 signed Les Paul to a licensing deal. In fact Chet, whose first high-class guitar had come to him by way of Les, through Jimmy Atkins, had been photographed for newspaper stories and PR shots with his Gibson. But Gretsch set its sights on him as a competitive endorsement figure. The company, run by Fred Gretsch Jr., son of the founder, Fred Sr., sent an executive, Jimmie Webster, to Nashville to get Atkins interested in a similar deal before Gibson could sign him as well.

As it happened, Chet had been thinking about doing what Les had, courting an endorsement deal. This was only natural since he had transcended the normal rhythm guitar status of singing guitar players, who didn't generally attract hardcore guitarists to follow them in the music trade magazines that ran ads by the guitar companies. Atkins was a whole new party flavor. The fingerpicking guitarist Pat Kirtley, who grew up in Kentucky in the '50s craving Atkins's records, vouched for the fact that Chet "actively avoided being cast in the role of sideman. He wanted to be the out-front star, and he wanted it from an early age." And he was in dire need of a new guitar. That year, his

D'Angelico was damaged when the Carter Sisters came back to town to do an Opry show. Rehearsing with them, he put it on a stand and June Carter accidentally knocked it over, causing the neck to break off. June, he recalled, "cried like a baby and I was devastated. That guitar was my most cherished possession . . . and I don't think she ever got over feeling bad about it."

He had a local music doctor repair it, but the D'Angelico was never the same. He made do with it, mainly as an acoustic with clunky pickups and other acoustic ephemera, but the incessant hum from the wiring drove him crazy. Still, the attention of the man from Gretsch didn't seem like a godsend. As with many in the guitar-maker crowd, he knew Webster, who designed and played guitars himself, from his appearances for the company at local music stores. But when Chet had played Gretsches, he told Tony Bacon, "I never liked them," especially the built-in, low-energy pickups and "sustainability," what the geeks call continuous surge power.

> I had seen people play Gretsch guitars—a couple of my friends played their archtop acoustics. . . . But back then I wasn't interested in Gretsch. . . . I didn't like the design, but [Webster] kept after me, and finally he said why don't you design one that you would like? Next thing I knew I flew up to New York, went over to Brooklyn to the factory over there, and visited with Mr. Gretsch.

To come on board, Chet said he would need to be the chief designer of Atkins models and noted that they wouldn't be cheap facsimiles but guitars he himself would play. He would have the final word on every tiny detail. But because he had no experience in the legalities and royalty agreements delineated in these sorts of deals, he called a man who knew better than anyone about matters like that. The man was Les Paul. He then signed a deal, without legal representation, that gave him a four-cent royalty per each guitar sold, and then got down to designing his eponymous guitar line.

That was a team effort, though what Chet wanted, Chet got. Treble and bass strings were to be plugged into separate outputs, something some amateur guitarists didn't even know was possible. Some of the ideas floating around made it onto the first Atkins 6120 models, the single-cut, orange-finish hollow body, and the brown semi-solid-body 6121—delivering the kind of electric current he had believed sounded too thin on previous Fenders. But when he would get back home and play the models presented to him by Fred Gretsch, he was not happy. Webster, he would recall, "was always coming up with ideas, like the Gretsch tuning fork and the pad on the back, the mute and all that bullshit. I never liked it! He said, 'You got to give them something different all the time . . . they want new features.' And I guess he was right."

He also accepted the bright orange color of the 6120, though he thought it was "hideous." But he wouldn't give in on other quibbles, such as the hokey "western" motif with engraved images of cows, cowpokes, and happy trails. Decades later, he recalled these designs as "junk," and overall, "I wanted more of a sturdy guitar, that was more sustained, and Mr. Gretsch was not into that at that time. He was into strictly acoustic guitars. What's more, the 6121, while supposedly a solid body, wasn't. Rather, it was hollow inside too but looked like a solid, with, Chet said, "kind of pockets inside it." Accordingly, he said, "I hated the sound of the pickups, at first, because the magnets were so strong on the string, you pluck a string and there was no sustain there, especially on bass strings. I was tortured pretty good until Ray Butts (an inventor who added a built-in tape echo to a guitar amp) built that Filter'Tron pickup (that Gretsch implemented as a humbucker). And then they were much more fun."

No matter the bugaboos, much of Chet's prickliness was eased by seeing his signature stylishly engraved into the Gretsch pickguards. The relationship was solid, and Chet got what he needed from the 6120 when he took it into an October 2 late session at the Thomas studio, recording two songs with old confrere Hank Snow, the first a cover of Edward Madden and Percy Wenrich's 1911 ragtime number "Silver Bell," with the two guitar masters having a ball adjoining sprightly passages on Chet's Gretsch and Hank's steel guitar. The song would be officially billed as being performed by Hank Snow and Chet Atkins as a "guitar duet," as was the B-side, a cover of country-western and blues songwriter Billy Hill's "The Old Spinning Wheel." These new singles would go out late in the year, when the first stock of Chet Atkins 6120 Hollow Body guitars began to trickle into musical instrument stores. The Gretsch catalog featured screaming prose about CHET ATKINS ELECTRIC GUITARS BY GRETSCH. The Hollow Body 6120, a 15½-inch, choice curly maple—"mellow tone with brilliance when you want to!"—would sell for $385, as would the 13½-inch Solid Body 6120—"for ultra-fine tone projection and sustaining power, this is your Guitar!" Earning their pay, the copywriters hogtied the guitar to its namesake:

> Every Chet Atkins appearance, whether in person or on T.V. (you should see and hear his reception at the Grand Ole' Opry!) and every new album he cuts for RCA Victor, wins new admirers to swell the vast army of Chet Atkins fans.

In the wake of this publicity gift, turning Atkins into guitar hero, Steve Sholes was even more curdled that he didn't yet have the state-of-the-art studio in Nashville that he yearned to have Chet go to work in, which seemed odd indeed given that Chet was being marketed on the same level as RCA stars like Minnie Pearl, Hawkshaw Hawkins, and Hank Snow; on gigs around town and in the hinterlands, he was being billed almost regally as "Chet Atkins and the RCA Victor Troubadours." The problem, as always in this penny-pinching business, was having a new market properly funded, and even with Sholes coming around to the new studio idea, he still couldn't get the money allocated to build new digs. In the meantime, he did what he could with what he could get, conscripting an existing studio that he thought was a better workplace than Brown, Thomas, or Castle. And he fibbed a little to make it easier for his man in Nashville to get with the company's corporate vibe.

"Chet," he told him, "how would you like to take over the new RCA studio we're building? You know the business and the people and the songs. It would be the perfect deal for both of us."

Chet didn't know if it would affect his own recording, but it was an offer he couldn't refuse, putting him in charge of the details of all RCA sessions in Nashville, with an appropriately larger salary. The studio was in a drab, three-story brick building at 1525 McGavock Street just off Music Row, owned by the United Methodist Television, Radio and Film Commission. The ground floor, shared with a coffee shop, was built for radio evangelists' radio shows and public service ads for the church, but some pretty big names came there for their own purposes, one being the droll, crewcut comedian "Lonesome" George Gobel, who broadcast the NBC radio show that vaulted him to national TV stardom.

But the first time Chet saw the new place, he stopped in his tracks. The studio was just as crimped as the previous ones. Deep bass notes were swallowed up by low, curved ceilings, and its dead spots and lack of bounce off thick walls made recordings thin. Worse, the Methodists' staff engineer, Jeff Miller, crimped any loud sounds by using a limiter, and employed just a couple of microphones, which would make it impossible to record in stereo, as was becoming a fashionable option in the industry. Chet convinced Miller to lay off the limiter and, despite the hardships, made it all work.

Two of the first songs recorded were for his works. On November 17 he laid down "Set a Spell," a satirically silly old-time country gambol cowritten by Chet and Louis Innis, with adenoidal vocals by Red Kirk, though Chet's brief, clangy solo on the bridge defined it. The flip seemed like a throwaway, "Mister Sandman"—the cutesy plea to "bring me a dream," written by Pat Ballard—which had already been recorded by Vaughn Monroe and would be, in 1958, by the Chordettes, reaching the top of three different pop charts. Sholes saw it as mere fodder. but Chet's simple-sounding yet technically complex arrangement was so ridiculously smooth it left Steve's jaw hanging. Chet had come to use an EchoSonic amp after Ray Butts traveled from Illinois to Nashville just to tout the amp for him; the effect, created by a small, plug-in tape loop, was that of another inventive idea in multitracking: a second track playing back sounds a microsecond later, the same effect Chet could rig with a physical second track but with much less work—basically the touch of a control panel button. Combined with the studio track and added echo, it sounded like *three* guitars playing at once, in a swirl, with bent notes and a gush of tremolo, giving Sholes a tight little guitar cantata on "Mr. Sandman," a smooth concurrence as Chet spun through key changes from A to D to G then back to A on the closing note.

Steve immediately earmarked it as the B-side for "Set a Spell" for which was scheduled for release in early January, after the concurrent release of an album Chet was hurrying to complete: *A Session with Chet Atkins*, a country-pop/jazz bridgement that was no less than a classic leap. The album, Chet's third, was replete with covers of some rather geriatric standards—"Old Man River," "Red Wing," "The Birth of the Blues," "Alabama Jubilee" (a number-one hit for Red Foley in 1951), "Honeysuckle Rose," "(Back Home Again in) Indiana"—spiced by two "race music" favorites, Duke Ellington's "Caravan" and Ray Charles's "South." Another prime cut covered Peter De Rose and Billy Hill's "Have You Ever Been Lonely? (Have You Ever Been Blue?)" Chet also enlivened "Corrine, Corrina," one of the most played standards ever, here spinning off a 1935 version by Roy Newman and His Boys (on which guitarist Jim Boyd is said to have played the first electric guitar part on a record), and there was a new arrangement by Chet of the traditional fugue of ill-fated lovers, "Frankie and Johnnie," as the latter name was spelled on the record.

The tracks were impeccably chosen by Sholes, Chet, and Fred Rose and produced by Chet, and the added touches are superb, such as the use of a celeste, a glockenspiel-like piano that bounced playful pings into the mix. The crew included Homer and Jethro, pedal-steel guitarist Bud Isaacs, lap-steel guitarist Jerry Byrd, drummer Jim Carney, bassist Bob Moore, and fiddler Dale Potter. However, its release had to coincide with yet more tragedy to absorb. On November 30, just days before

A Session with Chet Atkins went on the market, Chet walked into the studio and saw Fred Rose lying on a couch, his body limp, face ashen. He insisted he was OK, but the next morning, Chet opened the paper and on the front page, it said Fred Rose had died overnight at fifty-six from a heart attack he had likely suffered while in the studio. He was buried in Mt. Olivet Cemetery, with Chet and hundreds of other industry notables mourning at his graveside. But the business went on. Fred's thirty-six-year-old son Wesley, a licensed accountant who wore a slicked mustache and greased-up hair, took over the reins at Acuff-Rose.

A much harder-edged profiteer, Rose *fils* would be no less effective or peripatetic, bringing to life the Country Music Association, becoming the first Nashville publisher to be on the board of ASCAP, and opening Acuff-Rose offices around the world. As his father's assistant, he had signed off on Chet Atkins as the prime lever of Nashville's growing hegemony and continued on that locus when *A Session* went into circulation, Chet's first LP on the twelve-inch, long-playing, 33⅓ format, ensuring a crystal-clear exhibition of guitar mastery blended with snappy, finger-snapping rhythm. On the back cover was the kind of "country" artwork Chet would have deleted from the 6121 as well as extensive liner notes by the "king of country deejays," WCKY's Nelson King, hailing Atkins for having "built a bridge . . . that spanned the gulf between country and pop music," and noting, "There's always a feeling of suspense waiting to see what surprise Chet will have ready . . . all the definition you need of the word 'artist.'" On "Birth of the Blues," he wrote, Chet played the chorus "so high the guitar strings seem to have changed to tiny, tinkling crystals." At Chet's urging, the backing musicians' names were also printed on the back cover, a nicety that, like producers' credits, was rarely employed by record labels for another decade.

The reviews were quite positive, and while it didn't crack the album charts, the reaction was strong enough for RCA to release it as two distinct EPs—and for retro-reviewers to consider it the quintessential formative Atkins album, an AllMusic notice calling it a "joyful, yet sophisticated and controlled compilation of mostly standard pop and jazz tunes all decked out country-style." The word of mouth alone pumped up sales and prompted an immediate run on Atkins Gretsch guitars—thousands sold each week. As Chet would later boast, out of character, "I think if [Fred Gretch] were alive he would tell you the most important thing he ever did was to sign me, because they started selling the hell out of guitars. . . . No one here in Nashville played their guitars until I went with them. That makes me sound like a braggadocio, I guess, but it's true."

There would also be a postscript. Chet would produce Jim Reeves's version of "Have You Ever Been Lonely" in 1961, the same year that Patsy Cline recorded hers, produced by Owen Bradley. Two decades later, RCA would electronically create a "duet" of the two tragic superstars, which made it to number one on the country chart. Clearly, anything Chet and Owen produced had happy returns.

11

THAT DO MAKE IT NICE

Arguably, the happiest return was a surprise that earned Chet his first chart hit. After the single release of "Set a Spell" early in 1955, disc jockeys began to get so many listener requests for "Mr. Sandman" that they turned over the record, precipitating the rise of the song to number thirteen on the country chart. In a chain reaction, Chet's duet with Hank Snow, "Silver Bell," which had been released first, with Hank's name first on the label, caught fire and ran to number fifteen. This double-play was welcome indeed for Sholes, who had been pining for any country top-liner besides Eddy Arnold, whose Sholes-produced sessions with Chet as session leader unveiled the number-one country hit "That Do Make It Nice," which stayed at the top for two weeks in 1955, and the *Wanderin' with Eddy Arnold* album, the country album of the year. Yet Eddy was by now only semi-country, hosting his own summer replacement TV show from 1953 to 1956, produced by Si Siman in Springfield. His sleepy baritone and generic themes had led RCA to position him mainly as a major pop act with such easygoing heavyweights as Perry Como, Eddie Fisher, and Dinah Shore. He rarely had country acts on, and indeed, the most "country" was Chet, a regular in the show's band in '56.

Not long before this, Chet would have been content to be on the same level as Jimmy Atkins. Now Chet had surpassed him, even as Jimmy continued doing quite well, recording in the mid-'50s with his band Jim Atkins and the Pinetoppers, covering old groaners like "I'm a Ding Dong Daddy (from Dumas)" and "Juke Joint Johnny" on the Coral label. He would write songs for the Four Recorders and, in 1958, cowrote with Johnny Cash "You're the Nearest Thing to Heaven," an early Cash recording at Sam Phillips's Sun Records. But for as long as Jimmy would live, *he* would be in his kid brother's shadow, and grateful for brotherly alms, such as Chet getting the Carter Sisters to record "Columbus, G-A." In fact, Chet tried for years to record an album with Jimmy, and in the fall of 1958 it would happen when Jimmy came in from New York and they cut *My Brother Sings*, with Jimmy's soft, fluent vocals perfectly meshing with Chet's laid-back guitar rhythms.

The LP would be pressed and packaged with the cover of both Atkins boys, Chet with a guitar and a natty, bespectacled Jimmy with his arm around Chet's shoulder. However, Steve Sholes believed it would disrupt Chet's by-then-unstoppable momentum as a solo act and nixed it, to Chet's dismay. Indeed, though the word was that the masters were destroyed, Chet somehow whisked the tapes away and would include four of the tracks on his 1959 *Mister Guitar* album, two of them being covers of Johnny Green's "Out of Nowhere" and Willie Jones's "Even Though." And, years later, in 2012, when an original copy of the unreleased Atkins brothers album was found, it fetched $8,100 on the record market.

Even back in 1955, as Atkins' agenda for such personal deviations was being played out, it sometimes was not on a linear plane with Sholes's, which is why they usually happened when Sholes was absent from Nashville. As far as Sholes knew, whatever Atkins was up to, RCA Nashville was in good hands. He would make his way to town perhaps once every other month to formally produce top RCA acts with Chet all but calling the shots; during those interregnums, they would knock off three sessions a day. When Sholes was gone, Chet, with no record company barracudas to deal with, went on with more personally involved work, including sessions for non-RCA artists who he believed had merit. These included the Louvin Brothers, Webb Pierce, Faron Young, and the Carlisles, the common thread usually being that these acts sang songs published by Acuff-Rose, a neat little trick that would earn him some side money.

He also had commitments for gigs in and around Nashville and even produced live spots for the *Ozark Jubilee* radio show back at KWTO, at Siman's request. Chet was a dervish, in constant motion, barely stopping to take a breath. And for Sholes, he was well worth the deviations, not only in the name of Nashville solidarity but because RCA desperately needed a game-changer in its country division. Other than Chet and the top-line acts like Arnold, Porter Wagoner, and Hank Snow, RCA was mired below the other major labels' country fodder. Pierce had three number-ones in 1955 for Decca, two of them, "In the Jailhouse Now" and "I Don't Care," consecutively spanning thirty-three straight weeks. June Carter's husband, Carl Smith, the same year they became parents of future country star Carlene Carter and a year before they divorced, hit number one at Columbia with "Loose Talk."

Chet put another high card in the game for RCA and needed no string of massive individual hits to boost his reputation. What's more, he could do his work as a shadow figure who could walk through Music Row with sometimes not a single person knowing who he was. But put a guitar in his hands and they seemed to know, since that was now an established image on his album covers and single record sleeves. Little wonder Sholes would have him record at least four albums a year, plus singles. Because wherever one shopped for music, there was that image again.

Over at the Opry, meanwhile, he continued his ambiguous relationship, knowing that his rise in popularity obviated any possibility that someone in a suit would hand him a pink slip. He was a constant presence within any band that mounted the stage there, all but fusing into the Louvin Brothers act after having wowed the roguish Alabama brothers and cousins of the Nashville songwriter John Loudermilk. Chet enjoyed them because they were absolutely unpredictable. Charlie and Ira Louvin, who played guitar and mandolin, and brilliantly, were among the most ethereally odd people in a town of very odd people, their music an amalgam of bluegrass, gospel, blues, and craziness. Their songs preached austere Baptist homilies warning of sin and immorality, sung in precise harmony, but Ira was a drunkard and womanizer who blew through four marriages and was shot four times by wife three after he tried to strangle her with a telephone cord; he somehow survived but—in another case of the "country curse"—he was wanted on a DUI charge when in 1965 a drunk driver plowed head-on into his car, killing him and his last wife.

Chet, who produced their first country hit, "The Get Acquainted Waltz," nearly walked out on the future Country Hall of Famers because "Ira was a little difficult to work with. . . . He had a terrible temper. He didn't like anything you did. He'd get a smirk on his face and say, 'Well, I guess that'll do if you can't find anything better.'" He soon did walk, leaving Los Angeles country producer Ken Nelson to take over the brooding brothers, with great success and raised eyebrows. Their 1959 album *Satan Is Real* had them posed in front of a depiction of the devil, tires burning like fire and brimstone, the most unsettling cover ever, until Lynyrd Skynyrd's fire-bathed cover for their last album, *Street Survivors*, previewing the plane crash. Chet's place onstage and on sessions with the Louvins at the Opry would be taken by one of his early, and permanent, acolytes, Paul Yandell, who consciously copied his style as best he could. He'd come to Nashville when he was still in high school and first encountered his idol when he got a shot on WSM's *Friday Night Frolics* talent show at the National Life Insurance Building, which housed the company that owned the Opry. As he recalled:

> As I was roaming up and down the hallway I saw Chet taking a smoking break. I went up to him and asked him for his autograph. He had just started playing Gretsch. I was sort of upset because of the change in his tone and sound going from his D-Angelico to Gretsch. I said to him, "Chet, I don't think that Gretsch sounds as good as your D'Angelico." Chet replied, "I like it." I didn't say anything else.

Given the terse, taciturn manner Atkins had perfected, those three words seemed to Yandell to mean "get lost," aimed at a kid who had the nerve to criticize his playing. But he was taken back when Chet signed his guitar. Then, about a year later, Yandell had an audition for none other than "Judge" George Hay, who had founded the show back in 1925 and still handpicked performers. Crusty as he was, when Yandell's turn came and he said he'd need to get his guitar from his car, the crusty old Judge told him he had no time to wait. And there was Chet Atkins again. "Chet was on a break, standing out in the hallway. He came up to me and said, 'You can borrow my guitar.' That scared the hell out of me. Chet [got] his amp, a little Fender Deluxe, and brought it out with his guitar. It was a 6121 [with] a solid body. He plugged it all in, handed it to me and walked away." Yandell didn't hear back from Hay. But, he said, "I really didn't care anymore because I got to play Chet Atkins' guitar! Chet didn't remember that day but it was the greatest thing that ever happened to me." Until he died in 2011, Yandell kept the autograph Chet signed for him that day, in green ink.

As it happened, after Chet bowed out on the Louvin Brothers, the oddball siblings were seeking another guitarist. When they came to Yandell's hometown in Kentucky, a local disc jockey recommended Paul, who was later given an audition by the Louvins backstage at the Opry. Just twenty, the diminutive, bespectacled farm boy drove to Nashville and won the audition playing a Louvin song just as he'd heard Chet do it. A week later, he was playing on the stage on a night when Chet was also featured. There was something almost spooky about Atkins's presence, and Yandell still considered him a paragon, even trading his guitar at a music shop for a used 6120 of his own. He came back to Nashville, moved in with Ira Louvin when the latter's wife left him, and then shared an apartment with another young guitarist, Odell Martin.

Yandell recalled the rituals of emulating the Atkins style: "We'd sit up until three o'clock in the morning, trying to figure out what Chet was doing . . . when Chet started playing that solid top 6120 with the prototype Filter-Tron pickups, I had never seen anything like that before. Nobody had. Chet was light years ahead of everybody." He also believed Nashville's stable of guitarists were there on a sort of pilgrimage to Chet. "There were some fabulous guitar guys around town. All the great stars were young and in their prime. Hank Garland was playing the Opry with different artists as was Grady Martin. But Chet was on every Friday and Saturday night, and when he was, everyone who ever held a six-string would be at the foot of the stage or watching from the wings." Indeed, Paul was brazen enough to take his 6120 to Chet during a break and point out some problems he was having with it. Expecting a dismissive response, he was floored when Chet told him to come over to his home the next day so he could check it out.

Just like Chet, Yandell would himself spend an inordinate amount of time tinkering with his Gretsch, even having an updated 6120 sent to him when he was in the army a few years later. As impressive as Yandell would be—enough for Chet to subsequently hire him for sessions and as a backup on concert tours—Paul claimed he never quite got the hang of playing like Chet. "I would watch his hands," he said. "Seventy-five percent of it was in his hands. He used his hands and the ends of his fingers together when he picked the strings. He used a high action which let him get clear notes and sustain. Chet had really strong hands and his right hand was something else, as fast as he wanted it to be. I used to stand by him to try to figure out what he did . . . but I never did."

For Chet, it was the product of practice and invention that never took a day off. His self-study was so consuming that he had only one other interest that seemed to animate him. Nashville was being built and rebuilt. Entrepreneurs, investors, storefront hunters, and industry people were looking for property. And music publisher Jack Comer told Chet he should buy some of that potentially lucrative property on Sixteenth Street. Knowing nothing about real estate, he hedged. But he soon caught the bug. Another music publisher, Rick Sanjek, who became a BMI vice president in the early 1970s, worked with Willie Nelson, and recently authored the trenchant and highly relevant *American Popular Music and Its Business in the Digital Age*, stated:

> [Investments made by Chet] went on for years. He knew every inch of Music Row, and owned more than a few. In the '50s they were renovating all the old houses from the Black Bottom era and turning them into these duplexes and storefronts, and Chet and Jack Comer were snapping them up.
>
> When I got to town, he and Ray Stevens had gone in on some of them. They resold some land on 18th Street that became a big mini-market. Chet even bought some alleys *between* houses around 16th and 17th—it was so cheap and buyers wanted anything they could fit something into. Years later, Chet had an office down there for himself that he almost never went to, but the value increased so much he sold that off too. [*Laughs.*] I think people wanted to partner with him because he was like the magic man: everything he touched turned to gold.

Which of course is literally why Steve Sholes turned to Chet Atkins when RCA needed to make its move. The only hedge was holding off on a piece of property of its own, one that could house a state-of-the-art studio. It seemed the tight-fisted bosses up in New York needed one big reason to justify it. And when the new year of 1956 began, the reason arrived in Nashville, in a pair of pink britches.

12

ELVIS IS IN THE BUILDING

In November 1955, when Elvis Presley took a giant step and signed with RCA, it was both an artistic decision and a financial one, created by two of music's most memorable and off-the-wall characters—Sun Records' boss Sam Phillips and Elvis's beyond-odd manager/Svengali, the rapacious hustler who called himself "Colonel" Tom Parker, though he was neither a colonel nor named Tom Parker, a moniker he assumed to hide his status as an illegal immigrant from the Netherlands. Parker made Elvis a pawn as he rose to fame recording rockabilly blues at Phillips's Memphis studio, his first hit covering Arthur Crudup's "That's All Right"—originally released in 1949 by Crudup, the song had music's first guitar-solo break, though in an old story, Crudup was robbed blind of royalties and by the mid-'50s was working as a moonshiner.

But neither Elvis nor Carl "Blue Suede Shoes" Perkins, a criminally underrated fingerpicker who was the first rockabilly singer on the R&B charts, made enough for Phillips, who was eager to sell off his assets before rockabilly lost its glam. Offering Elvis around, he sold Elvis's Sun Records contract to RCA for a then-industry record $40,000, of which $35,000 went into Parker's pocket, in addition to another $5,000 to license Presley's incipient movie merchandising rights. For Steve Sholes, it was a gift that kept giving, the deal stipulating that Elvis would commit to recording as often as he could in Nashville—not incidentally, with Chet Atkins in the room, basically calling the shots for Sholes, the nominal producer. It was a challenge for both of them, having never been under such pressure to find new ground for any other performer.

As it was, 1955 was a typically busy year for Chet. He released four Chet Atkins and His Guitar–bylined singles—one was a cover of Freddy Morgan and Norman Malkin's "Hey, Mr. Banjo" as "Hey, Mr. Guitar," with the lyrics sung by the Anita Kerr Singers. The far more interesting B-side was an instrumental of one of the first releases of "Unchained Melody," Alex North and Hy Zaret's Oscar-nominated theme song from the B-movie *Unchained.* And while the most famous version is Phil Spector's literally unchained production with the Righteous Brothers' Bobby Hatfield, Chet's stripped-down take, with just his lead guitar and a backing rhythm guitar, is no less emotionally powerful as an instrumental, the almost fleeting notes seeming to tear up when leaving the guitar. There was also his Christmas record, "Christmas Carols" / "Jingle Bells," the rerelease of *Stringin' Along*, and his next album, *Chet Atkins in Three Dimensions*, showing off his non-country chops, conceptualized as tributes to evergreens, such as his rearranged "Londonderry Air," "Tiptoe Through the Tulips with Me," and the 1879 "Dark Eyes (Russian Song)"; pop hits like "Tenderly," Harold Arlen and Johnny Mercer's "Blues in the Night," and "Arkansas Traveler"; and classical compositions in two minutes or less, like "Johann Sebastian Bach Medley" and "Intermezzo."

Enormously intricate yet deceptively simple on the surface, Chet had recorded too many songs for one album, and RCA released them in three separate EP volumes. Another EP, *Pickin' the Hits*, featured more pop covers: "Tweedle Dee," "(The Wallflower) Dance with Me," "Cherry Pink and Apple Blossom White," and "Darling, Je Vous Aime Beaucoup." Despite none of the singles charting, though, Atkins's stock kept rising, and he was all but living on McGavock Street, producing songs for RCA like Porter Wagoner's "Uncle Pen" and non-RCA acts like Webb Pierce ("There Stands the Glass," "Walkin' the Dog"); Faron Young ("Goin' Steady," "If You Ain't Lovin'"); the hostess of New York's first country TV series Rosalie Allen ("Guitar Polka"); and his old confereres Johnnie & Jack ("South in New Orleans") and Kitty Wells

("Release Me," "Repenting"). But when the new year came around, he braced for what would be the most momentous session of his life.

That of course was Elvis being Nashville-ized. It became a plan when he was recording at Sun in early November 1955—Sam Phillips told him he'd been sold to RCA and to prepare for sessions there. When Elvis made his way to Nashville for his first session there, on January 10, 1956, he came in with his band, led by fingerpicking guitar man Scotty Moore, with bassist Bill Black and drummer D. J. Fontana. They would be met on the studio floor by Chet and Floyd Cramer, sitting at a Steinway piano. Elvis and his boys naturally knew of Atkins but had no idea how their internal chemistry with Elvis might be affected. Sholes in fact walked a thin line, wanting to re-create the energy and live feel of Elvis's early recordings but with a more controlled undertow and spit and polish.

Chet had briefly met up with Elvis the day before, but the real work went down on the tenth, beginning at two o'clock and lasting six hours, the musicians' union limit for a session. They would need every minute of it. Elvis's band, all terrific musicians, were accustomed to virtually winging it on recordings, playing by feel, letting Elvis's mood flow through with minimal aid. And Chet could certainly ease his way into musicians' trust; whenever he was asked if he knew how to read music, he would jive, "I do, but not enough to hurt my playing." His lead sheets, which replaced complex chords with simple numbers, were meant to keep things as simple as possible for session cats—and were modeled after an even more simplified system used for vocal arrangements by the Jordanaires, Elvis's backing group, who had been members of the Grand Ole Opry since 1949. Yet Moore and company were still flummoxed by it. Scotty, a classic noodler who paid scant attention to music sheets, bitched that the system was too "regimented," with engineer Bob Farris "call[ing] out everything by a tape number. We would sit around at Sun, eat hamburgers and then somebody would say, 'Let's try something,'" an MO definitely *not* the Nashville, i.e., Atkins way.

Chet and Farris had already resorted to sonic workarounds for the Methodist studio's curved ceiling, which smothered deep bass notes on the guitars. Soundproof baffles were erected to separate instruments and prevent bleeding. They also had erected an echo chamber by placing a speaker at the end of a long hallway, attached by a long cable to a microphone on the studio floor. The sound waves would arrive at the speakers with a slight time delay. And that also threw off Elvis's band. Stopping and starting, they got on Atkins's nerves, something Moore would confirm in future interviews, saying with exasperation that Chet had continually repeated "keep doing what you're doing," although Moore couldn't detect any meaningful difference each time.

Elvis had his own gripes. His compulsive need to do things *his* way included having the Jordanaires on recording sessions. Sholes, however, had hired only one of them, Gordon Stoker, along with Ben and Brock Speer of Nashville's gospel-singing Speer Family group. Elvis grumbled that all the Jordanaires would be required at all future sessions. He also insisted he be allowed to play his acoustic guitar, which without amplification would fade into the mix. And during the rehearsals, he would jerk his head, making it impossible for the microphone in the studio to catch every note. Atkins tried to gently remind him to keep his head still, but round and round it went, and Farris, doing what Sun Records' engineers had, taped an *X* in front of the microphone so Elvis could see it under his feet and keep still. When Elvis still couldn't keep still, Farris arrayed the entire studio with mikes, a time-consuming procedure.

The first song to be cut, "I Got a Woman," didn't have an acoustic guitar line and thus had Atkins in the booth alongside Sholes and Farris, both of whom had to elbow their way past some of Elvis's proto-edition of the clubby "Memphis Mafia," which unlike the later editions were mainly a couple of Presley cousins and former school chums. The first six takes of the song were rough and aborted. On the sixth, after a minute and thirty-two seconds, Sholes also said "cut!" On take eight—which by today's standards is barely getting started, but then actually long for an Atkins session—"I Got a Woman" made it through. Then came the song everyone had really come there to record—"Heartbreak Hotel."

Cowritten by Nashville songwriters Mae Axton and Tommy Durden, the song was based on a newspaper story of a man's suicide in a seedy Miami hotel, and him leaving a suicide note about "walking a lonely street." Axton played a demo of it for Elvis and he insisted on recording it, and being listed, per Parker's directive, as a faux cowriter, resulting in higher royalties for Elvis and the Colonel. He had first performed "Heartbreak Hotel" during a live show in December, while on tour, on the *Louisiana Hayride*. Now, Atkins was on the floor with his Solid Body Gretsch (on some other tracks he used his Del Vecchio Dinâmico wooden resonator acoustic), playing rhythm. Elvis at first seemed less than eager to embrace the outsider. He and his band gathered in a tight group around the microphone, leaving Atkins separate, an odd man out. Cramer sat at his Steinway at the front end of the studio, just inside the door. However, once the tape was running, Atkins and Cramer supplied a depth and subtlety that cemented the gritty, presuicidal ramblings of the song's heartbroken agonist, Chet playing as if telepathically, focusing—and bettering—Moore's electric leads and Black's rumbling bass, Chet's wrapped thumb firmly on his bass strings.

It was a profound layering of sound, beyond what Elvis had heard before, and Sholes knew as it unfolded that he had misjudged the song as too depressing when he first heard it, not expecting it to be sautéed in sensuality along with its obvious grimness—the effect being to make one wonder if there would be a last affair of the flesh at that lonely hotel. Elvis's cold open—"Well since my baby left me, well I've found a new place to dwell"—comes with metronomic *bah-bom* squeals from Moore's guitar. Then a rise in emotion comes in tandem with the mordant bass stream of Atkins and Black, and Cramer's piano canoodling. The middle-eight bridge—with a tingly solo by Moore followed by another solo by Cramer—has the feel of a desolate piano bar, or is perhaps one in the man's tortured head.

Though the chords of this song are pedestrian—it runs a C chord almost all the way through—one can almost taste it when Elvis does the repetitions of his nearly indecipherable blues mumbling: "They'll be so lonely baby, they'll be so lonely, they're so lonely they could die," adding the "baby" to the lyric on impulse, painting it more personally. The same refrain ends the song on a two-note stop. It all came together on take seven, which runs only 2:08, but with every second it sounds all too authentic, with a brooding quality that would serve Elvis well whatever song he would sing, similar to Chet Atkins's own multidimensional guitar licks. It had taken two hours to get it right, but in that room, history had been made. Chet thought so too. "He had Lamar with him, a big, fat boy, and Lamar would say, 'That's fantastic, Elvis. That'll see 3 million. Play that sumbitch again,'" he recalled years later. "Lamar finally got up to saying, 'That'll see 7 million,' and I thought, yeah, he's probably right."

Not everyone in the room agreed. Sam Phillips, who observed the session, pronounced "Heartbreak Hotel" a "morbid mess." Worse, sessions on the following two days, intended to provide filler for Elvis's first album, produced only two usable songs, "I'm Counting on You" and "I Was the One." Sholes then went back to his bosses far from confident he had overseen with Chet one of the greatest songs of all time, and terrified that all that loot RCA had thrown at Elvis and the Colonel would be the price of his own firing from the company. Chet had his own misgivings: he might have betrayed country music by contributing to a record that moved country too far "uptown" for it to survive—a fear confirmed by the record selling three hundred thousand copies in its first three weeks and surging to number one on the singles chart for eight weeks, going to number one on the country chart and number three on the R&B chart. It was the first of a record 149 hit singles, 30 going to number one and 54 going gold or platinum, in addition to 70 albums, 9 hitting number one (not including numerous compilations and numerous specialty, live, and posthumous releases that continue to this day). As with Atkins, sales of Presley's records are subject to divergent methods of counting, but Guinness World Records says his total sales are something like one *billion* units sold, by far the most of all time.

"Heartbreak Hotel," which has tallied ten million copies (even when rereleased in 1996 on the *Elvis '56* retro album, it hit number forty-five), indeed made Elvis not just a country star but a White R&B and rock star, though for many R&B purists, his R&B cred was suspect. As it should have been. As much as Elvis loved "race music," neither he nor any other White act that has ever sung the blues, especially in the '50s, came close to Black blues singers, or their rock counterparts like Little Richard and Bo Diddley; in a then-condensed, White man's world, anyone could get onto the R&B lists by selling well in the Black market, as Elvis did. But this became a thorn after Elvis returned to Nashville on April 14 to record his follow-up to the hits he had recently recorded in Hollywood: "Loving You," "Love Me Tender," "(Let Me Be Your) Teddy Bear," "Treat Me Nice," and "Jailhouse Rock." He came specifically to record the romantic blues ballad "I Want You, I Need You, I Love You," with Chet again on rhythm guitar backing Scotty Moore. They went through seventeen arduous takes in three hours, none of which suited Sholes. Chet agreed, believing that Elvis was less gung-ho than on "Heartbreak Hotel." All they could do was to hunker down with Bob Farris, scour the takes for usable bits and pieces, and splice parts of takes fourteen and seventeen. They did it so well that no one else at RCA knew it wasn't a complete track, and it was released on May 4.

Not only had Sholes and Atkins saved the song, it soared to number one pop, number one country, and number three R&B over the summer, giving Presley his second gold record and three hits concurrently in the top twenty; and its B-side, the Arthur Crudup "My Baby," ran to number thirty-one pop and number thirteen country. Yet lost in history now is that those R&B rankings carried forth Chet's initial nervousness about Elvis taking country out of its lane, which also applied to his next songs, "Hound Dog" and "Don't Be Cruel," recorded in RCA's New York studio, sans Atkins, and released as a two-sided single, "Dog" to become Elvis's biggest-selling record at that time, though today "Hound Dog" ranks seventeenth, well below "It's Now or Never," "Jailhouse Rock," and "Are You Lonesome Tonight?," which are all up in the twenty-million range. However, when Jerry Leiber—who with his famous songwriting partner Mike Stoller cowrote and produced the original, delightfully crude "Hound Dog" by gravel-throated Big Mama Thornton—heard the Elvis cover, he heard the opposite, dissing it as "a combination of country and skiffle. It's not black. He sounds like Hank Snow."

Except neither Hank Snow nor any other country singer ever unleashed the backlash Elvis took as a White man appropriating Black musicians' "acceptable" crudity—witness Big Joe Turner's "Sixty Minute Man," an even more freewheeling sexual metaphor. Ironically, Elvis happened to be a prude himself, who replaced Thornton's rawness with anodyne like "You ain't never caught a rabbit and you ain't no friend of mine," not that it appeased pandering politicians calling for "Hound Dog" to be banned. Perry Como's reaction was simpler—he said it made him "vomit a little." Caught in between all this now risible controversy was Chet Atkins in Nashville, trying to find the public's pulse without losing country music's pulse. As country music historian Bill C. Malone wrote in his valuable book *Don't Get Above Your Raisin': Country Music and the Southern Working Class*, "traditionalists resented the hedonism and sexuality of rockabilly" while "the music compromise [was] forged by Nashville's record producers to deal with the youthful music upheaval."

Atkins and Sholes had skillfully walked Elvis down the middle lane, making him viable as more than a curiosity, those pink britches soon traded in for hip suits or leathery hip-huggers. Whether rock, country, soul, or a whole lot of shlock—RCA shamelessly billed him as "The Nation's Only Atomic Powered Singer"—he was all over the media, on the big and small screen, making headlines when cameras avoided those swinging hips on an Ed Sullivan appearance. And he knew where the bread was buttered. Even being thousands of miles from Nashville most all the time, Nashville would carry him back. His next gig there was in June 1958 for a session including Chet and Floyd Cramer, at which he recorded "I Need Your Love Tonight," "A Big Hunk O' Love," "Ain't That Loving You Baby," a cover of Hank Snow's "(Now and Then There's) a Fool Such as I," and "I Got Stung." He would record around 250 songs in Nashville, though the next ones would have to wait three years while he served his army hitch, and by the time he got back, Chet Atkins would be so singularly entrenched that he could actually turn down the biggest musical constellation in the world without a second thought.

13

OH, LONESOME ME

RCA had no choice after "Heartbreak Hotel" but to go bigger in Nashville, finally moving ahead with the longed-for studio that would be on a par with Owen Bradley's Quonset Hut—though the giant label pulling in millions each year still cheaped out, sinking no money into the studio's construction or property ownership but rather simply renting it and collecting fees from artists. And there was no dearth of businessmen who made offers to finance the construction. The label gave Chet the power to choose who would build it, and late in 1956 he signed off on local businessman Dan Maddox, whose bid was about $40,000. In truth, RCA could have bought the property for that forty grand. Instead, still hedging on Nashville's potential, it entered into a twenty-year lease with Maddox. The location was chosen five hundred yards south of the Hut, on the corner of 17th Avenue South and Hawkins Street, later renamed Music Square West and then 1611 Roy Acuff Place.

As the building began to go up, Chet met with RCA's chief audio engineer, Bill Miltenburg, to draw out the plans for the studio on a dinner napkin. But he would have to wait for his new star chamber to be built. In the interim, his life was ever more hectic. With cause. Every day, it seemed, he was having more to do with rewriting the American songbook, which country music had entered long before but had only now grown up and found a place in the pop pecking order. The first number-one putatively "rock" song, in fact, would be recorded by a White, country-friendly act, the rockabilly Bill Haley and His Comets, who in 1955 recorded "Rock Around the Clock," a song lifted from Hank Williams's 1947 "Move It On Over" and that had a lot of Chet Atkins-style hoppin' and boppin' electric vibratos running through it.

That song and numerous copycats can be traced to the "Nashville Sound," the indelible phrase that Bill Monroe attributed to Tommy Hill, an engineer for the small Nashville label Starday Records in a 1961 interview. By 1957, when Patsy Cline's ballad "Walkin' After Midnight"—coproduced at the Hut by Owen Bradley for Decca —had captivated multi-markets, the blues-based country conjunction was becoming rock solid. A good decade before that, though, the ingredients in the country beaker were identifiable; as early as 1947, the entire cast of the Grand Ole Opry, led by Ernest Tubb, had performed at a sold-out Carnegie Hall concert. As well, the Sons of the Pioneers became the first western band to play Las Vegas. Kitty Wells recorded "It Wasn't God Who Made Honky Tonk Angels," a Southern-fried blow for women's liberation that opened the gate for "mean girl" country singers like Wanda Jackson and, in the '60s, for Loretta Lynn's daring "The Pill." But a different breed, led by Gene Vincent and Eddie Cochran, was in the late '50s spreading rockabilly-proto-punk with landmarks like "Be-Bop-a-Lula" and "Twenty Flight Rock"—the latter being what Paul McCartney would sing for John Lennon to get into John's first band. Rockabilly began in the South but now was a staple in Los Angeles, where Ken Nelson was the West Coast answer to Chet Atkins.

Chet meanwhile kept making strides with compelling instrumental coatings to the country beat. In November 1956 he recorded a new song at the Methodist studio he had written called "Trambone," a portmanteau for a song that actually had no trombone but sounded like it did, due to his sliding, low-string glissandos in a chugging, rockish glean. Musicologist Mark Reinhart identifies the "Trambone" chord progression as C–A minor–F–G—known to music mavens as "the '50s progression" of rock. Backed by the Atkins and Boudleaux Bryant "Blue Echo," the song didn't hit the charts but clearly did catch the ears of country fans and underground rockers, the latter most consequently across the pond, and specifically McCartney, whose early fascination with rockabilly and Atkins's influence was like cotton candy for British rockers. In his 1998 autobiography, McCartney mentioned hearing the sound from a group called the Remo Four, who he wrote "did a lot of Chet Atkins stuff, with clever guitar picking." Recalling a key Beatles milestone, Paul would recall that

> "Michelle" was a tune that I'd written in Chet Atkins' finger-pickin' style. There is a song he did called "Trambone" with a repetitive top line, and he played a bassline whilst playing a melody. This was an innovation for us; even though classical guitarists had played it, no rock 'n' roll guitarists had played it. The first person we knew to use finger-pickin' technique was Chet Atkins, and Colin Manley, one of the guys in the Remo Four in Liverpool. Later, John learned how to [fingerpick] folk-style from Donovan or Gypsy Dave, which he used on "Julia." I never learned it. But based on Atkins's "Trambone," I wanted to write something with a melody and a bass line on it, so I did.

In a roundabout irony, Chet would cover "Michelle" in 1965 on his hit Beatles tribute album *Chet Atkins Picks On the Beatles*, but "Trambone" was not generally noticed; it took decades before it and "Blue Echo" got onto an album, as bonus tracks on the 2006 CD rerelease of Chet's 1957 LP *Finger-Style Guitar*. Yet it opened the crate on what Atkins could do above and beyond the necessities of his mainline country repertoire, which was still clearly defined by his other singles that year, Harry Ruby's "Cecilia" / "The Lady Loves" and two more guitar duets with Hank Snow, covers of Bob Wills's "New Spanish Two-Step" and Clarence Snow's "Reminiscing." Those didn't make the charts either, yet people were listening—his early 1957 single "The Poor People of Paris (Jeans's Song)," a French stroll song sung melodramatically by Edith Piaf on Ed Sullivan's show and then covered as a sweeping instrumental by the Les Baxter orchestra, was one of the year's biggest songs and a far cry from Chet's back-porch simplicity, which took it to number fifty-two on the pop chart.

More significantly, the long strides taken by country music were altering the caste system in Nashville, to the benefit of both Chet and Sholes. Over the summer of 1956, Chet was moved upstairs, into the position of vice president of the pop music division and head of Nashville operations. Steve would still oversee the division from his New York office, but the day-to-day affairs of RCA Nashville would be solely in Atkins's hands. He had the authority to sign new acts or refer them to other labels, and approve the songs they would perform, choosing whether to be the producer or a session player, or take a pass. All he needed to do was keep the bottom line moving up, a sword he didn't really need hanging over his head but accepted in the line of duty, not to mention the slice of publishing rights he received from Acuff-Rose.

Sholes also stopped taking production credit on Atkins records after "Mister Sandman." He would roll out a new single and album of his own every four months or so, and a blur of records bearing his stamp at any time. In '56, following the Hank Snow duets, he recorded with another RCA act from Canada, sixteen-year-old Sholes protégé Myrna Lorrie, who would in the future be called "the first lady of Canadian country music," and then jammed two of his songs on one side of an EP with Lorrie, "Tricky" and "Peanut Vendor," under the name of "The Rhythm Rockers Featuring Chet Atkins." He had that wide a slack now, and in this new phase came the opening of the new RCA studio that would become the seat of his empire.

For Chet, it wasn't a matter of going too far but of whether he needed to go further, technically. Interviewed in the *Tennessean* in February 1957 for a profile titled "Lucky Chet Atkins Has a Secret!," the "mighty Chet," as the writer, Bill Maples, called him, was depicted as "a real shy guy," but one with a mission. "He drives an unspectacular 1955 car, and still recalls the lean days of his youth," wrote Maples, but the big "secret" was something that made Chet seem like a slightly daft lab professor. Said Chet: "Bob Farris and I have invented a gadget that'll baffle the science world. I've got a bass fiddle player with me, but you can't see him," meaning another gizmo for his endlessly modernized guitar.

At the same time, he went into his great-is-never-enough mode. "I have a horror of becoming a has-been guitar player. I go fishing once in a while, but not often, because I'm afraid I'll get to liking it too much and stop practicing on the guitar." He went on, "I want to become progressively better. I want to make the pinnacle at 65. People think I'm stuck up, and it's usually because I'm scared to death. Depression children are different, I think." Asked if he considered himself a success, he barked, "Heck, no! I realize that I'm not as hungry as I used to be, and I make a comfortable living. But I think that when you feel that you're a success, you're on the downgrade."

Yet, much on the upgrade, the new studio, and sanctuary, opened on October 29, 1957, with no bells or whistles or ribbon-cutting ceremony. Only hours after a McGavock session, Chet surveyed the RCA Victor Studio (which would resonate in history, confusingly, as Studio B seven years later, when the accompanying shop newly rented by RCA was called Studio A). The new digs were built to accommodate the overflow of sessions and would earn the moniker "The Home of 1,000 Hits," which probably isn't too far off. Still, this wasn't a hub in the strict sense. The staff consisted of Chet Atkins; his assistant, Juanita Jones; Bob Farris, the house engineer; and an outside hire to field calls from people trying to rent studio time. Atkins, who would need to sign off on each one, had an office in the bowels of the building that he rarely had the time to use outside of publicity photos.

The studio was completed for $37,515, Dan Maddox bringing it in under budget, whereupon the twenty-year RCA lease began. There was still much refining to do. It was plenty big, 40.5 by 26.5 feet, but had thin walls that provided no cushion for bass notes, though it did make some crackling high guitar lines seem to peel the paint off the walls. The thing Chet had wanted most, an echo chamber, was built on a substory just above the studio. All of this is still preserved as it was, as a tourist attraction, with old folding chairs and instrument stands with faint RCA circles on them strewn about. Floyd Cramer's old Steinway piano sits against one wall, a vibraphone nearby, a beat-up drum kit against another wall, amps strewn on the floor. And one can almost see the apparition of Chet Atkins moving in the shadows with his guitar, doing wondrous things with what were originally four tracks—state of the art at the time. Part of the lore was that Atkins always encouraged artists to offer their own ideas, one of which was Roy Orbison stuffing coats, tablecloths, whatever he could find, on a coat rack right behind him when he sang those mournful songs to keep springy echoes from bouncing off the walls and floor.

The first song Chet worked on at the new studio was on December 3, delivering to the label another sky-high hit with a performer it had all but forgotten, the beefy balladeer Don Gibson. RCA had gotten a top-ten country hit from him, "Sweet Dreams," in 1955 and then left him akimbo when he couldn't follow up on it. But Chet dug his laid-back burr and prevailed on Sholes to give him another try. Gibson had written two songs, "Oh, Lonesome Me" and "I Can't Stop Loving You," and he had sent Chet a demo of the former that employed a heavy bass drum riff. That was new for him, and he produced the tune—its title one that he may have thought applied to his own lonesome self—with it as a heartbeat-like thumping backbeat. Playing on the session, he added a ticklish electric guitar line on the bridge that kept a finger-popping tempo, and used the Jordanaires as backing singers. Gibson's lead vocal had him drawing out vowels into an almost painful yowl, famously singing the title as "*Ohhhh lonesome meee.*"

Paul Yandell, who by then had returned from army duty and started touring, backing Kitty Wells and Johnnie Wright, heard about Atkins-led sessions from the musicians who had a front-row seat at them—rumors of Chet's perfectionism that would be confirmed when Paul himself became one of the A-Team brigade. He was stunned by the complexities that Chet got them to play without ever losing the beat and tempo of essentially simple songs. And he was struck by Chet always starting with the guitar players strumming alone. No matter if the guitars would be recessed in the mix, they always led off sessions, setting the mood. Remarkably, Chet could play up-tempo with all downstrokes with his thumbpick, with which he played the fast notes in perfect time; the finger-played notes would even sound different from the picked ones. And he often would use Velma Smith, a terrific rhythm guitarist, for acoustic intros. Detail. It was all in the detail.

For "I Can't Stop Loving You," a pleading declaration of love, Chet played delicate flamenco-like accents. When a single with both songs hit the market early in '58, Gibson and Atkins would have themselves a two-sided hit. "Lonesome" topped the country chart for eight weeks and hit number seven on the pop list, while "Can't Stop" made it to number seven country and has been covered by around seven hundred singers—the most known of course being Ray Charles, who took it to number one and won a Grammy for it in 1963 as the best R&B song, with the industry pooh-bahs caught off-guard by a Black man's seamless entrée into country. Gibson's record propelled him to a career extension, striding on one more avenue that Chet Atkins had laid down in Nashville. And Chet would keep doing the same for as long as he could, even as his new responsibilities made him have to pinch every penny he could for Steve Sholes. That was the kind of thing that tore him up inside, and it would go on doing so for another two very long decades.

Without pause, he recorded at the new studio again only a day later, for his own catalog. The session he produced and played on was filled out by Floyd Cramer, Bob Moore, and Buddy Harman, and they led off with a cover of Irving Berlin's "You're Just in Love," from the Broadway show *Call Me Madam*. The song, a tricky one indeed, matched two separate melodies, which Chet knocked off somehow without using multitracking, just his quick fingers. Mark Knopfler, who like other British guitar giants came upon Atkins's records around this time, said years later, when he could record with him, that until then he believed only multiple tracks could have created those sorts of complex melodies. Atkins was so proud of it that he would reel at the simple conclusion that he always multitracked, which was logical once that technology became standard, partly because of Chet's experimentation. During their time together, Knopfler said, "Some folk worthy, I can't remember his name . . . who everybody thinks is amazing, said something about how Chet had obviously multitracked all this stuff. And that's the only time I've ever known Chet be upset. And he actually wrote in to this particular publication . . . and said there was no double tracking."

Amazingly, all that in-studio modernism began when the sclerotic Dwight Eisenhower was president and White pablum like Pat Boone songs and *Leave It to Beaver* on TV were Americana. In a still-stunted but itchy Nashville, "You're Just in Love" would open Chet's next album, titled *Chet Atkins at Home*, which was anything but Cleaver homestyle, incorporating a wide array of jazzy musicals (Duke Ellington's "Sophisticated Lady," Ernesto Lecuona's "Jungle Drums" and "Say Si-Si") and other highly *un*-country selections such as Friedrich von Flotow's main aria, "M'appari," from the German opera *Martha*; "Cielito Lindo," retitled "Ay Ay Ay"; Billy Hill's 1936 pop song "In the Chapel in the Moonlight"; Harry Warren's dancy 1928 Tin Pan Alley favorite "Nagasaki"; and one original Atkins song, "Yankee Doodle Dixie," cribbed from "Yankee Doodle Dandy."

However, probably not to the delight of his bosses, one particular non-RCA act became synonymous with Chet and, with his guidance, eased—oozed, really—country's entrance into mainstream rock 'n' roll. It happened because Chet Atkins's preeminence was such that people who barely knew him correctly perceived him as the ultimate transom to success. One of those people was named Ike Everly, a coal miner and struggling fingerpicking country singer from the Kentucky hills. He and his wife, Margaret, sang together, living like tumbleweeds for years, moving from one small country radio station to another in the Midwest, and back in Kentucky, their radio spots expanded to include their two string-bean teenage sons, who played guitars and sang perfect high harmonies, their nasal twang mixed with bluesmanship. Don, a superior acoustic guitar player, sang the main keys, a few octaves lower than Phil's near falsetto while he played almost as well on his guitar, their voices and strumming so tightly knitted that no one could tell who sang and who played what.

As kids, they had achieved a modicum of fame billed as Little Donnie and Baby Boy Phil, and when they reached teen-hood, Ike saw an opening when Chet Atkins played a show in Knoxville over the summer of 1954. Ike, whom Chet had met on the circuit but probably had forgotten, took his sons to the concert and afterward boldly approached Chet and began bragging on his sons, who were exalted Atkins fans and, though star crossed, promptly played some riffs on their guitars. As Atkins remembered one of probably hundreds of similar fleeting moments, "I can still see them lookin' up at me through the fence." Ike also made sure Chet knew that "they're writin' some good songs, too."

Not brushing them off, Chet told Ike to bring them to Nashville, where he could better evaluate them. As Don Everly would remember, "Chet, bless his heart, gave us his home phone number, which was like the key to the city, a treasure." Atkins indeed had the power to move mountains, and once they came and he listened, things moved fast. Don had written a few songs, and before he knew it, Atkins was sending demos of them out to industry people. One of them, his old friend Kitty Wells, decided to record one called "Thou Shalt Not Steal" as a B-side. The brothers then rejoined the Everly Family on a Knoxville radio station owned by grain salesman Cas Walker, who also gave the precocious, ten-year-old Dolly Parton her first radio exposure. However, when Walker judged the teenagers to be too rock 'n' roll, he fired the whole family.

Worse, when Chet tried to sell Steve Sholes on the Everlys, Steve wasn't interested. Don and Phil faced having to work like Ike in the coal mines when Chet got another of Don's songs recorded by Anita Carter and talked to no less than Columbia Records to sign the brothers in 1956. They even got to record at Owen Bradley's famed studio, but their first records, produced by Columbia's Nashville head Don Law, failed, and the label gave up on them. But Chet struck again. He convinced

Wesley Rose to sign them to Acuff-Rose as writers and performers. Then, early in 1957, when Don was twenty and Phil eighteen, Rose got them signed to another label, Cadence Records, owned by Archie Bleyer, bandleader and former music director of Arthur Godfrey's TV show. Bleyer had been sent one of the Bryants' songs, "Bye Bye Love," and slated it for the brothers' debut recording. A few days before, they were jamming in the Opry alley, where Nashville wannabes gathered, hoping to attract attention from the Opry bird dogs. As Atkins recalled, "Don said, 'We just signed a deal with Archie Bleyer.' I knew how happy he was because he said, 'Won't you join me? Let's play some Bo Diddley.' And I said, 'yeah, man, just call me. We'll do it.'"

He kept his word, booking the session at the McGavock Street studio on March 1. Bleyer was the nominal producer, but Chet would lead the band, which included the Everlys on their acoustic Gibsons backed by Chet, guitarist Ray Edenton, Lightnin' Chance on bass, and Buddy Harman on drums. Unlike the static nature of Elvis sessions, the Everly Brothers, raised by a musical father not unlike Chet's own, were as anal about recording as he was, especially Don, and Chet, as when he first heard them singing through the gate in Knoxville, was immediately struck by the compelling layers of sound and feel that rose within the room. The Everlys, he would say, "filled a void. They had a different arrangement: the Nashville Sound combined with Bo Diddley beats." With no intro envisioned by Bryant, Chet let Don improvise one, which was indeed Bo Diddley-like, a chugging *ba-da-da-da, chicka-chicka-chicka* riff. Just two seconds long, the riff of an uncomplicated kiss-off song forged the Everlys' sound, a country blues that set the feet tapping and head bobbing, and Chet added the rock sauce with electric vibratos tickling false-bravado teen male lines like "I'm a-gonna cryy-y, so bye-bye my love good-byy-y."

That and their heavenly harmonies, which were only faintly Southern and never too loud, amounted to nectar for teenage girls, who'd identify as either the victors or victims of puppy love in succeeding Everly songs, lighting a fire almost as fervid as Elvis's records had. "Bye Bye Love" zoomed to number two on the pop chart, number one on the country, number five on the R&B, and not incidentally number six in England. Expressing a young, White, and self-consciously cool wellspring, the records were instantly bankable and "safe," and thus lifted the freshly minted brothers onto both teen-aimed and mainstream TV shows, on the latter as reassuring symbols of changing culture without any real sacrifice. And even a kerfuffle that arose upon the release of their second single, "Wake Up Little Susie," didn't slow them down, registering a clean sweep of the big three charts at the same time, though it's a canard that, as some have claimed, this was the first time that ever happened, since Elvis had done it twice within a few weeks two years before with each side of "Don't Be Cruel" / "Hound Dog." (And, in any case, the same retroactive caveat applies as with Elvis's conscription of the R&B chart, that neither act, nor any other White one, was in the same corridor as the Black blues acts.)

The kerfuffle was that the record wasn't in fact about teens falling asleep at a drive-in and not waking up at 4:00 AM, knowing "our goose is cooked, our reputation is shot," but about *doing it* in the dark. Even Elvis didn't go there. In the '50s, this was about as metaphorical as a mainstream act could get about sexual license, and Chet had no qualm that it might interfere with the Everlys' assumed innocence; to be sure, adult country songs had dealt with cheeky themes forever. More important, the sound was buttery smooth and an easy turn into the rock corridor. The Bo Diddley tie-in was not just cool talk. The session for "Susie" embedded it. As Chet remembered, "We just experimented around. [Lightnin'] Floyd would suggest that I play a lick or something or I would. But Don and I were both big on Bo Diddley and what a great sound that was."

Bleyer recognized that Atkins turned the key on such invention, always putting just enough tang into a simple country-rock song to unleash the Everlys' vocal stream. The fail-safe was the brothers' image of button-down, neatly attired conformity. That saved "Susie" from disbarment when radio stations in Boston and New York ludicrously took it off their top-forty playlists for a time, which lasted only days against the demand to hear the song all the kids were singing. The Everlys' eponymous first album rose to number sixteen on the pop chart. Their third release, "All I Have to Do Is Dream"—their first recording at the new RCA digs, more easily creating the dreamy essence of jangle pop—rode the same bullet train to the top of the three major charts simultaneously. The fourth, "Bird Dog," hit number two on the pop and R&B lists in 1958.

The Everlys clearly worshipped Atkins, his sense of coolness and indifference feeding their own. While they also were a popular act at the Grand Ole Opry, their sights were set far above that, on the mainstream of coast-to-coast American pop music. Like Elvis, they would never give any commitment to the Opry, spending much time in New York and on the road with the national bus caravans on which they became tight with Buddy Holly. And while Jim Denny was so turned off by Elvis that he told him to go back to driving a truck for a living, the Opry suits all but begged Don and Phil to play more than the two shows they did at the Ryman—where on the latter Archie Bleyer came onstage and presented them with their gold record for "Bye Bye Love"—and even gave them coveted Opry membership, something otherwise reserved for those who played a couple dozen times there. But unlike Chet—who would never accept membership but played there to keep faith with the audiences—the brothers would never come back and were officially excommunicated from the "church," a fate they greeted with yawns, gladly joining Elvis, Jerry Lee Lewis, and Johnny Cash in Opry purgatory.

Even so, though they would soon move from Nashville, they would return like Elvis to have Atkins shape their records, which would for several more years stream from Boudleaux and Felice Bryant's bobby-sox and lipstick cantatas—"Problems," "(Till) I Kissed You," "Let It Be Me," "Cathy's Clown," "When Will I Be Loved," "Walk Right Back," and "Crying in the Rain." Chet would prioritize not using the same formula for them, always suggesting a surprise chord or tempo shift, making each record seem completely fresh. On "Wake Up Little Susie," the snappy acoustic guitar intro, similar to the one on "Bye Bye Love," would win Don the Riff Award shortly before his death in 2021, and both he and Phil's Gibson J-180 Flattops would be exhibited at New York's Metropolitan Museum of Art. Chet could listen to the Everlys rehearse and know how to take a line like "Never knew what I missed 'til I kissed you" and instruct Buddy Harman to kick into his bump-and-grind *ba dum da dum* drum roll after "kissed you," setting up the brothers to harmonize with a knowing *aha*. In truth, Chet was envious of *them*, for what they could get away with as young, bold rebels who never had to care about business matters.

What Chet could do was use his time on the Opry stage to induce subversive change. For example, he faced down the idiotic taboos by including in his solo act violin players and drummers who hit the snare not with brushes but with hard-edged sticks. Soon, fiddles and banjos were gone and background singers were in. Not that he needed anything other than his guitar to rock the house. On May 23, 1959, he played the traditional bluegrass folk tune "Old Joe Clark" on an acoustic Gretsch, and the popcorn-gulping audience broke into applause before the song even ended. The host, Rod Brasfield, then oozed, "Aw, thank you, Mister Chet. That was *realll niiice*."

Given this protective cocoon, being Chet Atkins seemed a simple enough job. Certainly, RCA valued him, albeit far beyond what they were paying him. In Nashville, people would say he always seemed to get the best out of whomever he believed in—if they could find a way to see him. Not even Ray Charles could in 1959. When Ray, in his ultracool country progression, heard Hank Snow's "I'm Moving On," he told Atlantic's producer and honcho Jerry Wexler to somehow arrange for Chet to play on the session Ray scheduled to record the song himself. But RCA sent word that Chet was unavailable, even for Ray Charles (though they would collaborate down the road). As RCA's fulcrum, Chet had responsibilities—some that he hated. But for as long as he could stomach it, he played A&R man, making RCA even more money by doing the job well. It was a fair trade to play his music his way, but the job was already making him a little nuts, and would soon become self-torture.

14

THEME FROM A DREAM

The backbone of Nashville as it grew from a one-horse town to a music utopia was Chet Atkins's A-Team, which for many stood for the "Atkins Team," of studio sidemen. These gifted musicians were almost telepathically tuned to his thinking and instincts, and as a result were some of the most well-paid sidemen in the country, most of them never to leave. Almost like clockwork, Nashville albums on Chet's watch were by the late 1950s a business franchise, some being cut in a day. This would not change for decades, and for all that time, fresh-faced guitarists would have identical tales to tell of his technique and studio system. After Chet died, the members of his Certified Guitar Players (CGP) clique would be interviewed separately and together about him, all with the same observations that the older wave of A-Teamers had a half century before, as when John Knowles told of how Chet would interrupt a take only when he couldn't abide by someone screwing up. "He would say, 'That's too much work. Look at this.' And he'd show me better fingering."

It wasn't what he said, it was *how* he said it, and that alone could prevent any more slipups. Even when rushed, Atkins found the feel he was after, always bending notes geometrically into a new sound, which he had learned from Maybelle Carter's guitar licks—the art of hitting a note and sliding almost simultaneously to another note, creating a melancholy sound that one could borrow a line from Roberta Flack's

"Killing Me Softly" to define—"strumming my pain with his fingers." If a song had vocals, he would have the singer do it live even when it became de rigueur to add vocals to a prefab rhythm track. Chet would expect all instruments to "sing," which another future CGP club luminary, Tommy Emmanuel, would learn was part of Chet being "a great improviser. . . . he approached melody like a singer . . . by imagining that my guitar is actually the vocal." Knowles concurred. Chet's axiom, he remembered, was that "the words are where the melody and the phrasing and the breathing come together."

Emmanuel can boast that he discovered Chet Atkins when he was around seven. As he related on his website,

> I think it was 1962 or 63 when I first heard Chet. I can't remember the tune, but I remember the feeling that came over me. I got butterflies, and my heart was thumping, and I wanted to tear my teeth out. I didn't know how to express it, but I knew that I loved it, and I knew that it was really special, and I said "I want to be able to do that . . ." In those days, in Australia, if anybody wanted anything from America that was exceptional like Chet Atkins or Les Paul, it was like "Oh it's all recording tricks." Everybody tried to put it down. But I didn't listen to any of that. I knew in my heart there was no question that Chet was the real deal and that he was doing it all at once. Every time I heard him on the radio I'd be glued to the set, and if there was any distraction I'd shout at someone! Then I got "The Best Of Chet Atkins" album and "Reminiscing" with Hank Snow, and I wore them out, then I went and found other albums. In the outback and in small country towns, you've got to order a record and wait six months for it to come through.

He would teach himself the Atkins method much like Chet had done with the Merle Travis method, a fingerpicker halfway across the globe. He got up the nerve to write Chet a fan letter when he was eleven.

Expecting no response, he got a letter back with a signed photo. It took another decade for Chet to hear a tape of Tommy's, in the '70s, and he wrote back that he hoped to meet him. By then, Emmanuel will swear, he had a supernatural experience only an obsessed guitarist could have.

> I had reached the stage where I was playing quite a few of Chet's tunes and I wanted so badly to be able to play harmonics, and I couldn't figure it out. No one in Australia knew how to do it. And I had had a dream, and in the dream Chet comes out on stage in a tuxedo, with a Gretsch guitar and he sits down and starts playing some of his greatest harmonic licks, and he walks off, and that was the end of the dream. The next morning I woke up and I could do it. I don't tell many people that because they think I'm crazy but it's a fact. Yeah, he showed me how to do it in a dream. The next day I called a friend and said listen to this, and I played him the harmonics and I could hear him yell on the other end.

This brings to mind another song title apropos to Atkins—"You Can Do Magic." But Emmanuel didn't see the spell cast until he could see the Atkins method up close, after he was invited to meet him in 1980. "I remember working on the arpeggio Chet calls the 'super lick.' It was on the tune 'Cast Your Fate to the Wind.' I kept stacking coins on the tone arm until it was slow enough to hear the notes, and I said 'That's what it is!' When you hear that for the first time the top of your head nearly pops off!"

Even in his forties, Emmanuel was a student; he would describe how Chet seemed not to be moving his long fingers, yet they alternated between slow and fast movements like a piston engine. It was, he said, "like a mariachi guitar was being played, but if you play it like Chet, you sound like the Everly Brothers." The rub was, nobody *could* play it like Chet. Which explains why, as late as 1972, Don and Phil Everly came back to Nashville so he could produce and play on their return-to-country album *Pass the Chicken & Listen*. Atkins relished being the core of Nashville, but even he never quite understood how ridiculous it was that what he did in the 1950s still blew other top musicians away in the 1990s. Emmanuel, at almost seventy and a guitar master for decades, was still saying that Chet "has been my main influence all my life and he still probably is," and that "it's such a pleasure to play the style that Chet developed . . . I play 'Lady Madonna' and people's jaws hit the ground and they say 'What is that?' and I say Chet Atkins did that 25 years ago—or I play 'Yankee Doodle Dixie' and I get a standing ovation. And I say [Chet] did that in 1947."

By 1960 Chet was on his upward trail, and a good soldier. He still did radio shows at WSM, played at the station's shows around town as well as RCA-sponsored concerts, made appearances at meetups with radio sponsors and industry muckety-mucks at conventions, and gland-handed his fan clubs on their treks to Nashville. He and Faron Young even hosted a Miss Tennessee ball. Now that checks from these sorts of commitments—which included a guest spot on the NBC morning show *Today*—had put some good money in his pocket, he could buy Ida and Willie a new home in Luttrell. James Atkins Sr., however, was typically hard to find, having all but vanished from his son's life.

Chet, anticipating that he would be spending as much of his time at home on music as he would in the studios, sank $5,000 on a home studio built in the basement of his permanent home, a two-bedroom ranch house on a sloping hill on Lynnwood Boulevard. As he had in his previous home, he furnished the studio with high-tech control boards and equipment many studios wouldn't even have for another decade. But it looked more like the workshop of a madman: benches with unidentifiable pieces of equipment, vacuum tubes, pages filled with notes only he understood, jars with pens and pencils, and for no reason, badminton birdies and a quart of Quaker State motor oil. Leona's joke was that at least she always knew where he was, though she might not have been able to find him in all the mess down there. Steve Wariner, who would later spend hours down there with him, referred to it as Chet's "man cave." There was even, he said, a slot machine to break up the monotony of playing, with an extra bonus for Chet—he kept all the money. "I lost a lot of money in that machine, man. I used to play it between takes and when we were just hanging out."

But this grease monkey paradise was where Chet would record tracks and upgrade his guitars, which he never seemed to think were made well enough by Gretsch, even though the company meticulously followed his requirements. Each year, Atkins models were refined and reintroduced. Even back in 1956, Gretsch introduced a double-cut design with a fake f-hole painted on under the strings, a simple solution that somehow cut down on unwanted feedback buzzing. There would be two new models as well, the Country Gentleman and the Chet, neither of which he had input on, then the Tennessean. Not that Gretsch always waited for his input. "They would just steal the ideas from the 6120, use my ideas on other guitars, and just change the name, call it a Country Club or something, and sell the hell out of them," he once said. While he would play them all, he would stick mainly to the original 6120 and 6121, not only out of loyalty. To earn his loyalty, a guitar had to be uniquely suited to his internal chemistry; it had to work right, feel right, in his hands.

In a sense, that was how he approached his ambivalent relationship with the Grand Ole Opry. Despite the changes he had engendered at the Ryman, it never became a part of his chemistry, or his soul. Playing there in the name of Nashville solidarity was a job, no more, and he never could warm to it, given the cold shoulder of the brass who knew he had them over a barrel and mainly kept a distance, something that played right into his primary instinct, to entertain people and then go home. Indeed, he was able to separate himself from the Opry crowd even during the shows there. When he wasn't onstage, he would often slink out the back door and across the alley to the back entrance of Mom's, which in 1960 would be known as Tootsie's Orchid Lounge, but the drinks would taste just as good.

Truth be told, he was more at home in the ring of honky-tonks on Fourth Avenue, within walking distance of the Opry, turf known as Printer's Alley for the newspaper offices, print shops, and publishers with office space in the area, which had been joined by red-light attractions like strip joints, whorehouses, and underground clubs where jazz was played by Black musicians who needed not apply at the Opry. This sacred turf for Nashville's bourgeoisie, which was also called the "Men's Quarter," was borderline dangerous and would remain so. David "Skull" Schulman, who owned the Rainbow Room, an aboriginal music and strip joint dating back to the 1940s, would be murdered in the club in 1998, and people claim his ghost haunts what today is called Bourbon Street Blues and Boogie Bar. But for Chet, the Quarter was more true to life than cartoon cowboys stomping around at the Opry. Sitting in the dark bars chugging drinks and listening to blues men was much like the Harlem music scene he had experienced in New York with Jimmy during the war.

At Mom's, he hung with a changing cast of musicians, one of those being the young but much traveled, trouble-prone, and easily detourable Johnny Cash, who followed Elvis out of Memphis when he signed with Columbia in 1958. Stories followed him around, such as the one where he had gone on a drug-stoked rampage, using his expertise as a demolition man in the army to blow up every road sign between Little Rock and Nashville. To Chet, Johnny was a classic example of art imitating life. "Johnny," he once said, a little enviously, his neutrality about other people's morals not his concern, "was a lot wilder" back when they were both dealing with their own pressures and compromises. Chet of course was nowhere near the wrecking ball Johnny was. He had some antisocial aspects, but he also had business duties. And as Paul Yandell confirmed, Chet's uneasy peace with the Opry never fooled the musicians about his real feelings. "Chet was never a member of the Opry," Yandell said. "He just played on it. [Eventually] he would quit the Opry altogether." But even during his run at the Ryman, he could drop in a little dig. In 1956 he recorded a song he wrote with country pianist-singer Del Wood called "Intermission at the Opry," though no one knew of his fondness for those interludes. Two years later, when the Everly Brothers played their second and last Opry gig, on March 28, 1958, Chet did a solo turn, singing "Please Don't Talk About Me When I'm Gone," though again, what he meant was his inside joke about the Opry not being on his long-term itinerary. Don and Phil knew the score; in fact, he was their role model for their who-cares aversion to the Opry.

For the time being, Chet would still keep his commitment to the Opry, and would never publicly renounce it, periodically making less frequent return engagements. And back when he was still gaining ascent in Nashville, if he wasn't in the studio, he would loiter in the Opry alley and play guitar with people he didn't know. Guys who knew his name but not the face would show up there and ease into jams. Once, when a guitar player was being ragged by the others, a normal part of the scene, he had the perfect comeback line—"Screw you, I have an appointment with Chet Atkins!" He had no idea that a guy who was standing five feet away was the same Chet Atkins, who had never met him. But then Chet, for the most part, never knew their names. All he knew was that they were lost souls, just as he had been once.

His torturous schedule had kept him from recording albums for over a year following his late-1957 LP *Hi-Fi in Focus*, another buffet of rearranged Tin Pan Alley and Broadway standards like Bach's "Bourée," Jerome Kern and Otto Harbach's "Yesterdays," Fats Waller's coy "Ain't Misbehavin'," the Dixieland favorite "Tiger Rag," the movie theme "Anna," Al Dubin's "Shadow Waltz," "Portuguese Washerwoman," and jazz guitarist Johnny Smith's "Walk, Don't Run"—and Chet's intricate chords were the prospectus for the Ventures' 1960 electrified version of Smith's song, with amped-up Fender guitars, that became a number-one hit instrumental. *Hi-Fi in Focus* had that sort of premonitory power for emergent musicians. Its cover design, by artist A. M. Baunach, depicted a guitar lost within concentric circles, floating against a black background that looked like endless outer space. On the back cover were quirky illustrations of studio equipment, right down to the tubes and reel-to-reel heads, and it featured liner notes by *New York Times* camera editor Jacob Deschin, who wrote about Atkins's music creating colors for sounds. The LP didn't chart but is a modern classic, rereleased as a CD package on its fiftieth anniversary with thirteen new "colors."

The next Atkins album was a year later, when Steve Sholes, who was spending most of his time producing Elvis's movie songs in Los Angeles, wanted Chet to come out west and sit in on some of them. While there, curious to see what sort of effect the airy L.A. environment would have on his own recordings, Chet made the album an impressionistic musical palette of the Hollywood movie legacy of orchestral music, adding a string section that would sound similar to the high-string dreamscape of Percy Faith's 1960 instrumental "Theme from *A Summer Place*," the longest-running number-one instrumental in history, nine weeks, and the first to win a Grammy. For this effect, Chet worked with orchestra leader Dennis Farnon, RCA's West Coast A&R head and a founder of the National Academy of Recording Arts and Sciences, which created the Grammy Awards. They stitched together movie iconography such as Charlie Chaplin's theme ("Eternally") from *Limelight*, George Duning's "Theme from *Picnic*," and a new version of Chet's 1951 cover of "Meet Mister Callaghan" with standards like "Greensleeves" and "Santa Lucia" as well as Boudleaux Bryant's misty "Theme from a Dream."

When it was done, Chet came back to Nashville and dove into two of the biggest songs he ever produced. One was an adaptation of a French folk song called "Les Trois Cloches," sung by Edith Piaf in 1946, which had been recorded in America as "While the Angelus Was Ringing" by various artists, including Frank Sinatra. Another English version, titled "The Three Bells," had been released by both Piaf and the Andrews Sisters, with middling success. Then, in '59, one of the country-folk trio the Browns, an Arkansas brother and two sisters who had been with RCA without a major hit since their 1955 cover of the Louvin Brothers' "I Take the Chance," heard it on the radio and implored Chet to produce it for them. He did, intrigued by their tight, sharp harmonies, and came away with uncharacteristic optimism; as Maxine Brown remembered, he boldly foresaw it as "the biggest hit ever."

While it was being prepared for a release, Chet also discovered another French song he wanted to cover and add to *Chet Atkins in Hollywood.* It was a French ballad, "Je t'appartiens," written and recorded in 1955 by Gilbert Bécaud, with original lyrics by Pierre Delanoë. Although it was covered with English lyrics in 1957 by American singer Jill Corey and called "Let It Be Me," it sold mildly. But Chet was entranced by the original and its uniquely lachrymose French strings and swelling emotional arpeggios, so he recorded it as an instrumental for *Chet Atkins in Hollywood.* He just did get it onto the LP, which was released in July 1959. And while neither the album nor its sole single, "Meet Mister Callaghan," made it to the charts, the LP left another vibrant Atkins mark, the more open and airy L.A. sound and glistening strings unveiling what retro-reviewer Richard S. Grinnel called "one of the great makeout records of its time."

Chet could live with that. However, the real bonus was "Let It Be Me," which would have been merely fascinating album fodder had not Don Everly also discovered it while playing the album over and over, something he did as a rule with Atkins albums. He would call "Let It Be Me" "one of the great songs of my lifetime. I said to Chet, 'I love that melody. Is there a lyric?' He said, 'Yes, and it's a great one.'" The result was that the Everly Brothers ran with it, recording it at a grand session not in Nashville but in New York, with Chet and backed by Archie Bleyer's orchestra. It would rise to number six on the pop chart, though for Bleyer it was bitter fruit, as the brothers would walk on Bleyer just after the new decade rang in to sign their then-unheard-of million-dollar contract with Warner Bros. Records and move to the coast—stipulating to their new bosses that they would still record in Nashville under the watch of Chet Atkins.

There seemed no reason why not. The West Coast was on the rise as a recording colony but was fairly dependent on the rockabilly of Eddie Cochran and the Chicano rock of Ritchie Valens—the latter of whom tragically died on February 3, 1959, when the tin can of a plane he was riding in with Buddy Holly and J. P. "the Big Bopper" Richardson crashed in frozen Iowa, preceding by fourteen months Cochran's death in a car crash while touring in London at the same time the

Everly Brothers were also touring England. Don and Phil would have to restart L.A. rock, but one suspects that the brothers would have flown anywhere in the world to work with Chet. And Chet himself had no desire to resettle. Despite the cover of *Chet Atkins in Hollywood*, which had a giant guitar hanging over the twinkling vista of an L.A. hillside view, Nashville was home, and his dominant figure only gained more heft after the new year, when the Browns' soft and buttery "The Three Bells" zoomed to the top of the country chart for four weeks and the pop chart as well, and reached number ten on the R&B chart as well as going top ten in many countries worldwide.

Chet thought too much of the Hollywood album to let it go. He cut the entire album again—in Nashville—and released it in 1961 as *Chet Atkins in Hollywood with Dennis Farnon and His Orchestra.* It was cleaner and sharper, and the cover was the coolest and most uncountry cover ever for a Nashville album—the guitar now hung on a lamppost at Hollywood and Vine, a blonde starlet in a gold pantsuit grinning nearby—but it was given no PR support. Still, it was a guilty pleasure for serious Atkins collectors and in make-out sessions. For the nerdy guy from Smoky Top, that wasn't half bad.

Having come to believe he needed a more technologically aware engineer than Bob Farris, Chet hired Bill Porter, a young engineer for WLAC's TV shows, to man the board for "The Three Bells." Porter was just out of college when he got the job and thought he might have blown it when, mixing the record, he accidentally stretched the tape of the opening, ruining the pitch. Without telling Chet, he edited in an alternate take of the intro—again, a taboo for the time—and sent the master tape to RCA in New York. Nobody was any the wiser, not even Chet, who admired the kid's chutzpah. Porter would make key refinements at the studio, such as installing a three-track recorder and lining the hardwood floor with acoustically beneficial tiles. The lesson was clear: when you worked for Chet Atkins, you worked *hard* and virtually all the time. Porter refloored the still-new studio with tiles more acoustically beneficial. He had the walls curved for a swirling bounce-back effect that became haunting in the echo chamber. Most famous were the triangular-cut panels hung from the ceiling at different lengths, dubbed the "Porter Pyramids," and he taped Xs on the floor at points where sonic resonance was most propitious. The sweet spot was found to be just inside the door, and that was where Elvis and the Everly Brothers would sing their vocals.

Lloyd Green, a pedal-steel player on sessions there, said that this aerie made music recorded in the room feel "like a dance. The changes were so subtle that you didn't pick it up consciously, but subconsciously you felt this swing." Chet would record his next singles and albums with the clarity and mood he craved, and racked two more albums. The first, *Hum and Strum Along with Chet Atkins*, was a singalong based on the concept of Mitch Miller's albums and TV show, with an enclosed songbook. The playlist is dizzying, including "Cold Cold Heart," "In the Good Old Summertime," "Bill Bailey," Arthur Smith's "Beautiful Brown Eyes," Pee Wee King's "Tennessee Waltz," Lead Belly's "Goodnight, Irene," the mordant folk song "Birmingham Jail" (which had been sung by Lead Belly while in a Shreveport jail), and the grim '20s plaint "The Prisoner's Song." Also included, with the lyrics sung by the Anita Kerr Singers, was "John Henry," the folk tale of an ill-fated runaway slave that had been recorded by Merle Travis on his 1947 album *Folk Songs of the Hill* and adopted as a protest song for labor unions and civil rights marches.

While the album again resonated mainly with Atkins fans, the crossover reach of "Oh, Lonesome Me" and "The Three Bells" elevated Atkins and Nashville to their highest ground yet. And Sholes suggested that Chet's next album make the jump to rock 'n' roll. It would be called *Teensville*, which was similar to the nascent Motown Records' subtext as "The Sound of Young America." The LP would be a tad offbeat, its single release being Buddy Harman and John Loudermilk's "Boo Boo Stick Beat," from an industrial term for the heavy cardboard lining that musicians copped to describe a scratchy percussion sound, which Chet turned into bongo rock. The flip was a cover of Django Reinhardt's "Django's Castle," a down-tempo stroll full of Django-style hooks and reverberating notes—and, a real change for an Atkins song, a swaying horn introduced by sax man Boots Randolph, who like Floyd Cramer would now be virtually joined to Chet Atkins's hip in the studio. "Boo Boo" was a surprise hit, rising to number forty-nine on the pop chart.

Another intriguing track was the title tune by rockabilly/rock writer Wayne Cogswell, with Chet's guitar as rousing as Duane Eddy's "Rebel Rouser," and "Teensville" also went on the market, backed by a cover of the Clovers' 1952 R&B hit "One Mint Julep," Chet shifting into a Mills Brothers-like rhythm with a funky electric guitar riff in tandem with Randolph's fleshy sax solos and Cramer's slip-sliding piano runs. Nothing like these rocking riffs came out of Nashville, and it led Ray Charles to record his own instrumental of "Mint Julep" in 1962. Impressively, both sides of the Atkins single would place on the pop chart, "Teensville" at number seventy-three, "One Mint Julep" at eighty-two. And the album scored as well, having included Chet's instrumental take on "Oh, Lonesome Me" as well as covers of the Santo & Johnny soft-rock instrumental "Sleep Walk" and the show tune "Till There Was You" (which the Beatles would croon on their first Ed Sullivan appearance). The Bryants' "Take a Message to Mary" would be covered by the Everly Brothers. The album's peak at number sixteen pop made it Chet's first chart placing since *At Home* hit number twenty-four.

He wouldn't take any great bows for it, but he knew he was doing exactly what Sholes wanted, which was to make country-rock an RCA property. In a province of music where the Grand Ole Opry forbade any of its performers from singing anything close to a rock song—not only at the Ryman but *anywhere* they performed—suddenly there was a quiet culture clash happening in Nashville. And no one who knew Chet Atkins believed he would give an inch.

15

"HOW THE HELL DID HE COME UP WITH THAT?"

The tip-off that Atkins's way was superseding the old country rubrics was that the Opry was quickly becoming almost vaudevillian. The borders of the new country music were bending beyond Nashville. The L.A. franchise was looming just behind, with Ken Nelson's numerous country-rock hits for Capitol Records, like those from Ferlin Husky and the young Merle Haggard. Of course, Elvis was the main shape-shifter for these newer stars, another being Nelson's newest find, in *their* former truck driver, disc jockey, and part-time actor Husky, whose enormous hit "Wings of a Dove" elevated its writer, Bob Ferguson, into a job in Nashville as Chet's assistant A&R man and, soon after, producer of such hits as Porter Wagoner's "The Carroll County Accident."

On a technical level, this colonization of country music led back to Atkins. The Ventures' "Walk, Don't Run," which had revamped Chet's version into a number-one rock song and instrumental gold, was followed by Johnny and the Hurricanes' "Red River Rock." Chet had no compunction covering others, like the Brooklyn brothers Santo and Johnny Farina and their aforementioned "Sleep Walk." Indeed, instrumentals in general were the hottest records of non-gentle rock—witness Duane Eddy's "Rebel Rouser," Link Wray's sinister "Rumble," and the Ramrods' "Ghost Riders in the Sky," as well as the twin-Fender unit the

Fendermen, who covered the old Jimmie Rodgers classic "Mule Skinner Blues." And when Elvis came home after his three-year army hitch ended in 1960 and faced a crisis, needing to update to a '60s musical flavor, he was right back with Chet in Nashville.

By then, Atkins had been moved up to officially coproduce Elvis with Sholes, and on March 20 and 21, the crew at the RCA studio included Elvis's old regulars Scotty Moore and D. J. Fontana along with A-Teamers Floyd Cramer, Buddy Harman, Hank Garland, and upright bassist Bobby Moore, along with all the Jordanaires. The first round of songs was highlighted by "It's Now or Never" and "Stuck on You," which would be Elvis's first post-service number-one hits, and he banked the album *Elvis Is Back!* One cannot underestimate these crucial sessions, and surely RCA had not. At the studio, Bill Porter's Xs on the floor kept Elvis from shifting around, and Porter's new three-track recorder and Telefunken U47 condenser microphones had a sensitivity capable of capturing the quietest breath to the loudest, without any distortion or volume increase or decrease. The comeback work was well received, with Elvis buffs finding a new variety of more-adult songs, like his simmering covers of Little Willie John's "Fever," Lowell Fulson's "Reconsider Baby," and Jesse Stone's "Like a Baby"; a hat tip to the army, "Soldier Boy" (not the Shirelles' 1962 hit); and another taken from Leiber and Stoller, "Dirty, Dirty Feeling." The LP went to number two, and critics praised the new depth in Elvis's deeper, less frenetic voice and the sophistication of the material. However, the postscript was that it would be the last significant studio album Elvis would record, as he resumed movie projects, whose usually mundane soundtrack albums claimed his priorities, and those of Sholes, who flitted to Hollywood to produce them.

For those less than depthful projects, Sholes wouldn't disturb Chet from his other work, and the difference showed, explaining why he would call Chet back into Elvis service when the latter's star began to dim by mid-decade. Indeed, it was the terrifying prospect of flaming out that made Elvis keep on paying his dues again to Nashville and Atkins. Yet Chet faced a similar problem, since putting in overtime with Elvis began to burn him out. For one thing, Elvis had become nocturnal, not emerging from seclusion during daylight hours, partially because he would be mobbed wherever he went. This forced Chet, who liked to consider himself a nine-to-five working stiff, to spend all day on other, less stressful projects and then turn to the rigors of Elvis work. After a while, though, he walked away from the high-voltage night work and went home to Leona and Merle.

Thus, after producing the *Kissin' Cousins* soundtrack, Chet began to drop off, but it's unclear whether he was in the studio here and there, or not in there even on session sheets that say he had been. For example, in January 1964, according to a website run by Keith Flynn that charts every Elvis session in detail, Chet was listed as producer on a nighttime session for "Ask Me" and "It Hurts Me." But the engineer for that session, Ron Steele, recalled that Chet was not there. Yet the website notes that "someone who sounds like Chet Atkins can actually be heard after Take 4 of 'Ask Me' breaks down saying 'We got a pop on 'Possess,' and again after Take 8 saying 'one more please,' so it does appear that he was at the session perhaps on a drop-by basis for a short time." However, "Ask Me" was released with Elvis listed as the producer, and though "It Hurts Me," the flip side of the "Kissin' Cousins" single, was listed with Atkins's name, later releases again had Elvis as producer.

Chet did produce a March 18, 1965, session at which Elvis recorded an overdub for "Tomorrow Night." Still, he would clearly pull back, as would Sholes, whose health began to decline in mid-decade, and new Nashville producers like Felton Jarvis, Hans Salter, Fred Karger, and Gene Nelson, as well as newer musicians, would emerge. No matter—basically whatever Elvis recorded, including an increasing amount of gospels, it was guaranteed gold or platinum. But the lounge- and Vegas-based Elvis was a diminished, less dazzling creature, and while more gospelly, Chet might have remembered his initial worries about Elvis's popularity going through the roof but the country aspect crashing into the basement. That may have been on his mind when he covered "Heartbreak Hotel" as an instrumental in 1962 in a swingy cadence, reclaiming its original country derivation. The irony was that

Elvis was now pondering the same thing, worrying that he had strayed too far from his roots. If so, losing Chet fairly ended the endearingly snarling charm of the Elvis who had been crafted by Tom Parker and perfected by Sholes and Atkins. And so Elvis would drift from Nashville to Memphis, his waistline and drug habit growing. He would vow to re-establish his ties with Chet. Sadly, it never happened. Because it might have saved his life.

In the summer of 1960 Chet had segued to his favorite idiom, jazz—although that route landed him in an unfortunate chasm at the Newport Jazz Festival on July 4. It happened when he, Floyd Cramer, Boots Randolph, Buddy Harman, Hank Garland, violinist Brenton Banks, bass man Bob Moore, and vibrato player Gary Burton were booked at George Wein's annual jazz fest in Freebody Park. Billed as the Nashville All-Stars, the reputation of Chet Atkins made them the top attraction on the Sunday show, which also was to star Muddy Waters. But on that day, hundreds of inebriated young fans shut out of the show went on an alcohol-fueled melee, throwing rocks and beer bottles at police, leading Wein to cancel it. National Guardsmen had to quell the mob with tear gas, arresting 200, and there were 160 injured. In reaction, the city canceled the following year's festival. Yet the aftermath produced some delightful residuals. Muddy would turn a poem called "Goodbye Newport Blues," written by Langston Hughes, who had attended the festival, into a song that he performed later at a free concert. And the All-Stars, who hightailed it back to the old mansion RCA had rented for them, did an impromptu recording there that became *After the Riot at Newport*, a low-key gem with liner notes by Wein, that RCA released shortly thereafter, which included some of what their set list was to have been: Thelonious Monk's "Round Midnight," the Gershwins' "'S Wonderful," Horace Silver's "Opus de Funk," a redo of "Frankie and Johnny," Jimmy Guinn's "Relaxin'," and two allusions to the contretemps, Hank's "Nashville to Newport" and the Randolph-Garland "Riot-Chorus."

Still feeling the vibe—which made the album a guilty pleasure for jazz and country buffs but which drew some criticism for being too much of one and too less of the other—eight days after he was back in Nashville, Chet was in the studio to record an instrumental ballad, "Last Date," written by Cramer to reflect the jazzy skew of his piano technique. The song derived from another Chet had recently produced for Hank Locklin, "Please Help Me, I'm Falling," written by Don Robertson and Hal Blair, which spent fourteen weeks atop the country and went top ten on the pop chart. But what impressed Chet most was Robertson's piano runs on the demo, similar to Floyd's slip-note patterns but, as Chet described it, bending notes a full tone rather than half, sounding "something like a slur." Chet gave Floyd the demo so he could bend his own notes just that much further, and Cramer played it on Locklin's recording perfectly. And those tinklings would become, Chet estimated, the basis for "about fifty percent of the Nashville songs" over the next decade, not least of which was "Last Date."

Atkins is credited as the producer of the song but, as with some Elvis songs, his role seemed limited. Originally, he was so busy that he handed the job to a ubiquitous Memphis songwriter and producer, Jack "Cowboy" Clement, who had been the engineer at Sun Studio for the legendary 1956 Million Dollar Quartet session combining Johnny Cash, Jerry Lee Lewis, Carl Perkins, and Elvis Presley and then came to Nashville as a producer. But when an arranger he had hired for the Cramer session didn't show up, Chet himself had to step in. He called in Anita Kerr to write an arrangement, but with time ticking down, he went without one, later ruminating that the improvised nature of this last-minute decision was a blessing, given that he believed arrangers often overwrote, losing the basic simplicity that the "head arrangement" on "Last Date" preserved.

Floyd was knocked out by the simplicity and happy keyboard hooks set against slow-dance, hip-swaying strings and light background humming, and Atkins always was amazed that Cramer on keys could bend notes not a half tone but a full note. It was, he said, like "a piano player imitating a pedal steel guitar. That's what gives this record that peculiar sound." It carried the record to number two on the pop chart, kept from the top only by Elvis's "Are You Lonesome Tonight?"—also produced by Atkins—and helped make Tennessee the crossroads of rock, with Booker T. and the M.G.'s' soul-drenched "Green Onions" concurrently coming out of Memphis. As country-pop, "Last Date" would become for many the theme song of Nashville, and soon was covered with added lyrics by Skeeter Davis.

Chet, meanwhile, stayed on his mark. He rolled out singles that had little in common save for their unconventionality as country songs, like "Marie" and "Tammy" along with "Goofus" and "Slinky." There were also more rock-friendly tunes like "Hot Mocking Bird," backed by a light pop version of "Whatever Will Be, Will Be (Que Sera, Sera)." Another, "The Slop," was so infectious that RCA released it three times on various album and EP packages. No one ever knew what to expect from Atkins, and he was more than happy about it, since no one else seemed to possess the innate ability to turn sometimes nothing into something. Mesmerizing as he was, the spell he cast made it impossible to know if and when he messed up on the guitar, though he was self-effacing enough to admit that yes, he did, not often but too often for him.

During one appearance on *Nashville Now*, he misplayed a chord, not that anyone knew. When that happened, he had the same fix—playing the same wrong chord next time it came up in the song, then glancing back at the house band and winking. Another time, playing a Flatt and Scruggs song, he murmured under his breath in self-admonishment, "Lester [Flatt] didn't play it like that." But these instances were extremely rare. Normally, he was a perfect totem, uniting different formats with not a blip. This was apparent when he recorded *The Other Chet Atkins* and stirred into the mix a nylon-string Dobro, the first time he played that resonator "singing guitar," which had been brought into country music in the '30s by Bashful Brother Oswald, a member of Roy Acuff's Smoky Mountain Boys.

The future multi-Grammy-winning fingerpicker Steve Wariner was then still a decade and a half from becoming an Atkins protégé and CGP member—he would also write Garth Brooks's "Longneck Bottle" and "Katie Wants a Fast One," and Clint Black's "Nothin' but the Taillights." He recalled that his father would "play me a Jim Reeves record and say, 'Chet produced that.' He'd play a Don Gibson record [and say] 'Chet produced that.' Everything was connected to Chet. I can't even imagine my world without him." Yet the irony was that Atkins didn't think he was doing anything worthy of such a fuss. Rather than setting off a flame, he once said, he simply "tried to make good records that had a pretty sound. The only playing I have to go by is what I like, and luckily I'm kind of square—and if I like a song it's pretty sure that the public will, because I'm square." And:

> I've always felt that any records you make you gotta get a hook in it somewhere and get something different. We weren't sitting around and saying, okay, let's start a Nashville sound or anything like that. . . . I was a country musician. And I was into jazz a little—Fifties jazz, what I consider to be a great era of jazz—so you know I could use little progressions and these things that I've heard and do it in a country way to where it wasn't offensive. I think that is the great advantage I had.

There was also the matter of actualizing songs in the semi-hostile environment of Nashville's publishing and marketing elites. Cowboy Jack Clement, who flitted back and forth from Memphis so regularly that he was dubbed the Pied Piper of Nashville, never could find the breathing room or feel the "family" vibe. In 1980 he lamented, "Country music used to be free. But the business in Nashville inhibits that free flow of music. Nashville has never been a place where people invented music, like Memphis was when I was young. So my philosophy is to go my way and to invent what I can, to make life flow from music and not the other way around."

Cowboy Jack could appreciate that Atkins kept on shape-shifting in this stranglehold, while sorting out daily business for RCA, auditioning musicians and singers, signing acts, and making spreadsheets he tried to keep under budget while paying musicians union scale. He hated most of it—especially billing artists for studio time, which he disliked as much as billing himself for it—and had to keep time on sessions so he could move out one act and move in another. This teeming overflow would have him on the phone to Sholes in New York already asking about RCA building a companion studio, which took as long to get the green light on as had the last new studio. And so life went on, same as it ever was, although, as with Elvis and his nighttime sessions, Chet had to get more selective about whom he could produce, assigning Clement to produce the sessions he couldn't accommodate—a job that became so problematic for Jack that he later downgraded such work as second-string fodder Chet saw as inferior. But he hung around Chet enough to know what he could do for a breakthrough talent. Indeed, Clement had turned the key for Jerry Lee when the splintery wild man from Louisiana, whose early rockabilly records had failed but who pitched himself in 1955 to Clement, by using a magical two words.

"I was at the studio one day piddling around and Sally Wilburn, who worked the front office came back into the studio and said, 'there was a guy here that says he played the piano like Chet Atkins,'" recalled Clement. "I asked her to bring him back. He came in and sat down and played 'Wildwood Flower' on a little piano, and he sounded like Chet Atkins playing the piano." That alone was enough to go ahead with Jerry Lee Lewis. And soon he would serve Chet another one for the ages.

Recording in Nashville had become a haze of sound and tempered fury, along with the promise of an Atkins sensibility—and salability—with each new record. Remaining true to his ethic of loyalty to Nashville as a whole, he dropped pending business when the Everly Brothers came cross-continent for new sessions, despite RCA's feeling that making hits for them was short-changing its own rock acts. To be sure, Chet was more loyal to Acuff-Rose than RCA, and Wesley Rose continued funneling songs to Don and Phil. This formula paid off mightily in 1960 when the Everly Brothers signed that ten-year, $100 million deal with Warner Bros. Records, a then-struggling adjunct to the Warner movie studio that seemed to have no idea how to make rock 'n' roll records or who should sing them.

For Don and Phil, the living was easy in L.A., and perilous, stoking more fussing and feuding. Don, a chronic cheater and abuser of women, was on a path to drugs and dissipation that would lead him to try to kill himself twice while on a tour of England. Yet the Everlys were wise enough to keep returning to Nashville, no matter the cost of doing so and the rent they paid for being in the studio with Chet. The result was a chain of hits that would keep Warner Bros. Records from going under. Their debut record for the label, "Cathy's Clown," was technically produced by Don and Phil but was guided by Atkins, who had Buddy Harman center the rhythm with a strip-joint drum shuffle, and Bill Porter again found ways to add sass by running a tape loop through four playback heads, which made it seem as if two drums were playing at once, keeping time with Chet's pointed electric accents.

The song climbed quickly to number one, earning the Everlys another gold record, its sales to date having accrued to around eight million. The follow-up records, "When Will I Be Loved," "Walk Right Back," and "Crying in the Rain," were tricky matters for Chet, since the Everlys in a personal snit had fired Rose as their manager and producer, prompting Wesley to deny them from recording any songs by the Bryants or other Acuff-Rose writers—or even their own songs. And Chet, too, became something of a lost connection when they began to bypass him for the airy L.A. studios, trying in vain to lead the rising tide of Hollywood soft country-rock. But when they would come to a detente with Rose, they would have one last rodeo with Chet and Nashville.

Chet's own works meanwhile moved on, now issued in mono and stereo as Nashville caught up with the big recording power centers. His assembly line of albums continued with the late 1960 *The Other Chet Atkins*, on which he played a single nylon-string Spanish guitar, ripping through tracks like "Begin the Beguine," "Sabrosa," "Siboney,"

"El Relicario," "Marcheta," and "Tzena Tzena Tzena." The next album, *Chet Atkins' Workshop*, was a buffet of pop fodder such as "Tammy," "Theme from *A Summer Place*," "Marie," "In a Little Spanish Town," "Hot Mocking Bird," and "Lullaby of Birdland." The album cover is particularly notable, the liner notes written by David Halberstam, then a columnist for the *Tennessean*, who sized up the Atkins mystique as being mostly a man living in a personal cocoon: "This is the lonely man's room and Atkins when he is working is a lonely man. 'Can't take my time in the studio. We're making money there and when you are making money you can't really take your time.' Here he can retire for days on end to be handed an occasional sandwich through the door by his wife Leona, but here to stay with his guitar, and his sound."

The album surged to number seven on the pop chart, the highest ranking he would ever attain, and the follow-up, *The Most Popular Guitar*, veered again, taking him back to converting big-band show tunes into guitar-primed spaciousness, layered in strings and an ornate chorale backing on evergreens including the Gershwins' "It Ain't Necessarily So," Mack Gordon's "Stay as Sweet as You Are," Georges Boulanger's "My Prayer," Books Bowman's "East of the Sun (West of the Moon)," and Atkins's own "Goin' Home," a plaintive rune on which he alternated loud and soft, high and low streams into a mini-acoustic symphony (one that he would redo as a duet much later with Lenny Breau). It hit the chart as well, for ten weeks, but peaked only at number 119.

The next, *Christmas with Chet Atkins*, came out for the holidays in 1961 and broadened the holiday pigeonhole genre Gene Autry introduced and Owen Bradley made frothy with Brenda Lee and Bobby Helms. (Steve Sholes had also scored with *Elvis' Christmas Album* in '57, recorded in Hollywood, the top-selling Christmas album in history at over thirty million.) Atkins's takes on "White Christmas," "Deck the Halls," "Little Drummer Boy," "Silent Night," and the like had a traditional, around-the-fireplace feel, and he played with a single acoustic guitar and his electric Gretsch while covering Elvis's "Blue Christmas" and "Jingle Bell Rock." It was also the first time he played what he called "cascading arpeggiated harmonics," meaning the notes of a chord played individually instead of all in a single strum, a technique he had learned from listening to Django Reinhardt in the '40s. The album ran to number twelve on the Christmas album chart, giving Phil Spector the notion to do the same concept with a greater bow to rock with his Wall of Sound two years later, though retro-reviewers cite the Atkins entry as one with more peaceful ruminations while the *really* revolutionary Spector work made for an ear-splitting Christmas party.

Staying in that more restrained, native pocket, Chet began 1962 with the brilliant, Library of Congress-enshrined *Chet Atkins Plays Back Home Hymns*. Timeless as it is, it combined a mosaic of gospel songs, including "Amazing Grace," "Will the Circle Be Unbroken," "Take My Hand, Precious Lord," "The Old Rugged Cross," "Just a Closer Walk with Thee," and "Just as I Am," setting a spiritual tone with quiet tufts of both acoustic and electric melody embellished by either toe-tapping nobbing of harmonicas and brush strokes or arching string overdubs reminiscent of the almost subconscious spell of "Last Date"—the album cover being a disembodied guitar perched against a tree in front of a small-town church.

Eclecticism seems hardly sufficient to describe Atkins's appetite for subsuming music by its every root and vine. That year, he had no reluctance to try country-calypso with *Caribbean Guitar*, taking his Gretsch across the idiom of the islands, covering "Montego Bay," "Mayan Dance," "Jungle Dream," "Bandit," and the Tarriers' original version of the later Harry Belafonte hit "The Banana Boat Song (Day-O)," and adding Boudleaux Bryant's "Wild Orchids," Joe Burke's "Moon over Miami," the Tin Pan Alley "Yellow Bird," and Nacio Herb Brown's "Temptation." Chet's crew in the studio included some new faces—guitarist Ray Edenton, pianist Tupper Saussy, bassist Henry Strzelecki, drummer John Greubel, and a four-piece violin section—and they followed him into the calypso and classical Spanish guitar lines, with Chet perfectly reproducing the chordal cadences of "Mayan Dance" that both Segovia and Antonio Lauro had played when they recorded it.

Next he reared back into country swing and jazz with *Down Home*, on which he covered Merle Travis's "I Am a Pilgrim" and "Steel Guitar

Rag," Glenn Miller's "Tuxedo Junction," Red Foley's schottische dance tune written by Papa John Gordy, "Salty Dog Rag," and the Greek baglama-based movie theme from *Never on Sunday.* As well, there was a Paul Yandell song, "Give the World a Smile," and John Loudermilk's "Windy and Warm," which the writer brought to Chet with only one verse done. As Loudermilk remembered, "The damned guy finished the song perfectly by himself, and I wrote it!" Then there was the daunting *Our Man in Nashville*, assimilating seeming odds and ends such as Roy Acuff's "Streamlined Cannonball," Irving Berlin's "Alexander's Ragtime Band," Lead Belly's "Goodnight, Irene," Loudermilk's "Old Double Shuffle," Jerry Leiber and Phil Spector's politically incisive "Spanish Harlem"—and Chet's redux of the traditional folk song "House in New Orleans," a swingy take on the folk song of unknown origin usually called "The House of the Rising Sun," the legend of the house of ill repute that had been recorded by Woody Guthrie, Joan Baez, and Bob Dylan on his debut album, and soon to be the Animals' snarky worldwide hit. Chet's more jazzy approach incorporated a wa-wa trumpet by A-Teamer Karl Garvin and harmonica lines, but the album is more notable as the entry of Chet's soon-to-be main man, Jerry Reed.

Still just twenty-five, Reed, a garrulous guitarist-singer-songwriter from Georgia, had been a mild rockabilly teen idol at Capitol, when his swinging "That's All You Got to Do" was covered by Brenda Lee. He came to Nashville in 1961 after a two-year army hitch and fused into the nexus of studio session cats. A fingerpicker of distinction, Chet—who seemed to be aware of *every* record made—heard Reed's version of "Goodnight, Irene" with a fleeting rock band and conscripted the two Reed songs he would do as instrumentals, "Scarecrow" and "Down Home," the first a smooth blues roll with a two-one drum beat and overdubbed strings; the second, named after the preceding album's title, a bouncy trip up the fretboard with a tangy Boots Randolph sax. As opposite as could be from Atkins, the garrulous, rubber-faced Reed, who could play amazing licks but had no reason why and stored his guitars as if they were piles of junk, would become a kind of alter-ego of Chet and would soon have a career as a good-ole-boy character in the archetypal redneck *Smokey and the Bandit* movies. Without saying a word, that was the sort of door Chet Atkins could open if he took a liking to you.

Chet's own timeline had proceeded as if he was in sync with a youngish and galvanic president with a "new frontier" ideology. Only weeks after John F. Kennedy took office, he invited Chet to play at the White House, both similarly entrenched in the fable of Camelot, two youngish men from completely different economic and cultural backgrounds, yet immensely popular symbols of a new America that was still facing enormous countercultural and political tensions. Indeed, their rising stars could not separate them from terrible tragedy. By 1963, country music had to face its most grievous loss since Hank Williams's death, which came as the idiom had begun to turn inward, channeling Hank's throbbing blues by confronting personal pain. This formula made Skeeter Davis a superstar when she recorded her sad elegy to her late partner, Betty Jack Davis, her crossover mega-hit "The End of the World," a world that, she sang so convincingly, "ended when you said goodbye."

The song, produced by Chet, channeled Patsy Cline's mournfully soulful blues, and it seemed to frame an interim in which death ended the world for many before their time. First, Patsy died, along with Cowboy Copas, Hawkshaw Hawkins, and Cline's manager Randy Hughes, in a plane crash just miles from Nashville, with Hughes at the controls. That same week another country top-liner was killed, Chet's longtime confrere Jack Anglin. But that was all just a prelude to an awaiting national tragedy, the irony of which being that Chet spent the year rolling strong, making his historic trip to South Africa as a kind of cultural ambassador on a tour with Floyd Cramer and Jim Reeves—who also would become a victim of what seemed like a country curse a year later, when his private plane crashed in a thunderstorm outside Nashville, killing the velvety singer at age forty. Atkins's treks through Africa and Europe helped build a foreign audience for country music, which, like with the rock 'n' roll labels, was critical, tapping huge markets that had been largely overlooked in the '50s but became so important that the Everly Brothers would find a bigger base of support in England than in America. Atkins's popularity as a non-rocker was astounding. Ralph Emery, the host of the *Nashville Now* cable series, told of visiting Paris and, unable to read French, picking up the only English-language newspaper. Opening it, the first thing he saw was a full-length story about Chet Atkins.

Chet had found the magic rings of Nashville, and they too found global fame. The classic examples were Floyd Cramer and Boots Randolph. Boosted by Chet, Boots had signed with RCA in the early '60s but failed as a solo act. Signed by Monument Records, he blew his horn on Roy Orbison hits like "Mean Woman Blues" and in 1963 tried again as a solo act. He chose a song that had gone nowhere with RCA, an instrumental virtually stolen from the wondrous King Curtis's blazing sax solos on the Coasters' 1958 crossover hit "Yakety Yak." Renaming it "Yakety Sax," it was produced by Fred Foster, who would later cowrite "Me and Bobby McGee" with Kris Kristofferson. "Sax" was re-recorded as a peppy blues riff with fiddle parts and stop-and-start movements. And while it reached no higher than number thirty-five on the pop chart, the song took on an unlikely afterlife as goofy backing music for the burlesque-like scenes of the slapstick British TV comedian Benny Hill, mainly when he was mock-chasing barely clad women. Boots got more residual value out of it with his *The Yakin' Sax Man* and *Boots Randolph Plays More Yakety Sax* albums.

Then there was the ubiquitous and half-crazy Jerry Reed. Chet had taken to him as a fingerpicker after Reed had a mediocre career as a rock 'n' roll band frontman. On Atkins's *Teen Scene* album in 1963, the title tune was cowritten with Reed, and Chet recorded it with Cramer on organ and Randolph on sax as a near copy of jazz man Bill Doggett's "Hold It." It would be the first of a long string of professional and personal collaborations with Reed, who profited mightily from it, and delivered a teenish flavor with his guitar, driving such tracks on *Teen Scene* as covers of Ray Charles's "I Got a Woman," Dale Hawkins's boggy "Susie Q," the folkie-styled "Walk Right In," and the cool-cat piano instrumental "Alley Cat," which here became a cool-cat guitar instrumental. The LP made it to number ninety-three pop. But Chet's follow-up, *Travelin'*—designed as an audio travelog of the trips he, Cramer, and Randolph had made across the Atlantic, dressing up already orchestrated pop hits like the "Exodus" theme, "Calcutta," "La Dolce Vita," "Volare," and the soft-rock hit "Wheels"—was a rare swing and a miss. Chet hadn't put much of himself into it, having Anita Kerr produce the album, which missed the charts and would be retro-reviewed as "no more than hokey easy listening ephemera," albeit "deserv[ing] a reassessment."

By now, just about anything Chet Atkins put on vinyl had a built-in cheering section of industry pros on the nominating board of the still young Grammy Awards. *Teen Scene* was nominated for Best Rock and Roll Recording in 1964, the entire album competing against five singles, including Sam Cooke's "Another Saturday Night" and Lesley Gore's "It's My Party." It was Chet's first such nomination and well deserved, though he lost to April Stevens and Nino Tempo's "Deep Purple."

His cache was only just beginning, opening the way for essentially whatever avenue he wanted to stroll down. The same year, he could even complete the circle that dated back to the unreleased album he had recorded with Jimmy Atkins in 1958 only for Steve Sholes to shelve half the ten tracks. Chet, who hadn't forgotten about it, knew that Jimmy had no more paydays left as a performer and unilaterally put the five orphaned tracks on an album called *Mister Guitar*, filled out by covers of "Heartbreak Hotel" and "It's Now or Never," pop hit covers of "Out of Nowhere," "Hidden Charm," John Loudermilk's "Blackjack," and Nico Carstens's "Daar's 'N Wind Wat Waat." (The 2016 CD rerelease of the original *My Brother Sings* has all the tracks, with liner notes by Pat Kirtley.)

Satisfied that he had settled family obligations—another of which was sending money to Ida back in Smoky Top, though not to the shadowy James Sr.—he would lurch in early November to a session producing the bearded, plump trumpeter Al Hirt, who had once been a soloist with Horace Heidt's orchestra. The forty-one-year-old Hirt had recorded several albums for RCA, produced by Sholes, but lived in New Orleans, where he owned jazz clubs and played Dixieland swing. Looking for a long-overdue hit single, he came to Nashville expressly to work with Sholes and Atkins on another instrumental album, *Honey in the Horn*. The tracks congealed classic pop (Ira Gershwin's "I Can't Get Started"); country (Boudleaux Bryant's "Theme from a Dream," Hank Snow's "I'm Movin' On"); and soul (Ray Charles's "Night Theme" and "Swanee River Rock [Talkin' 'Bout That River]")—with one New Orleans-rooted song written by the peerless Allen Toussaint, "Java," which as Chet knew had been recorded by Floyd Cramer in 1962. Chet and Sholes put a low-bass rumble under Hirt's bubbly horn, added the Anita Kerr Singers as backing, and Al went back to New Orleans with Chet having told him he had a sure hit, an Atkins ritual that had become common. And again he nailed it. Even at Hirt's ripe age, he was about to become part of the rock 'n' roll calling. But what almost no one in America, not even Chet, knew was that the entire industry, and America's innocence, was about to face a sudden, massive change that left them searching for relevance.

16

"BUT IT'S CHET ATKINS!"

Both *Honey in the Horn* and the single "Java" would climb the pop charts, and in early November Chet performed at a show at Vanderbilt University with Boots Randolph and singer Bobby Bare. On the morning of Friday, November 22, RCA ran a full-page ad in newspapers across the country pitching Chet's recycled Christmas album along with other holiday LPs by Elvis, Perry Como, Eddy Arnold, Mario Lanza, Harry Belafonte, and others. That morning, Chet was in his office at the studio when the convulsive news from Dallas broke on the radio that shots rang out in Dealey Plaza, killing President John Kennedy while on a political trip to Texas. Shaken, and still mourning the multiple deaths of Nashville's power-elite performers, Chet went back home and sat stunned with Leona and sixteen-year-old Merle watching the horrific news as the hunt for the assassin went on and then, over the weekend, watching the murder on live TV of Lee Harvey Oswald and then the burial of a president in Washington. On Sunday morning, "beautiful music" (and future alternative rock) FM station KFOG in San Francisco ran a four-hour block of recorded Chet Atkins mood music to calm the emotional tide of mourning and fear of what might happen next.

As in the rest of the country, recording was halted in Nashville and the Grand Ole Opry canceled its shows. For the next two months, the holiday season seemed lost in despair, new records in stores sitting unbought, concerts scuttled. It would take a virtual revolutionary act to break the pall of mourning, that being when the Beatles descended on America in February and appeared in living black and white on that fabled show of Ed Sullivan's. This was the moment when the industry was given an instant facelift, and not to the benefit of American record companies, which were left shaken by four lads with cereal-bowl haircuts rendering American music acts and industry norms instantly obsolete, or so it seemed.

As things stood, there were almost no self-contained American bands writing and performing their music in the studio, and the first reaction was to try and sound like the Beatles. Even Chet Atkins had to bend to this new order, producing the Everly Brothers' *Gone Gone Gone* album, which was filled with Fab Four-esque guitar melodies. It did little for the brothers, but country was moving deeper into rock, which caught the fever of the only American idiom that prospered during Beatlemania—soul music, which of course had begun the rock revolution and sparked the British wave. Now, theatrical country singers like Roy Head, a White Texan, assumed to be Black because of his histrionic 1965 hit "Treat Her Right," and the irrepressible "White Knight of Soul," Wayne Cochran, the show-stopping Georgian who clad himself in white suits and wore a gigantic white pompadour, found new audiences.

But Nashville had its own style that kept it in the game. Al Hirt's Atkins-produced "Java" bounded onto the charts, easing to number one for four weeks on the easy listening chart, and number four on the pop chart, while *Honey* rose to number three on the album list. Hirt won a Best Instrumental Song Grammy for it in '64 and would earn seven more Grammy nominations. Moreover, the Brit bands' affection for Atkins-style licks became the chassis of many of the Beatles' and Kinks' early hits. And Chet could pretty much stay in his lane. Indeed, his load was so heavy that Steve Sholes now gave the go-ahead for a second new RCA studio to accommodate the spillover. As he had with the first studio, Chet consulted with Owen Bradley to reel in investors to finance the construction of the building just across an alley, almost as an extension. The project would cost the entrepreneurs over a million dollars. The construction began in mid-1964 for the three-story building, and the studio inside was designed to be a larger room at ninety-five thousand square feet, big enough to fit a hundred people at a time, with a more sonically ideal curved ceiling and walls and an immaculate parquet floor able to fit full orchestras and choirs. The control board would have eight-track capabilities and mixing boards with direct connections to specific instruments and amps. A separate, enclosed space for recording vocals had a built-in, airtight echo chamber. All of it made Bill Porter's pyramids and Xs on the floor unnecessary. So much was going on during sessions that it took a mile of color-coded cable to hook up twenty microphones.

Again, RCA did not own the studio, though it would routinely court recognition as if it did—as one typical headline in the *Tennessean* had it, RCA OPENS $1 MILLION CENTER HERE, without specifying that the money was paid by the investors—and would rent the place, shifting the name RCA Victor Nashville to it from the other, still-active studio, and there would be confusion, to this day, that the new studio was being called Studio A and the older one Studio B. Its sweetheart lease stipulated that rent paid for non-RCA sessions would come to the label, at elevated fees, with Chet's approval and, frequently, his participation. He was the king of the castle, and when the plain-looking three-story building opened on March 30, 1965, large crowds lined the street outside, hoping to get a look at some of the music stars who came by to celebrate with him. As revelers partied to Al Hirt's trumpeting on the stage of a top-floor living room with cushy couches, a chandelier, speakers, and a life-size statue of Nipper, the RCA Victor dog logo, Chet lifted a glass to the occasion, saying of the studio, "It's a good manifestation of the faith the music industry has in Nashville as a recording center."

Sholes was not well enough to attend, but RCA vice president George Marek came in, pledging that Studio A stood as "equal in beauty, modernity and technological advance to any recording facility anywhere." The label put an office there, and Chet took one he tried to avoid, and both Studio A and Studio B would be in operation continuously until 1977. But the mid-'60s years were his apogee. He could clear his head by taking to the road at his convenience for major venues around the country, one being a gig in the Hollywood Bowl, where the Beatles had played twice, before fourteen thousand people late in 1965. He was also back on the Grand Ole Opry stage and gave concerts at the Nashville Auditorium, often with Cramer and Randolph, whose informal bonding led them to form their booking and promotion company, ARCO—which was known by the more breezy name of "the Big 3."

Chet held the line on spending as well as he could and paid due diligence to the paperwork that accrued in that office when he would find time to sit at his desk. It was surely a conflicted existence, personal versus company, and few knew how he could ever have pulled it off as he did. He even took a principled stand as a musician rather than a label apparatchik when a US Senate subcommittee would hold hearings in 1967 about reforming copyright laws and establishing intellectual property in the music industry. Atkins didn't hesitate to join with Floyd Cramer, jazz pianist Stan Kenton, and Nashville promoter Hubert Long to go to D.C. and testify in favor of increased royalties for performers. It would take another decade to happen, but this testimony helped extend copyright laws for artists up to seventy years, though it would take decades more for artists and music-business suits to be on roughly even ground, and many were able to hire accountants and lawyers to claim profits stolen from them. Yet as well paid as he was, Chet never believed he wasn't used and manipulated. And on this count, he was probably right.

By mid-decade, American rock had stayed the course, and Nashville was crawling with studios, musicians, and producers cut in the Atkins mold. RCA's stable had been put together by him, his circle all but running the place. His adjutants as staff producers included Felton Jarvis, Bob Ferguson, and Cowboy Jack Clement, with Ferguson his executive assistant. Each would cut his own cloth in the studio working with acts that Chet had signed to the label. And during this interim, three of the biggest names to ever hit country music joined the fold—Willie

Nelson, Waylon Jennings, and Charley Pride. Willie, who had come out of Texas in the late '50s and, while knocking around and deejaying, wrote and played on his acoustic guitar almost painfully personal songs like "Funny How Time Slips Away" and "The Party's Over," and then came to Nashville as Ray Price's bass player. Nelson was already in his thirties, still looking conventional but his quavery, semi-spoken song vocals unconventional and his somewhat disheveled, proto-"outlaw" guise mirroring the hard-knock drug, booze, and jail tortures of Johnny Cash and Merle Haggard, who had cultivated large fan appeal among younger country audiences. In truth, this was a replay of Hank Williams, which was what worried the Nashville hod carriers. The saver was that Chet was no outlaw, and he could frame a naturally likable, introverted guy like Willie to draw out this new subgenre of less formal and formatted country rebelliousness that could reach the mainstream.

After signing Nelson to RCA in 1964, Chet produced his cover of the Hank Williams-like "Blue Eyes Crying in the Rain," an enormous milestone for country music. Then another hardscrabble Texan, Waylon Jennings, arrived. Like his longtime buddy Willie, the onetime juvenile delinquent had been around the block and back, traipsing around the country writing, singing, and playing, lucky to be alive—after being taken into Buddy Holly's band, he'd given up his seat on the ill-fated plane to J. P. Richardson before it crashed. Signed to RCA in '65, it was the first conjunction of the nobly ignoble sub-idiom of Outlaw Country, taking traditional pining and regret to a down-and-dirty realism that resonated less with optimism and emotion than with inevitable, even acceptable gloom.

Chet had seen the dawn of this movement, and he loved Waylon's sense of dare. But he was darker than Willie, and thus Chet was hesitant to take Nashville too deep into his outlaw shade, which was far afield from the Nashville Sound. He did make a glaring exception to the RCA house rules at first, allowing Jennings to use his own touring band in the studio, but mandated that the debut album not be hard-edged country but rather folk-country, and *polite* folk-country, embellished by Jerry Reed, Floyd Cramer, and Buddy Harman. Chet would title the work just that, *Folk-Country*, going with only four original Jennings songs. And Waylon didn't press the issue. As he said, folk was "the original country music, sung by folks, plain and simple." What's more, because Waylon was not and could not ever really be "countrypolitan," Chet was trying to get him a hit, always job one. Even so, he left a mildly harder edge to the songs, which is why the first single, the toe-tapping "Stop the World (and Let Me Off)," remains a Jennings classic and harbinger of things to come—introspection with a groove.

Folk-Country was indeed a hit, going to number nine on the country album chart, and "Stop the World" hit number sixteen. Waylon progressed faster than Willie and would soon furnish some of the greatest antiheroic country music of all time, recording nine albums in five years and standout interpretations of songs like "Walk On Out of My Mind," Jimmy Bryant's "Only Daddy That'll Walk the Line," Mel Tillis's "Mental Revenge," Haggard's "Today I Started Loving You Again," Harlan Howard's "Yours Love," and Roger Miller's "Lock, Stock, and Teardrops," as well as a hell of a cover of Neil Diamond's "Kentucky Woman." He also recorded versions of Bobby Bare's "Woman, Don't You Ever Laugh at Me," John Hartford's "Gentle on My Mind," and even Lennon and McCartney's "You've Got to Hide Your Love Away" and Chuck Berry's "Brown Eyed Handsome Man."

To be sure, Atkins cautiously moved away from the folk flavor and scoured country and rock for apt material for him. Jennings's reputation, and the depth of his songs, would grow, and the still-nascent umbra of the outlaw movement would only expand when Kris Kristofferson entered in the '70s, having come to Nashville to work as a janitor at the Opry to make connections, landing in 1965 with Monument Records, where he was managed and produced by Fred Foster. The trouble was, Willie and Waylon were, well, trouble, neither believing Atkins was letting them be in charge of their own direction; Waylon rode high but soon was forbidden from using his band, frequently leaving Nashville with Johnny Cash, with whom he roomed, to tour. It didn't bode well that, even after being made famous, country's new leading edge was too self-possessed to cede even an inch, not even to Chet Atkins.

Still, Atkins's hold on country would last as long as he wanted it. The polar opposite to Willie and Waylon, the third member of the great '60s country triumvirate would all but worship him. His arrival was more complicated and in many ways endemic to the conditioned racism within the country sphere. He came through Cowboy Jack Clement, who in 1965 started his own production firm, Jack Music Co., renting an office in Studio A next to Chet's. Clement checked the mail one day and found a demo sent from somewhere in Montana by an unknown singer named Charley Pride. "I sent for him to come to town," Clement recalled with the timing of a comedian. "He arrived. He was black." Which was enough to turn most everyone in the Nashville country arc off to Pride. It was just a year since the Civil Rights Act was passed, which in the Jim Crow South was largely ignored. Clement knew what he was up against, but he loved Pride's voice, which was soothing and every bit country, and agreed to represent him, the hardest sell anyone ever attempted in Nashville.

As it was, Pride was thirty and unknown, and had failed in the late '50s when he auditioned for Sam Phillips at Sun. Born in Sledge, Mississippi, in 1934, he was not a singer by trade. His main occupation for years was as a "mud ball" pitcher in the dying Negro leagues from 1953 to 1956. Then, after being drafted into the army, he relocated to Helena, Montana, of all places, where he married and had a son, pitched for the local semipro team, and worked unloading coal from railroad cars. He also began singing in local bands, the rarity of a Black man singing country music attracting minor attention, and during a tour in the sticks, Red Foley encouraged him to travel to Memphis and audition for Sam Phillips at Sun Studios. Nothing came of it and he returned to Montana, but his tapes made it to Nashville, where a talent manager, Jack D. Johnson, started sending them to people like Cowboy Jack, sans the rather significant detail that Pride was Black. And when Clement sent out feelers about the singer, he too kept it mum, figuring he could sell Pride based solely on his talent. Thus, when Cowboy Jack played the tapes for Chet next door, he was interested enough to have Pride's manager bring him to Nashville.

Even a color-blind man like Atkins could not automatically be assumed to make such an invitation. According to Rick Sanjek, the Pride matter was a delicate maneuver. "Clement never mentioned to Chet about Charley being a Black man. He only said that Charley was 'tall, dark and handsome.' That's all Chet knew. He was going to New York for an A&R meeting and told Jack he would bring up Charley Pride as a guy he wanted to sign, calling him a 'country cowboy.'" Days later, a session was arranged at Studio B, under the supervision of Clement. By then, the little white lie had broken through the deception, and the pressure of it fell completely on Chet. Said Clement: "When word got around that some idiot—me—was cutting a black country singer, the studio was packed with half the music business in town, waiting to see if I would make a fool of myself." No one left the session believing he had. Only learning now that Pride was Black, Chet, who for all purposes produced the session, immediately rejected idiotic suggestions such as dressing Pride in colonial garb under the name George Washington Carver III. Instead, Chet realized Pride was the ideal Jackie Robinson candidate for the all-too-long-unfilled position of Black Nashville singer.

To be sure, like Jackie, he was indeed tall, dark, and handsome, and wise enough to blunt the racial issue by never making it an issue himself. Some might have called that selling out, but in '65 he, Clement, and Chet reckoned that understating an utterly important progression was the only way forward. As it was, Nashville's musicians were all for it, having waited forever to play in an integrated studio. On their own time, they would spend much time living in the world of Black music, as had Chet when he was rummaging through the sticks. They would watch the local dance party shows on WSM-TV, like *Five O'Clock Hop*, on which country acts alternated with soul stars such as Tyrone Davis, Al Green, Sam and Dave, J. J. Jackson, and Garnet Mimms and the Enchanters; another after-school teen show, the syndicated *The !!! Beat*, hosted by Nashville deejay Bill "Hoss" Allen, was a blues paradise, the house band including Clarence "Gatemouth" Brown and David "Fathead"

Newman and its guests including Otis Redding, Etta James, Freddie King, Lou Rawls, Sam and Dave, Little Milton, and Percy Sledge. On the show featuring Redding, an unknown left-handed guitarist named Jimi Hendrix played in the band, and he also made live appearances at Club Del Morocco on Jefferson Street. Sanjek remembered that White producers would say Black musicians looked "bored," a canard similar to the old racist baseball owners' claims that Black players would damage the image of their supposedly more professional all-White teams.

Chet, to his credit, didn't pull away from Pride; rather, he was all in, yet all involved remained cautious about when the truth would be revealed to country fans as Chet and Bob Ferguson turned to making Pride's first records. The first, written by Mel Tillis, was a curveball, "Snakes Crawl at Night," a dark and, considering the stereotypical assumptions about Blacks and crime, daring, as a confession of a man who murders the killers of his wife and is sentenced to death. There were reservations from the producers and label superiors, but the song itself was sonically up Pride's alley and so it went ahead, with the vocal smooth, swingy—and White, which seemed to matter to RCA most. Charley sounded like Jim Reeves, and to some listeners it might have been, since RCA released his early records with no images of Pride's face anywhere on the record jackets or in publicity photos. "Snakes Crawl" missed the charts, as did the follow-up single, "Before I Met You." But the third, Clement's "Just Between You and Me," made a mark by riding into the top country ten, which necessitated that Pride tour to support it. That meant he would be seen for the first time by country fans—a real historic moment, with real uncertainties.

The decision was made to have Pride tell the story of his ascendance on the stage when he made his first appearance, with spectators eager to see the man whose records they were buying, sight unseen—and which had quickly earned him a Best Country & Western Performance Grammy nomination, the first of his thirteen. And so it was that Pride strolled onto the stage at a late summer concert headlined by two stalwarts, Buck Owens and Merle Haggard, in Detroit's cavernous Olympia Arena before ten thousand fans, most of whom still thought he was White. Coming onto the stage in a hail of flashing lights, his caramel color and short Afro haircut brought the cheers to an end. He then walked to the front and, having hated to go along, affably said, "Friends, I realize it's a little unique, me coming out here—with a permanent suntan—to sing country and western to you. But that's the way it is." This sort of wry truth-telling was all that country needed to position its first non-White star; not again would racial sidestepping be a consideration, though the first real exposure in the press given to his story, in the September 14 *Detroit Free Press*, bore the awkward headline Charley Pride, Negro Star in White Man's Music.

But that was all that was needed. Pride's first album, *Country Charley Pride*, coproduced by Atkins, Clement, and Ferguson, would stay on the country chart for twenty-three weeks, peaking at number sixteen, countrifying and expanding Pride's sunny affability with a mélange of country covers of songs written by Johnny Russell, Bill Rice, and Jerry Crutchfield, and covering Hank Williams. The next four albums made the top ten, with one, *The Country Way*, going to number one. Pride also made his debut at the Grand Ole Opry, as tough a task as he ever faced but one made possible by Chet's insistence to the mandarins that Pride deserved the honor. At first there was resistance, but the Opry burghers could only put it off until New Year's Day 1967, when Pride was brought onstage by Ernest Tubb. He became a favorite there and would often return, firmly erasing one of the country arc's worst omissions. Pride would record for RCA for twenty years, with Chet stepping aside from producing him in 1969—whereupon Clement would produce twenty of Charley's albums over six-and-a-half-years as Pride was en route to winning three Grammys and cementing twenty-nine number-one country hits and a Lifetime Grammy Achievement Award before he died in 2017. And he would do all of it with a circumspection about race, leaving it as a silent reality. When Nashville songwriter Red Lane in 1996 offered him the song "Blackjack County Chain," a hard-bitten tale of a Georgia sheriff killed by a chain gang, Charley turned it down as too inflammatory.

The real problem, though, was that although being a good soldier worked for Pride, no other Black artist would be accepted; it would take until 2012 before the next Black Opry member was named: Darius Rucker, the former Hootie and the Blowfish frontman who segued to country and also had an easy smile and nonpolitical tendencies. That said everything necessary about country music's original sin, and how well Nashville kept it alive even as it only marginally gave in to necessary realignment. Even as late as 2024, some in the country establishment and fandom blanched when Beyoncé, a native Texan, digressed from hip-hop to record a well-received country music album. Country would make important cultural strides, but deep in the well of Dixie, exclusion never seems to fully evaporate.

The metaphoric dynamite of Charley Pride's career paved the way for Clement to open his own recording studio in Nashville, where, among other notable assets, Ray Stevens recorded his self-produced 1969 monster hit "Everything Is Beautiful." This reinforced the fact that Chet Atkins could launch careers virtually on his word alone, including for those who ruled behind the scenes.

Bob Ferguson would take the reins of Porter Wagoner and Dolly Parton's duet act, which vaulted Dolly to mega-stardom and won Ferguson a Grammy for Wagoner's version of "Carroll County Accident." Bob Johnston would ease in as Bob Dylan's and Leonard Cohen's producer in Nashville as well as write songs for Elvis movies. Of course, Chet's role model, Owen Bradley, was himself a legend, and other veteran producers were now propagated all around Nashville. Epic's Billy Sherrill would break out Tammy Wynette and then George Jones. Mercury's Shelby Singleton, who had produced veteran R&B singer Brook Benton's "The Boll Weevil Song"—another step forward for a more racially diverse country idiom—hired Jerry Kennedy at the label, the fruition of a career that began when Chet recorded Kennedy as a kid singer; Jerry would later win Grammys for his Dobro playing and for producing Jerry Lee

Lewis, Elvis, Roger Miller, and Reba McEntire. Even Capitol Records, synonymous with the L.A. scene, opened a studio in Nashville.

Tourist traffic into the city was heavy, with a diverse music crowd up and down the boulevards of Music Row, where one could find shows by Otis Redding, Little Richard, and Etta James, who recorded her live *Rocks the House* LP at the New Era club on Jefferson Street. Through all this growth, Chet Atkins only grew more legendary, his matched set of the 1964 *Guitar Country* and 1965 *More of That Guitar Country* albums—both of which he had Ferguson produce—were virtual audio overviews of the new Nashville. The former, the title track penned by pop royals Johnny Mercer and Willard Robison, was buttressed by effortlessly shifting treats. Chet wrote one song, "Dobro," with Cy Coben, who had written for Peggy Lee and then fell in love with Nashville, composing hits with Charles Grean for Eddy Arnold when Grean became Eddy's manager. The classic "Kentucky" was joined by the folk revival "Freight Train," a favorite of Lennon and McCartney, and "Copper Kettle," formerly sung by Pete Seeger and Joan Baez. There were three songs by Chet's new protégé Jerry Reed—"Winter Walkin'," "Yes Ma'am," and "A Little Bit of Blues"—one by Merle Travis ("Nine Pound Hammer"), and Hank Garland's "Sugarfoot Rag." The LP hit number one on the country charts and number sixty-four on the pop, and was nominated as Best Country Recording, losing to Roger Miller's "Dang Me" single.

After *Guitar Country*, the only other LPs Chet recorded in '64 were *Progressive Pickin'* and *My Favorite Guitars*. *Pickin'* was another Atkins jazz dive, including Mercer's "I Remember You," the Gershwins' "Summertime," the Duke Jordan standard "Jordu," Johnny Smith's "Satan's Doll," Steve Allen's "Gravy Waltz," Toots Thielemans's "Bluesette," Edward Heyman's swaying "Love Letters," and, oddly, two Jerry Reed country-rockers, "Kicky" and "Early Times." There were no singles and it missed the charts, as did *My Favorite Guitars*, another one of his around-the-world-in-forty-minutes trips, using his Gretsch, Del Vecchio, and Juan Estruch classical to perfectly segue from "Wimoweh"—Pete Seeger's 1951 adaptation of the native South African chant that a decade later was renamed "The Lion Sleeps Tonight"—to the Japanese "Sukiyaki" to Duke Ellington's "It Don't Mean a Thing (If It Ain't Got That Swing") and Fred Carter Jr.'s "Say It with Soul" to Chopin's Waltz no. 10 in B Minor to Jobim's "One Note Samba"—along with some more Reed, this time "Rose Ann." Chet also had a song of his own, "El Vaquero," cowritten with Nashville session guitarist Wayne Moss, who played on Roy Orbison's "Pretty Woman" and would play on Dylan's *Blonde on Blonde.*

This was followed by the first of his compilation albums, *The Best of Chet Atkins.* Released late in '64, it is a curious "best of" because Chet chose eleven songs he believed he had performed best. Some were his own compositions, such as "Trambone" and "Yankee Doodle Dixie"; two were cowritten with Boudleaux Bryant, "Blue Ocean Echo" and the symbolic "Country Gentleman"; and also included was the redoubtable "Django's Castle." Neither this album nor another compilation, *The Early Years of Chet Atkins and His Guitar,* made the chart, but this was when Chet would bound onto it with his biggest hit.

He owed that plum to Boots Randolph, who with Chet had made the memorably goofy "Yakety Sax." Chet was working on new riffs when the unusual stop-starty patterns of "Yakety Sax" recurred in his head. Taking the sax out of it for a semi-cover was a challenge, and he handled it purely on instinct. As Mark Reinhart notes, "Yakety Axe" departs from all other Atkins songs, with every note played as "single-note soloing," with no accompanying pattern or harmony lines. It fell quickly into place, and the public reaction to the song was just as much a surprise as it had been for Boots, who with Spider Rich earned out again as the writers when "Axe" outsold the original, climbing to number four on the country chart and ninety-eight on the pop, and winning Grammy nominations for Best Country & Western Single (beaten out again by Miller's "King of the Road") and Best Instrumental Performance, Non-Jazz (losing to Herb Alpert and the Tijuana Brass's "A Taste of Honey"). The song would be the anchor of both *More of That Guitar Country* and, in 1966, *The Best of Chet Atkins, Volume Two.* And Chet was not quite through with it even twenty years later. In '66 the song could also give a kick to part two of the historic pairing capped by *More of That Guitar Country.*

That work amalgamated Chet's "My Town" and rearrangement of the traditional "Back Up and Push" with Dylan ("Blowin' in the Wind"); Donovan ("Catch the Wind"); Johnny Cash ("Understand Your Man"); John Loudermilk ("Cloudy and Cool") and Boudleaux Bryant, with whom Chet cowrote "How's the World Treating You?" It also reached back for Hank Williams ("Alone and Forsaken") and snuck in one more traditional country pill, "The Letter Edged in Black," with Chet's own updated arrangement. The album zoomed to number four on the country album chart and number sixty-four on the pop.

It would be beaten out as Best Country Album by—who else?—*The Return of Roger Miller* but is a much better mirror of the times. In truth, trying to choose Atkins's cream of the crop is all but impossible given the voluminous output. But anyone who needs to feel what country is, all the way into its soul, would be well served buying the 2001 dual CD rerelease of *Guitar Country* and the 1965 *More of That Guitar Country* by Collectables Records, which added four other tracks.

By 1966, in fact, Chet was of such loftiness that the Grammy people thought nothing of nominating him for *four* awards, though he was shut out in all the categories and would release his newest LP, broadening his purview with the title *It's a Guitar World*, which was a wide world indeed. The tracks were a forty-five-minute diversion that included the somewhat overlooked Lennon and McCartney song "For No One," Paul's baroque companion to "Yesterday" on the Beatles' progressive "acid" album *Revolver*, which, with its subtle and delicate classical-style descending chords, was right up Chet's alley, or one of them. Chet's one song on the LP, "January in Bombay," also followed the Fab Four's path into Indian musicology, gingerly integrating a George Harrison-type sitar played by Indian-born guitarist Harihar Rao, who recorded his own fusion album, *Raga Rock*, that year. Combined with Chet's acoustic Gretsch, they accounted for the most surreal country blues ever, with Chet throwing in some of the oddest percussive-like guitar clacking to ever jump off an Atkins record. More conventionally, some of the other songs tapped Ray Charles's "What'd I Say" and Jimmy Wilkerson's "Pickin' Nashville."

The work, which was all too typical of Atkins albums, stalled outside the top hundred album rankings, yet there seemed to be a logical reason for this—considering how frequently Atkins albums rolled out, few had the time to rise on the charts before the next one was released. As the head of A&R at RCA Nashville, he had the final call on this schedule and, with so much created on a whim, gave little heed to the charts. To be certain, none of them are not worth hearing all these years later, preserved in the personal collections of Atkins-philes. But in real time, one could never know which ones would make the charts, and if the better ones would be left out in the cold. One of his '66 albums was the attempt to profit from Beatlemania *Chet Atkins Picks on the Beatles*, yet this too is a must-hear. Chet and Ferguson crafted intriguing, scaled-down re-creations of "I Feel Fine," "Yesterday," "Can't Buy Me Love," "Michelle," and "She Loves You," and as Harrison wrote on the liner notes, the remake of "Yesterday" "gets far more out of [it] than some of the people known as 'class' singers do with a full orchestral arrangement to boot!" All the redos, he wrote, "have a country feeling about them [and] lend themselves to Chet's style of picking, which has inspired so many guitarists around the world (myself included, but I didn't have enough fingers at the time.)"

The LP, with a shot of Chet on the back cover smiling sheepishly and wearing a prop Beatles wig, caught its share of derision, and still does in retro-reviews, one calling it "disposable," but it also caught fire during the British Invasion, going to number 6 country and number 112 pop. However, once the Fab Four had moved on to sophisticated and introspective melodies and skillful arrangements, Chet ceded them their unique ground; the last time he covered the Beatles was with "Lady Madonna" on his 1968 album *Solid Gold 68*, winning him another Grammy nomination, for Best Instrumental Performance (Other Than Jazz), though the record was beaten by the Tijuana Brass's *What Now My Love* album.

The real lesson of Chet's expansion of country music was that he would not be able to skip past the more complex world outside Nashville.

He and his avatars now had to deal with music that reflected the younger generation's anger and angst about racial flames burning in America and napalm searing through the jungles of a far-off war. In 1965 President Lyndon Johnson was at the polar ends of both, having pushed through the Civil Rights and Voting Rights Acts and committed the country to victory at any cost in Vietnam, a place most Americans couldn't have found on a map but that he insisted was essential to capitalist freedom. Suddenly, the placid America of the '50s was on the edge of a match, with Barry McGuire's "Eve of Destruction" vying with "Ballad of the Green Berets" for sales dollars. The conjunction of psychotic division, psychedelic diversion, and the reincarnation of the onerous Richard Nixon would be all too real by decade's end, with a festival of peace and love to be followed by another begging for shelter.

Down in sleepy Nashville town, the match stayed unlit, though there were rifts—such as when three activists were arrested for throwing themselves before Johnson's limousine when he came to give a Vietnam pep talk—and country songs began to infiltrate the subculture, such as Johnny Cash's "Singing in Viet Nam Talking Blues," recasting the "living hell" he saw when he went to play for the troops there, and the pro-war "Hello Vietnam," sung by Chet's old confrere Johnnie Wright backed by Kitty Wells, which spent twenty weeks on the country chart. Other such yin-yangs were Loretta Lynn's moving "Dear Uncle Sam" and Ernie Tubb's "It's for God, Country, and You, Mom (That's Why I'm Fighting in Vietnam)." Pro-war sentiment seemed to be dominant, as if being Southern demanded it—witness Stonewall Jackson's "The Minute Men (Are Turning in Their Graves)" and Mother Maybelle's "I Told Them What You're Fighting For."

Chet on his part took no stand and in '61 killed the release of his own production of Jim Reeves's "Distant Drums," a sentimental plea by a soldier to his girlfriend to marry him before he shipped out, the inference being that he might not make it back. Touching as it was, Chet took a pass releasing it, believing it would stir up anti-war sentiment, just as he voided songs of fervent pro-war themes. However, RCA released it after Reeves's death, and in 1966, with soldiers playing it on

Armed Forces Radio in the jungles, "Drums" hit number one country and number one in England. Moreover, other Atkins songs whose titles they didn't know but were unmistakably homespun were also favorites of the GIs, the quiet instrumentals prompting them to ponder their loneliness and isolation. One story told was that a GI tried to get a buddy to shut off the radio, lest the enemy know where they were, whereupon the buddy told him, "But it's Chet Atkins!" This wide swath of popularity was more trenchant to Chet than siding with any political bent. Ray Stevens—who arrived in Nashville in the mid-'60s and, like Jerry Reed, fused into Chet's inner circle—described him years later with the rather blurry circumspection that Atkins clearly had carved out for himself:

> I'm sure there are other things the public is not privy to that may or may not be important. I know he always tried to conduct himself like a gentleman and he was a thoughtful person. Nobody had to ever call him down for not being politically correct and that was before it became such a big thing. He was always trying to say and do the right thing, and to my way of thinking that's a sign of somebody who is very intelligent and just a good person.
>
> Oh yes, he got angry, but he didn't often let it show. In fact, most people didn't know it; they didn't know he was upset. But I could often tell depending on the situation. If we were sitting in a group, most of the other people wouldn't know, most could not tell that he was not happy but I could—and I usually knew what it was about too. I guess when you hang around somebody a lot you figure out what different looks and reactions mean.

There are nonetheless intriguing side roads within this cover story of a man who never seemed to be disturbed by the foibles that complicated other men. For all his reluctance to be tagged with any political or musical direction, he was a fan of Bob Dylan's protest folk-rock and was delighted when Owen Bradley brought Dylan to Nashville to record. Nor did Chet take any moral stand when the Beatles' continual experimentation and drug references demanded change of moral and artistic norms by everyone within the industry. As much as he would have been happy simply playing old country, reality demanded what it always did—keeping up with the trends. And he wouldn't just copy; he would innovate. The days were over when Sinatra and Martin could score a pop hit and the Tijuana Brass were relevant.

He would define his role in cultural change this way in 1974: "We were consciously trying for pop sales . . . because at that time you couldn't get a record played pop if it had steel on it," noting the exception of Dylan's "Lay Lady Lay." He concluded with one of those cynical truths that always made it rewarding to hear him when something got under his saddle: "They're like sheep. I just follow whatever they think is the in thing."

Of course, even while going "uptown," he never said *he* was a sheep. And with a new thing erupting every day in music, even in his forties he would have to lead, not follow.

17

"CHIT ATKINS, MAKE ME A STAR"

In 1966 Chet cut his first album in collaboration with the patrician-looking Arthur Fiedler, the two men of opposite breeding sharing the same intention to broaden their often straitjacketed domains. Indeed, Fiedler, who had brought pop and rock into classical themes, bent considerably on the project, the title of which, *The Pops Goes Country*, perfectly characterized the ensuing twelve tracks of country fare. Arranged by Richard Hayman, the Boston Pops chief arranger for fifty years, who also arranged movie scores and pop records for mainstream singers like Barbra Streisand, the massive orchestra—the Pops' A-Team—recorded it at classical music's Opry, the cacophonous Boston Symphony Hall, playing not a single classical tune but country-folk, several having been recorded by Chet, such as "John Henry," "Country Gentleman," "Windy and Warm," "Tennessee Waltz," "Alabama Jubilee," and "Cold Cold Heart."

The result of Chet's reconnoitering with classical gas while sitting in with various orchestras—which he did five times with Fiedler at Carnegie Hall—was not always perfect synergy. The vibe was often one of mutual contempt. When things didn't go well during the sound checks, Chet would tell the orchestra conductor to "tune 'em up." According to Paul Yandell, whom Chet later took on the road with his own band as a creature comfort on such gigs, said that "most of the musicians in those symphonies are snobs. . . . If you live in Nashville they think you go around in overalls, barefoot, swinging a jug." Despite the irony that Chet saw himself as much more than a country player, he and his homeboys were snubbed. "[They] wouldn't even speak to you or make eye contact." Yandell remembered one such engagement with the San Antonio Symphony, when Chet gave a directive to tune up.

> Well, that did it! They all got an attitude! They really turned against us. You could have cut it with a knife. This got Chet a little upset so it was rough. I just wanted to get up and leave. [And] they never did get in good tune. When we got home, Chet wrote the newspaper there and told them how he had been treated by the symphony. He let them have it! That was the worst time we had in all the years I was with Chet, I think.

But what came out of the Fiedler album was worth the effort. It was a thread of ear-filling, sometimes hypnotic sound, with glockenspiels, crashing cymbals, and all the rest, though one wonders if Chet's more minimalist playing was a bit too obeisant to the orchestra. The public had no problem identifying with it—the album hit number sixty-two pop and number thirty-six country, and sparked a less-popular country-classic jam three years later, *Chet Atkins Picks on the Pops*, with some more intricately played guitar lines distinguishing more modern hit tunes, like Jimmy Webb's "By the Time I Get to Phoenix" and "Galveston," Burt Bacharach and Hal David's "This Guy's in Love with You," Bobbie Gentry's "Ode to Billie Joe," and another go at Jerry Leiber and Phil Spector's "Spanish Harlem." But the most startling aspect of these diversions was their own competition with the ever-shifting Atkins albums recorded, in some cases, only weeks apart.

Before the Fiedler project, Chet had joined in on one of the nuttier RCA specialty record projects, a two-volume limited-edition set of ten album compilations presenting dance crazes—the Watusi, hitch-hiker, frug, twist, cha-cha, slop, etc. What was nutty was that the whole thing was overseen by the geriatric TV dance instructor Arthur Murray and titled *Wurlitzer Discotheque Music*, with arrangements by the Claus Ogerman Orchestra on one side and already-released songs by known artists, including Duane Eddy and the Isley Brothers, on the reverse. Murray chose the songs and on volume 4 picked Chet's "Alley Cat" (as swing), "Back Home Again in Indiana" (frug), and "Sweetie Baby" (monkey). Then, the Fiedler diversion done, came *From Nashville with Love*, the title song written by John Loudermilk. Other selections included George Barnes's "Something Tender," Cole Porter's "I Love Paris," Stanislav Binički's "Drina," and Carlo Donida's "Al Di La." It went to number twenty-six country.

Another step was the similar wide berth of idioms that he put on *Music from Nashville, My Home Town*. There would then be eight more albums by decade's end, three of which landed in the top thirty country albums, with Chet having a crack at mostly soft rock fodder. On *Solid Gold 68*, the one with "Lady Madonna"—which he slowed down to accommodate his easygoing, long-held, and bent-note tremolo riffs—he also took on the Doors' psychedelic "Light My Fire," though it was more a cover of the bluesy José Feliciano redo, with Chet and Ferguson adding strings and horns. All the while, he was producing more noncountry topliners who caught Nashville fever and came in so he could weave hits for them. New was in, with both young and not-so-young arrivals scoping new ground. Dolly Parton had first come in from the Smoky Mountains when she was eleven. "I used to come to Nashville with my uncle [and songwriting partner] Bill Owens," she recalled, "and we used to run around after Chet Atkins, try to get on the Grand Ole Opry, and Chet said, 'You need to go on back home, and finish school, and then when you finish school you should come on back and talk to me.'" She did and, one day after graduating high school in 1964, came in again with tapes of songs, some of which were rather ripe for a teenager, and a killer figure. "He was the first person I looked up when I moved here."

Audacious as she was, she even had the nerve to reject his advice to "tone it down," which one could understand given that his daughter,

Merle, was just a year younger. And Dolly was one of the very few who rejected *his* wisdom and still won his allegiance; he signed her to RCA in 1967, and wearing the tightest of outfits and tallest of wigs, her soprano trill instantly became profitable when she teamed with Porter Wagoner on the latter's TV show and on a series of records produced by Bob Ferguson. And when Chet would speak of her, he would with a laugh remind everyone how wrong he was that one time. Actually, he was wrong a few other times too. But once sounded about right to him.

Atkins getting it right was a common adage, and that reputation stuck to him. During the '60s, it drew some mainstream eminences to town. The biggest were noncountry warhorses Perry Como and Rosemary Clooney, both of whom had been hit leaders on the RCA pop roster for years, Como since the '40s, Clooney since the '50s. Both had hit a rut, and Steve Sholes suggested that they take the midnight train to Nashville to see Chet Atkins. Both were preternaturally noncountry and Clooney, the jazz-singing on-screen bombshell, had long made waves with sexually dripping, Italo-centric come-ons like "Botch-a-Me" and "Come On-a My House," the sort of winking sexual come-ons Chet was uncomfortable about. But at thirty-five in 1963, she was a physical and mental wreck, hooked on drugs and hollowed by a depression that would soon cause a nervous breakdown and confinement in psychiatric hospitals for eight years. Indeed, the album she cut with Atkins, *Rosemary Clooney Sings Country Hits from the Heart*, would be her last one for RCA but a lifeline she could cling to.

She had dabbled in the idiom in 1961, releasing a cover of Don Gibson's "Give Myself a Party," and the album was partly recorded in Hollywood—produced by Dick Peirce and arranged by the veteran jazz conductor Marty Paich—but completed in Nashville. Wisely, Chet didn't try to force an unreal country flavor from her but mellowed and slowed her roll on mainly old country hits like Hank Williams's "I'm So Lonesome I Could Cry," Gibson's "Love Has Come My Way," Alton

Delmore and Arthur Smith's "Beautiful Brown Eyes," and Don Robertson and Hal Blair's "Please Help Me, I'm Falling," once a Hank Locklin hit, as well as "How's the World Treating You?," written by Chet with Boudleaux Bryant back in 1957 and recorded by Elvis, Locklin, and Wanda Jackson. These songs seemed meant for her and put her vulnerability on full display, backed by preening acoustic guitars and wispy strings. To be sure, her raw sexiness was still an immediate turn-on, most raw on "So Lonesome," with a pulsating piano by Cramer, and the cover was Rosemary posing in a haystack in sheer pajamas. But more deeply, the album is an astounding human portrait of someone falling through the floor, which she did after signing with Reprise Records and recording *Thanks for Nothing.*

As for the congenial Mr. C, Chet employed a smallish A-Team crew, with Floyd Cramer and Boots Randolph in place of Como's longtime backing by the Mitchell Ayres orchestra, and the Anita Kerr Quartet in place of the Ray Charles Singers. The objective was to massage Como's yawning big band pop into easy listening country hash, and in February 1965, Atkins produced the aptly titled *The Scene Changes* album. The song list included two sentimental songs by Willie Nelson, "Funny How Time Slips Away" and "My Own Peculiar Way," Don Gibson's "Give Myself a Party," John Loudermilk's "That Ain't All," Bill and Dottie West's "Here Comes My Baby," Don Robertson's "I Really Don't Want to Know," and Tompall Glaser's "Stand Beside Me." Also on the LP was Jan Crutchfield and Fred Burch's "Dream On, Little Dreamer," which was slated to be the main single, recorded as an easygoing blues stroll with a harmonica line and a finger-snapping beat, yet in line with the almost visual, hay-dangling country mien, on which Perry sounded like Bing Crosby harmonizing with the Anita Kerr Quartet.

While the album was almost perfunctorily regarded as a novelty, it gave Como a reset; after not releasing a single in two years, "Dreamer" rose to number three on the easy listening chart and number twenty-five pop, and set the path for his next three singles, recorded back in New York, one, "Stop! And Think It Over," going to number one. Moreover, the album would have lasting value, an AllMusic review calling it "an ideal match for the Nashville Sound" and "as warm and inviting as an old pair of slippers" when an expanded CD version was rereleased in 2016. Spared from the rack, Como's biggest record would come in his old age, something that he would credit to Chet, whom he would form a personal friendship with and again record with in the '70s—the decade he had his biggest hit—when they would have another round of recording sessions, both of them codgers but far from finished.

Already established as a miracle worker in Nashville, Chet came to the aid of Eddy Arnold, as well. Eddy in 1965 had also fallen into a slump as he aged and had Chet produce him, leading to Arnold having his first number-one record in ten years, the one that would be enshrined in the Library of Congress. This was *My World*, which Chet recorded in what RCA called "Stereo Dynagroove," utilizing computers to auto-equalize bass and treble. Chet—by no surprise—had already used the method on "Back Home Again in Indiana" on the 1963 album *The New Sound of the Stars*, as he had on Arnold's "The Streets of Laredo," and Eddy seemed especially clear and captivating on *My World*, weaving his soft country-pop into reflective moods on tracks like Harlan Howard's "Too Many Rivers," Al Stillman's "The Days Go By," Billy Reid's "I'm Walking Behind You," and "If You Were Mine, Mary," an early song by Chip Taylor, who had also written rock classics like "Wild Thing" and "Angel of the Morning." Chet also turned Eddy's single of Carl Belew's "What's He Doing in My World" into a number-one country hit, which would be Arnold's first chart topper in a decade, and Chet would make another number one with Eddy's cover of Hank Locklin's "Make the World Go Away."

The album, released in October, became the biggest-selling of Arnold's majestic career, spending seventeen weeks atop the country chart and forty-four weeks before falling off it. And Eddy knew where the corn bread was buttered. His next spate of albums, *The Last Word in Lonesome*, *Somebody Like Me*, *Lonely Again*, *Turn the World Around*, and *The Everlovin' World of Eddy Arnold* were all produced by Atkins and incorporated material by pop poet Rod McKuen, the writing team of Henry Mancini and Ray Livingston, and soul man Bobby Hebb, and all went to number one country. The next albums, *The Romantic World of Eddy Arnold* and *Walkin' in Love Land*, fell short—at number two. And Atkins did all this while concurrently working with Jerry Reed, turning him into one of the most unlikely stars in Nashville. In 1967 Reed played Chet a demo of his semiautobiographical, Johnny Cash–style life of playing dive bars. Chet encouraged Jerry to add what would become his trademark garrulous grunting to the breakneck pace, and it became the tone of Reed's first hit single, "Guitar Man." Released that fall, it hit number fifty-three country and forty-three pop, and went on Reed's debut LP, *The Unbelievable Guitar and Voice of Jerry Reed* in the fall, led by Reed's equally garrulous fingerpicking, with Chet and his other protégé, Ray Stevens, playing harpsichord. The cover played to form, with Reed flapping about like a dodo, guitar nearly flying out of the hand.

For Chet, the album had a family-like feel, the back cover having Reed and Atkins strumming beside each other while sitting atop a massive amp, with brief liner notes by the now twenty-year-old Merle Atkins, who had begun her college years studying religion at a local convent but switched to studying music. Merle, seeking to be a delegate of a younger America, swooned that "Jerry Reed is a whole guitar case full of soul" and "the strongest force behind Daddy's style." There would be thirty-two albums to come for Reed, and he was given a virtual hall pass at Studio A and B, as well as the Atkins family's dinner table. Chet spared no cost pushing him, running RCA ads in the papers with the blurb "When Chet Atkins says 'Jerry Reed's Guitar Man is the greatest' . . . who's gonna argue?"

Even Elvis was fascinated. He tried recording "Guitar Man" but couldn't get it right, so he had producer Felton Jarvis call "that redneck guitar player" to lay down rhythm guitar with Scotty Moore; the Elvis cover then hit number one on the country chart, and he would open with it on his comeback-special TV show the next year, with Chet one of the veteran musicians who famously ringed Elvis onstage. Elvis would also cover Reed's "U.S. Male" and "Big Boss Man," and Chet recorded a song for his own use written by Jerry's singing wife, Priscilla Hubbard (Jerry's surname), "Prissy," which won a Best Instrumental Grammy nomination in 1968. No one argued with Atkins's opinion of Jerry Reed—whose early, Atkins-produced material also included three gonzo country albums, *Nashville Underground*, *Alabama Wild Man*, and *Jerry Reed Explores Guitar Country*—and these two men from completely opposite ends of musical and personal scales took on the personae of the Odd Couple, Jerry as blithely unregimented as Chet was indeed prissily anal. For Atkins, however, Reed was but one cog in a continuum that never stopped moving, and before he knew it, the endless conflict between being creative and corporate would be sucking the life out of him.

Much like the continual gush of musical true believers into Nashville, newspaper and magazine writers seeking to find America's answer to London's new hegemony stopped at Chet's door. One wide-eyed reporter from Australia, Lillian Roxon, flew in, interviewed him, and wrote a story titled "Nashville: The Town with the 'Fresh Sound,'" lionizing it as "the star-spangled home of the fastest guitars in the country, a lively glittery town booming so fast that land values have tripled," something she may have learned about from Chet, whom she likely meant in writing about "a man who paid $39,000 for a corner lot on record row last year [and] recently refused $160,000 for it." Never entirely diplomatic with reporters, he groused to her that the musicians he had groomed into near cult status had become a bit too comfy in Nashville.

"You can take these fellows up to New York to record and they freeze up," he said. "It's not like being home," perhaps a barb that they were limiting themselves from a big, wide world outside the city's borders.

His own boundless sights and influence were beyond reproach, and had been since Country Gentleman and Mister Guitar became eternally applied appellations for him. In 1964 there was an inevitable tribute on vinyl when country comedian Don Bowman recorded "Chit Akins, Make Me a Star." For Charley Pride, that could have been the bottom line of his career, even a daily mantra during a career that mainly became a reality because of Chet. The Statler Brothers' "Chet Atkins' Hand" was waiting down the road. And Chet was willing to accept the spotlight, in his own tempered manner. In the mid-'60s, he had caught the golf bug and was hitting the links around town with Jerry Reed, striking up relationships with pros who wanted to play a few rounds with him. In '65 he got the funding together to stage the Chet Atkins Celebrity Pro-Am, starting in 1966 at the Nashboro Village club, which saw a rarity when pro Vernon Thwaites and jockey Bill Boland made eagle threes on a long par-five hole. The prize money was $10,000, and the event drew large crowds to gawk at Reed, Eddy Arnold, Charley Pride, Homer and Jethro, Floyd Cramer, local TV personalities, and not least of all Chet. Most years it was held at the Deane Hill Country Club, which was owned by Jack Comer, the publisher who had sagely advised Chet long ago to diversify, and who was on the board of directors at Deane Hill. Comer and Chet would greet Perry Como when he flew in on a private plane, and though Comer got himself into hot water for underpaying minimum wage salaries to employees, the pro-am carried on for twenty years at a host of high-toned clubs.

Ray Stevens, who had never played golf in his life, felt compelled to join Chet out there. As Stevens recalled,

> Hundreds of guys would show up and we would have a great time for 3 or 4 days, play golf and raise money [for charities]. I still have some of the souvenirs—bags and hats and things that they gave out at these events that say "Chet Atkins" on them. I'll tell you something funny about Chet and golf. I remember once we were at Hillwood and I was driving the cart, on about the 4th hole I think. I had hooked my shot left off the tee and Chet of course hit his into the middle of the fairway. We were heading up to the balls and were going

> slightly uphill. We were moving pretty fast when I thought I saw my ball over in the rough so I shouted "Oh there it is!" and I made an abrupt left which launched Chet right out of the cart. He didn't speak to me for several holes. I was really embarrassed about that.

Atkins, perfectionist that he was, shot regularly in the low eighties, and being isolated on a fairway was his idea of serenity now. Indeed, after Leona had also taken up the game and played with him, he said he only would play solo "because we fight," either one of his rim-shot-type jokes or a possible hint that things may have gotten a bit rough between them at times, given his need for isolation—though some Nashville elitists who bounced with him on the course would joke that his eye was more trained on pert blondes in the gallery than irons and putters. Rick Sanjek believed this was strictly a look-but-don't-touch situation for Chet, unlike his boss at BMI, senior vice president Harry Warner, who was, Sanjek said, "a great guy and a real womanizer," adding with a giggle, "and Chet's pimp," probably meaning *intended* pimp. The furthest Chet would go on the subject was writing in his 1974 memoir that "nothing stopped my girl watching," which clearly was no secret, since the same year he admitted in a *People* profile that what really mattered to him was "playin' guitar, playin' golf and girl-watchin'." Neither was he averse to a prurient story now and then involving some flirtin' but nothing more with high-level blondes—one being no less than a handsy Dolly Parton.

"She grabbed me by the ass three times last year," he once related to writer Nicholas Dawidoff, clearly taken with himself for it, provided it even happened, and adding his easy wit to the tale. "I was gonna sue her for sexual harassment, but only for fifty dollars 'cause I kind of enjoyed it, you know."

To be certain, his unabridged fealty to Leona was an act of faith. They were one of Nashville's great love stories, befitting his image as a fine family man with controllable urges. Nor did anyone ever dispute whether he was godly, and as such, he could be intimidating when disinterested in the usual maw of glad-handing record pooh-bahs in Nashville. Rather, unless he had formed a personal bond, he drew back, as if, like Paul Simon's proverbial rock, he had no need for outside friendship, laughter, loving, or the pain of caring. Sanjek tells of the coldness he felt when he first met him:

> I was only twenty-six when I came to Nashville from New York and Harry hired me at BMI. I was a young guy, a hot-shot. I played a little guitar, and I worked with big people like Cowboy Clement. And I revered Chet and was thrilled when Harry took me to lunch one day and none other than Chet was there! I couldn't wait to talk to him, pick his brain, but the whole time Chet never said anything to me, and truthfully I was a little pissed off. I was like, "Who in the hell is this guy? He doesn't even care about me." But then you'd hear things. Like when Pete Drake, a great pedal steel player I represented at BMI, who played the "talking steel guitar" on Bob Dylan's "Lay Lady Lay" and Tammy Wynette's "Stand By Your Man," got lung cancer and needed an operation he couldn't pay for. I never knew until Pete's wife Rose told me later on that Chet paid for the operation. And every musician had a story about how Chet put them on sessions to get some money.
>
> Truthfully, it's cathartic for me to talk about him now, because back then I figured he didn't like me but that was an assumption on my part and it wasn't true. He just didn't have a way of showing emotion, which was sad because I don't think he knew how much we loved him and we wanted him to love us back.

Few ever got as close to him as Harry Warner or Jack Clement, and, Lord knows, Jerry Reed, but many musicians were welcome to visit him at home. That would put local cops in quite a bind, having to keep unwanted strangers from wanting to show up there and meet him from those he invited over, naively unconcerned about the security concerns, which alarmed Leona. One of those caught in the middle was Rick Foster, a fingerpicker Chet had met out on the road in Georgia, where Rick was also a minister at the First Baptist Church in Thomasville. They began mailing each other letters and, recalled Foster, Chet offered, "If I can ever help with your recording in any way, let me know. I could always add echo or any of those things."

Foster went on:

> Chet invited me to come see him anytime I was near Tennessee, so the next time I was in Nashville I called and was invited out to the house. I headed there only to be pulled over for going the wrong way on a one way street. I was ordered to park my car, and then hauled to night court in a squad car. After informing the judge that I was on my way to the home of Chet and Leona Atkins, he [believed me and] immediately dismissed the case and ordered the patrolman to get me back to my car. When I finally arrived at Chet's house five hours later than expected, even though it was after midnight Chet and Leona were waiting up and welcomed me with Southern hospitality. Leona, who was a gracious and a perfect hostess, was also a personal friend of the police chief. She threatened to call and let him know that was no way to treat visitors.
>
> The next morning, Chet sat at the breakfast table practicing while he watched TV and Leona cooked the eggs. It seemed like there was a guitar in his hands all the time. He kept one near the phone and did finger exercises while he talked. He was always wanting to hear me play, although to this day I've never figured out why. And in later years after our family settled in Oregon, Chet kept in touch. He sent us tickets to his concert at the Britt festival in Jacksonville, Oregon, and invited me to play a tune at his concert at the Hult Center in Eugene, Oregon. He even had me open a concert for him at the Lobero theater in Santa Barbara, California, and gave me the Gibson guitar he played as a gift.

Foster, who has called Atkins "greater than the legend," would see some remarkable things at Chet's house. One involved Christopher Parkening, the classical guitarist and educator who at the time had withdrawn from the rat race to live in isolation, fly-fishing in Montana. Parkening was also an admirer of Atkins, and when Foster came to Nashville to perform with the Nashville Symphony, he invited Parkening to come with him. During the visit, they dropped by Chet's house. Within minutes Chet, who mutually admired Parkening, was showing him the rudimentary process he had perfected of manually cutting tape with a razor blade and splicing pieces together with no trace of any edit. Parkening was impressed but insisted it would be easier to re-record a full version. Such discussions were like debates between Plato and Aristotle, and hanging with Chet could be a peek into his guarded psyche.

Another time, accompanying the Atkinses to Sunday-morning church services, Foster was startled when Chet pulled out a hundred-dollar bill and gave it to him, saying, "I'll put some more in when the plate comes by so they won't think I'm cheap."

When Rick began quietly singing biblical hymns, Chet remained silent. Foster then asked him if he believed in God.

"I believe in something," Chet said, "but don't know what it is."

Out on the fairway was basically the only place where most people could get physically close to him. Chet would walk haughtily about, perfectly clad in dashing gold attire and two-tone shoes like James Bond in *Goldfinger*. But he was often nowhere to be found, having sequestered himself in a private room of the clubhouse, not practicing his putting but playing a guitar, which he always stashed in his locker. It was weird to see him doing what he played golf *not* to have to do, but for Atkins the golden rule was to practice guitar every single day, no matter where, including hotel rooms on the road. But when he would come out of the clubhouse, the "square peg" seemed to get more comfortable as a celebrity, which had its own public demands.

For example, on the twentieth anniversary of his signing by Sholes, and his tenth as head man in Nashville, the industry bourgeois arranged an elegant tribute on May 28, 1967, at the Municipal Auditorium. Tickets for one thousand in the double-decker hall were sold for twenty dollars each, the VIPs shelling out much more for a seat adjacent to the stage where Arthur Fiedler would conduct the Nashville Symphony and Jimmy Dean, who had left Columbia to sign with RCA just to be on the Atkins roster, would be the emcee for a show featuring Randolph, Cramer, Pride, Mother Maybelle and the Carter Sisters, and Merle Travis. The label also bought a twenty-five-page special insert in the June 3 *Billboard*, timed for the event, selling space to music people, promoters, politicians, and priests for personal encomiums. Gretsch bought a page that combined congratulation with a sales pitch for each of the Atkins signature models—"even if you can't play like Chet, you *can* play better on a Gretsch Chet Atkins guitar." Dean took an entire page to say "Congratulations Chet, and 20 more."

Photos of his life and career festooned the pages, and in a blurb, Sholes cited his favorite thing about Chet—that "he's quite a buy" and "every year [has been] profitable." Or as RCA's vice president and general manager Norman Racusin put it, Chet oversaw "a smooth running, profitable operation." Fred Foster quoted Sir Walter Scott to frame the Atkins mythology—"One crowded hour of glorious life is worth an age without a name." Skeeter Davis's message was "Chet, luv ya!" A full Atkins discography, even then an omnibus, took up several pages.

At the tuxedoed festivities, attended by everyone who mattered, the sponsors brought in Ida and Willie Strevel, the elderly but still cantankerous James Arlie Atkins, and Jimmy and Lowell, all resplendent in tuxes, as well as Archie Campell and Lowell Blanchard. Leona and Merle would sit in the front row with Lois and Homer Burns, along with other Atkins family relatives. The tributes came in waves for three hours, and Racusin gave Chet an award calling him the "laid back relaxed" Atkins, "one of the genuine pleasures we enjoy at RCA Victor Records." When Chet was called to the stage, he quietly thanked everyone for coming, including the patriarchal but distant father he had barely spoken with for decades, and after a short turn with Jimmy Dean, performed with the Carters on "Country Gentleman," "Alabama Jubilee," "Wildwood Flower," and "Tennessee Waltz," after which he was given a ten-minute standing ovation.

These rites of laudation were long overdue, and the timing was especially right. In 1967—by coincidence, the year of the axiomatic Summer of Love—he had been nominated in two categories at the inaugural Country Music Awards, held at the Ryman and telecast by ABC-TV, and won Instrumentalist of the Year (as he would for the first three years, and be nominated for it every year through 1988, winning the last five times in a row; he would also be named the CMA's first Musician of the Year in 1988). Already swathed in Grammys, he won another, Best Instrumental Performance, for *Chet Atkins Picks the Best*, one more eclectic tour that melded songs as diverse as "You'll Never Walk Alone," Django Reinhardt's "Nuages" and "Tears," "Battle Hymn of the Republic," the movie theme of *Run for Your Wife*, and a cover of Marty Robbins's monumental "El Paso." He was going full bore. But what he couldn't know was that, within months, his purview would be stretched even broader, which he took with an ambivalence that proved well founded.

On March 11, 1968, less than a year after he had helped pay tribute to his youngest son, seventy-nine-year-old James Arlie Atkins awoke with chest pains in the home in Corryton, Tennessee, where he and his wife Jewell still lived. Taken to St. Mary's Hospital in Knoxville, he lapsed into a coma, could not be revived, and was pronounced dead of a heart attack, leaving his widow Jewell, his three children with Ida, his daughter with Jewell, Jeanne Williams, nine grandchildren, and two great-grandchildren. Through the years, James Sr. had carried on as a piano tutor and church choir leader, only occasionally feeling the need to see or speak with his children, never for more than a few minutes. Chet, who often wished he could mend the broken fences with James

Sr., never did so, and his mixed feelings about James picked at him when he, Jimmy, and Lowell, as well as Ida and Willie Strevel, went to Knoxville for the service at Ailor Funeral Home in Maynardville and the burial at Rocky Dale Cemetery. On that early spring day, Chester Burton Atkins tried to focus his thoughts on the balm of music James Sr. had established for him, and how James had taken him to Georgia so that his lungs could function, allowing his son to find his future in high school. He hoped he could now put the childhood abuse and betrayals of his mother in that casket with him. Speaking with an AP reporter, he said, "He sang me to sleep when I was a baby and played the violin when I was in the cradle. He instilled a desire in me to be somebody musically. . . . He was a tremendous influence on all us kids." But Chet left with the same inner emptiness. Indeed, he may have felt a far greater loss when, just over a month later, his real mentor prematurely took the last exit.

On April 22 Steve Sholes had just landed in Nashville for a meeting of the Board of Directors of the Country Music Foundation, of which he was president. He rented a car and headed to a concert to be held by Homer and Jethro at Vanderbilt University when the car went out of control and crashed into a bridge railing. When an ambulance arrived at the scene, Sholes was pronounced dead at fifty-seven of a heart attack. This latest early demise in the country ambit seemed part of a cycle of death most foul, only eighteen days after Martin Luther King Jr. was gunned down in Memphis and forty-four days before Robert Kennedy would be in Los Angeles. For Chet it hurt like hell, as Sholes had all but built the Nashville identity that he put in Atkins's hands. Sholes had campaigned to finance the Country Music Hall of Fame and was elected into it. Chet's loyalty to him never wavered, his standard line being, "I worked for Steve, I didn't work for RCA."

But now he did only work for RCA, this newest tragedy in his life meaning an even deeper shift in the power structure. After Sholes was buried not in his home state of New Jersey but in Nashville, at Woodlawn Memorial Park and Mausoleum, Atkins was duly promoted by RCA to Sholes's vice-presidency and given complete authority over the label's country division, meaning more papers would be on his desk, and more headaches. As a good company soldier, he accepted the job, which included a raise and a base salary of $2,000 a week, bigger bonuses for each hit, and increased royalties on his own work—though one of Atkins's failings was that he never hired a lawyer or accountant to check out the little details of his contracts, a gross irony given that part of his job was to sign artists to contracts with, by industry custom, clauses essentially screwing them. No one ever blamed him; after all, he made sure they would get the best possible recording advantage—having him there. Being on the back end of such matters, however, made for some inner debates that he couldn't resolve, not to mention that, while he was doing well enough financially, he suspected even he was being screwed.

His once-heralded endorsement deal with Gretsch created more ambivalence. While he was profiting from its periodic unveiling of newer-model Country Gentleman axes, he would years later explain that he gave both Gretsch and RCA too much leeway and benefit of the doubt, for the same reason:

> Yeah, I got pretty good royalties. . . . I would get about $100,000 a year off my records, because I was selling all over the world, even though my royalty rate was really low. I don't know what I would have gotten if I'd have had a good contract where I got a lot of royalty, but back in those days probably the maximum I made was about five per cent, and I was probably getting three or four per cent. I don't know if they paid me all that was due me, either. Those accountants are clever that way. . . . They have all kinds of ways of charging things against you. I never did that, never pestered them. I'm kind of naive about things like that.

Still, within his double life, he wasn't naive enough to ensure other RCA artists weren't subject to those same pincers, and while he was also discontented with his Gretsch paychecks, he made no issue of it except for some snippy comments he would inject into interviews, though he always remembered to pay the company the highest praise for its workmanship. Yet by the new decade and mindset of the '70s, the underbelly of these issues became more swollen, and both RCA and Gretsch would have to live with the very real consequence that Chet would no longer be the good soldier, and worse, wouldn't need to be in order to keep moving forward.

18

OUTLAW MEN

Nashville in the late 1960s had to contend with competition by L.A. country-rock bands, a trend that Atkins had foreseen back in the '50s and that Nashville had a hand in when Bob Dylan migrated from folk to electric rock, bringing it to Nashville. And Chet dug the groove as a county subsidiary, while keeping the Nashville Sound distinctive rather than derivative rock. Clearly, the old guard was changing as new musicians became A-Team players, and he kept his finger on the pulse of business in his little office back of Studio A, ever more troubled that this was taking the edge off his guitar playing. He did release typically impressive work—his final album of the '60s, *Solid Gold '69*, another tableau of pop faves like "Both Sides Now," "Son of a Preacher Man," "Blackbird," "Hey Jude," "Folsom Prison Blues," and "My Way." It had liner notes by the British folk-rocker Donovan and, although a profusion of singles like his "Mrs. Robinson" cover faded away quietly, the album was nominated for a Best Country Instrumental Grammy.

But the proudest day he had came far from the grind, in Scotland, when he walked Merle Atkins down the aisle to marry an Irish-born doctor named Will Russell, whom she had met while working in a Nashville hospital. When they became engaged, Merle agreed to tie the knot in Will's homeland on January 9 at the Bansha Parish church. Merle wore a full gown with a pearl-beaded choker and three-quarter veil, and the ceremony was performed by Canon Thomas O'Byrne, with the maid of honor being an Atkins family friend, Gemma Hughes. A hundred and fifty guests had flown in from America, and at the reception at the Cashel Palace Hotel in Tipperary, they had the distinction of hearing Chet get up and play country songs with Floyd Cramer and Boots Randolph, whereupon the happy couple would buy a house back home, not far from Chet and Leona's spread in Nashville.

The wedding seemed like a fable, aptly, since Chet was at the stage where royal raiments were being given to him. He had already been awarded the sort of honors usually reserved for high officials, one being the National Humanitarian Award from the Conference of Christians and Jews, and he could organize events himself, such as a nonprofit Chet Atkins Guitar Festival, whose proceeds, and those from his golf tournament, he donated to charity. His bona fides included a place on the Board of the National Chamber of Commerce and as a board member for the National Jewish Hospital and the Boy Scouts. A standard joke around Nashville was that Atkins was really ten men sharing the same name, and that his close friendships with Jerry Reed and Ray Stevens meant they had special powers.

Both benefited mightily from it; Reed, produced by Chet, cashed in with "When You're Hot, You're Hot," in which he uttered a nasty line about there being no one to "pay for my welfare Cadillac" if he went to jail, though his knack for a nifty line was best shown in "Amos Moses," about the Louisiana alligator-baiter Amos who was named after "a man of the cloth." Reed was, by his own design, a savvy redneck, and by the '70s would be coproducing with Chet on albums like *Me & Jerry*, a harmless country/pop gander blending and soloing finger licks with no vocals, covering songs like "Bridge Over Troubled Water," "MacArthur Park," "Ol' Man River," "Something," Merle Travis's "Cannonball Rag," Jimmy Driftwood's "Tennessee Stud," and three offbeat Reed originals, "Nut Sundae," "Stumpwater," and "The January-February March." The album noted playfully that "on your stereo set, Chet's on the right—Jerry's on the left," and one could palpably feel how good a time they had, and the Grammy people gave it the Best Country Instrumental award. Two years later, they did a follow-up, *Me & Chet*, which Reed coproduced with Chet, tearing up some left-field numbers, including Liszt's "Liebestraum," Junior Parker's "Mystery Train," Hank Williams's "I Saw the Light," and Reed's delightfully polar "Good Stuff" and "Jerry's Breakdown."

It went top twenty-five country and was nominated for the same award—one of the other nominees being *Chet Atkins Picks on the Hits*, one of those Grammy rarities when one performer is nominated twice in the same category, though Chet came up short on both. Reed would ride his many hits to higher ground, playing a part he seemed born to play, a chummy redneck, in Burt Reynolds's *Smokey and the Bandit* movies. He also opened his own publishing and management company, Vector Music, with help from Chet, who got Harry Warner to affiliate it under BMI's corporate umbrella. And, just as he had been a fountainhead for musicians and singers, Chet's power could build business careers; taking a piece of Vector, he chose a young song plugger, Tim Wipperman, to run the company, which would prompt Wipperman's long career as head of Warner Brothers' Nashville office, then as president of Warner Chappell Music for three decades. Another, David Conrad, was a roadie who set up Jerry Reed's stage microphone, then went into publishing.

Ray Stevens's huge-selling records for Monument and then Warner Bros., produced by another Atkins acolyte, Shelby Singleton, included comic novelties like his early hits "Gitarzan"—a comical answer to Reed's "Guitar Man," with Stevens doing Tarzan shrieks and "Jane" ordering him to "shut up, baby, I'm tryin' to sing!"—and "Ahab the Arab," which required a listener to understand that disparaging names for non-Christian foreigners was common in Dixie, and sadly all of America. His biggest song, the Grammy-winning "Everything Is Beautiful," preached that Jesus loves all the children of the world, but "Mr. Businessman" explained that everything isn't beautiful due to vacuous greed merchants, the same kind that he and Chet would pinpoint as avaricious ministers later, in 1987, when Ray recorded "Would Jesus Wear a Rolex?" which Atkins cowrote with Nashville singer-songwriter Margaret Archer, a member of the Cluster Pluckers, one of the greatest band names of all time.

These personal attachments seemed a way for Chet to keep a "family" feel within the soulless fraternity of music autocrats, and that feel led him back to the Everly Brothers—or, to be accurate, the brothers back to him. Despite having saved Warner Brothers' skin in the early '60s, their contract was not renewed in 1971, leaving them down and out in Beverly Hills. As attached to Don and Phil as he was, Chet offered them an RCA contract, albeit a conditional one, for two albums. He let them record in L.A. with the Doors and Janis Joplin producer Paul Rothchild, one of the many rock music movers who revered them and tried salvaging their career. However, after the first one, *Stories We Could Tell*, was a bust, Chet told Don and Phil to come "home" and record the second one in Studio B. The album, the bit too cutely titled *Pass the Chicken & Listen*, drew a large contingent of newer studio cats groomed by Chet, including guitarists Bobby Thompson, Dale Sellers, Pete Wade, and Paul Yandell, the plucker who had come a long way since his quick brush with Chet after coming to Nashville to meet him, and had been on the two Atkins-Reed duet albums. Chet also had pedal-steel players Hal Rugg and Weldon Myrick, Steve Schaffer on bass, Johnny Gimble on fiddle, pianist Dave Briggs, and drummer Ralph Gallant.

It was an all-out project, and it consecrated an evolved Nashville in twelve tracks written by Waylon and Willie ("Good Hearted Woman"), Kristofferson ("Somebody Nobody Knows"), Boudleaux and Felice Bryant ("Rocky Top"), John Prine ("Paradise"), Roger Miller ("Husbands and Wives"), and Buddy Holly ("Not Fade Away," which Buddy had originally written for the Everlys). The problem was that Don and Phil bridled under Chet's imperious choices and directions, which were to re-create the roots of country-rock with current flavors. As Phil would later say, he and Don were like serfs, not stars, and that "we were saying 'okay' instead of 'yes.'" Accordingly, there were no songs written by the brothers on the album, which Chet ran diligently and with tender mercy for the Everlys' wondrous high and lonesome harmonies. Most regard the work as a quite noble effort by two thirty-something ex–teen idols guided by an almost fifty-year-old producer to fit into a young man's world. But something about it seems missing in authenticity, and at times more sad than revivalist.

In the end, not even Chet Atkins could revive the Everly Brothers. As important as it was, the album failed to chart or make much noise, and the brothers' simmering rivalry soon broke up the act for ten years, before they reunited for a cash cow of regressionary touring, at times invited by Paul Simon and Art Garfunkel to tour with them, the undercurrent of their legacy being that they fell off the cliff when they abandoned Nashville for L.A. recognition that never really happened. For Chet, secure as he still was, that failure was just a passing train in the night. But that enduring status would take a different form in 1972, subject to the terrifying prospect that it might be the last year of his life.

Late that year, he had also gotten Perry Como to come to Nashville for some new recordings. After Chet positioned Como to remain viable in the late '60s, Perry hit his pinnacle in 1970 with the windswept, million-selling "It's Impossible," produced by soft pop hitmaker Don Costa in L.A. It spent four weeks atop the chart and won the Grammy for Song of the Year. However, Como's follow-up work trended down again. Now presumably headed for retirement, he had originally resisted Chet's invitations to produce him again, which led to some part-wry, part-cutting Atkins criticism, saying it was a chore to "get Perry off his fishing boat. He's so damned lazy these days, you never know." If that seemed a tad harsh about a man of Social Security age, he knew it would work on Como, who returned for the new sessions.

They chose songs by hip, young writers. Atkins's favorite was Don McClean, whose "American Pie" was more dramaturgy than a pop tune, and his Van Gogh quatrain "Vincent," about an artist whose swirls of clouds and colors were not fully appreciated in his time, was so resonant that Chet's instrumental of it was a personal coda that always melted Leona's heart when he played it as a valentine to her. Reaching back to McLean's 1971 debut album, Como chose to cover "And I Love

You So," which had failed as singles for Bobby Goldsboro and Bobby Vinton but flourished into one of the most peacefully introspective love songs ever, which mounted slowly from its acoustic guitar pings into a quiet storm of emotional peaks, perfectly metered by Como with a subtlety missing from "It's Impossible." Stunning in nature, it could even make grown men weep, and when the single hit the top of the easy listening chart early in '73 (and number two in Britain), RCA had him record a version for foreign consumption in Spanish. It then released the Atkins-produced album of the same name, with other heartfelt tracks including Mac Davis's "I Believe in Music," David Gates's "Aubrey," Kris Kristofferson's "For the Good Times," and the song about Don McLean that Roberta Flack went to the top with, "Killing Me Softly." The album also made the bathetic "Tie a Yellow Ribbon Round the Ole Oak Tree" convincingly romantic.

Those sessions helped to keep Como around for another seventeen years, with another album to be produced by Chet in '75, *Just Out of Reach*, with remarkable covers of Kristofferson's "Loving Her Was Easier" and the Beatles' slow-burning emotional flame "Here, There and Everywhere," no easy task for any singer. However, Chet's biggest task was getting through the sessions. As it was, his chain cigar-smoking had befouled the air at the unventilated Studio A and B, leading some musicians to avoid sessions, and Chet came in less himself, doing most of his recording in his basement. Moreover, he began feeling increasingly queasy, with sharp stomach pains he passed off as the toll of another habit, junk food. In fact, when the alarmingly clean-living Como saw that Chet was suffering, he scolded him about his addiction to the candy-filled vending machines in the hallways.

Those who knew him well believed he had a supernatural bearing. Paul Yandell saw him tumble off a stage while rehearsing for an appearance on Glen Campbell's summer variety show in 1968, a terrifying moment. "They called the doctor and we got Chet to the dressing room. The doctor put a bandage on [and] he went ahead and did the show," after which they had dinner, with Chet not the slightest bit in pain. Having generally avoided doctors, he kept his stomach problems even from his family, including his doctor son-in-law. But he finally had his personal physician, Dr. Joe Robertson, come to the house and examine him. Robertson did a rectal exam while Chet leaned back over a piano and diagnosed him with colitis. He prescribed some medication, and Chet soon after left town to perform concerts in Denver and Oakland. But he didn't quit junk food, and when he got home after a round of golf with Jerry Reed, he was unable to eat without searing pain streaking through his innards. After more tests, the bad news came back that he had colon cancer, but he was told that it hadn't spread and was operable. An emergency operation was scheduled a few days later, on April 23, 1973, and Chet and Leona, he recalled, "had a good crying jag." And when he was flat on his back and rolled into the operating room at Miller's Hospital Clinic, he would later admit, "I was afraid . . . I kept thinking: 'What if I don't come out of the operation? What if I die right here?'"

They took eighteen inches of his large intestine in a four-hour operation, which hadn't been kept secret, and during which a good part of Nashville prayed and followed the news on the radio. After the surgery was over, Chet was feeling "as if a Volkswagen had run over me." The surgeon assured him the cancer was excised, but Chet, the classic half-empty-glass type, didn't necessarily believe it. As he recovered, he was back in the well of chronic depression, the surest sign of which was that although Leona had made sure to bring a guitar to his bedside, it just stayed propped against the wall. He was bedridden for nine days, during which Roy Acuff, Archie Campbell, and others came to visit. Gradually, though, he was practicing on the guitar, and by early summer he was up and ready to be Chet Atkins again. He was back on the golf course and at the office. However, he kept in mind the statistics about colon cancer's five-year survival rate of just 2 percent. Worse, his reward for surviving was walking back into the thornbush that had already soured him, his executive role, which he now began to construe had put him on that hospital gurney in the first place.

While his name remained on that office door, however, he was boss. And when the Outlaw Country movement he had helped spark carried into the 1970s, he had studio control over its main protagonists, Willie and Waylon. Nelson had recorded eighty-two songs produced by Chet between 1964 and 1969, chosen from a pastiche of country writers both old school, like Merle Travis and Willie Cochran, to new country sources like John Hartford and Eddie Rabbit, with Willie's own tartly romantic songs thrown in. Willie took his signature to be, "The Party's Over," to number twenty-four on the country list, and six of the seven albums they did charted high on the country album list. Also pertinent is that Willie went where Charley Pride refused to, recording "Blackjack County Chain." However, there were serious missteps, such as his *Good Times* album, the cover of which had him in golf clothing clutching a sexy woman golfer's hips as she was putting. These attempts to normalize an abnormal spirit were doomed and relegated him as an outlaw only in name, and Chet faced criticism from within the Nashville cabal for toning down Willie's bristly persona.

Willie couldn't disagree. Not accustomed to following others' advice, he had begun letting his hair and beard grow and was more concerned with going—as the title of another album put it—*My Own Peculiar Way*. And Chet did help him find his way by turning him on to a Martin N-20 classical guitar, which Willie fell in love with, for its "human sound, a sound close to my own voice. Didn't take long for me to pick a hole in it. That's 'cause classical guitars aren't meant to be picked. But that hole . . . seemed to deepen its soulful tone." But as the '70s began, unable to get out of his RCA contract, he lingered on, though without Chet, who in paring back his production duties had switched Willie to the less meticulous Felton Jarvis. Willie and his N-20, which he dubbed Trigger, kept recording in mass quantities, but sales never really picked up. At the same time, his life was a mess. He had by then gone through a bitter divorce, and then his Tennessee ranch was razed by a fire. In '71 the RCA power plane—in which Chet Atkins was no small player—tried to pull a squeeze play on him. With his contract about to expire, he was told that unless he renewed, the label would not release another album by him until it ran out.

Not playing along, in June 1972 he quit RCA, insisting he was retiring. Some believed his increasing cocaine use and lack of impressive songwriting had put him in crisis, his plea being his emotional rendition of Kristofferson's "Help Me Make It Through the Night" on what would be his last RCA album, which he fought to have released. Back out on the road again, he wore rumpled jeans and a black T-shirt, openly smoked pot, privately snorted cocaine, and found a post-hippie philosopher rubric. No longer at the mercy of the Nashville Sound—which he and his apologists would blame for his stagnation—he soon unretired and hired Neil Reshen as his manager, who got him out of the RCA contract for $14,000, and then was signed by Rick Sanjek, who had moved into the front office of Atlantic Records, as the label's first country artist. Willie recorded the milestone albums *Shotgun Willie* and *Phases and Stages*, then would move on again, to Columbia in 1975, where he really took off.

Waylon Jennings, on the other hand, would hang around at RCA with trepidation. Years before, Willie had warned him, "Whatever you do, Waylon, stay away from Nashville. Nashville ain't ready for you." As Waylon correctly construed it, *Nashville* was a synonym for *Chet Atkins*, who had overseen an astonishing 125 Jennings songs until 1970, as well as three duet records with Anita Carter and one with Waylon's wife, Jessi Colter. That same year, Chet handed Waylon the first of his three lifetime Grammys during the show in L.A. for his and Colter's cover of "MacArthur Park," which won Best Country Performance by a Duo or Group. But one of the last songs Atkins and Jennings collaborated on, "Alone," ideally described both Willie and Waylon's intentions for recording and living—and with perfect symmetry, it was the song Chet was working on when his colon erupted on him. By the mid-'70s, Waylon had progressed robustly and was the hottest name in the country corral, despite endangering his health with his own unstinted cocaine habit and his financial future by evading hundreds of thousands in taxes.

After his classic *Ladies Love Outlaws* album in '72, Waylon became seriously ill with hepatitis. It happened when Chet was recovering from his colon cancer surgery, and RCA rejected Jennings's request for a $25,000 advance, mainly for his medical bills, to sign a new contract. Instead, RCA sent Chet's assistant VP, Owen Bradley's ambitious son Jerry Bradley, to see him in the hospital, armed with a new contract and a bonus of only $5,000. Telling Jerry where he could go, Waylon sicced Neil Reshen on the label and in the end wound up getting a $75,000 advance. But Chet, who felt relieved he hadn't been in the position poor Bradley had found himself, was so offended by Waylon, who smoked seven packs of Marlboros a day, going right back to coke, up to seven grams a day, and meth that he had it out with him. As Chet had progressed through the years of cultural change, the use of marijuana in the studio had become common, but he laid down the law, prohibiting coke and amphetamines. Willie, whose vice was weed, had no problem with that—"If you're wired, you're fired," he told his bandmates. Waylon also complied, but believed, as he would later say, unleashing a closely guarded secret, that "Pills were the artificial energy on which Nashville ran around the clock." But when he wanted to record a song about pill popping that was not expressly anti-drug, Chet wouldn't hear of it, prompting Waylon to say about him, "Chet Atkins thinks it's a sin to even look at [a pill]."

They did agree on some things, such as Waylon's opinion of the Grand Ole Opry, where he never was a member, and about which he said, "Who needs it?" But the bigger story was control, namely of material and studio composition, and more broadly, that for Waylon the fabled Nashville Sound was "too boring. They've got some great musicians, but I just can't get into that sound." The irony was that an Atkins session was always so easy to digest for musicians, given Chet's cool, confident command. RCA engineer Jim Malloy once said that during sessions "the worst that could happen is that [Chet] could pick up the guitar himself and play the whole thing. . . . Chet would rise up and hit the talk-back [say something] . . . and, sure enough, it was always better." But for Waylon, Chet's complete control was antithetical to *him*, and people close to him began to spread word that Chet was still grabbing trace royalties on songs he produced for others. And the royalty issue would bug Chet so much that as late as 1996 he would say,

> That's the biggest fuckin' joke I've ever heard. . . . I had a little publishing company before I went on the payroll. [But] I was making $50,000 or $100,000 a year in royalties off my guitar playing. So I didn't need that. Jim Denny would send people over and say, "If you record this, you get 10 percent." And I said, "You know, I don't do that."

Yet, as author Michael Streissguth wrote in his 2013 *Outlaw: Waylon, Willie, Kris, and the Renegades of Nashville*, "In the outlaw story, Chet had to be removed in order to liberate Waylon and Willie." This was a tall order indeed. Chet Atkins could still make or break careers, but he had agreed to accommodate Waylon before, as when he allowed him to record with his touring band the Waylors, guitarist Jerry Gropp, bassist Paul Foster, and drummer Richie Albright. This of course led to muffled accusations of favoritism, but Chet went out of his way to please Waylon again, pulling away and not producing him. That suited Waylon fine, and Jerry Bradley also gave him the leeway to play with whomever he wanted in the studio, and even to record outside of Nashville. Thus, while they coexisted on a very wiggly tightrope, Waylon wisely held his tongue about Atkins, not needing to offend him.

Indeed, when Jennings's 1973 LP *Honky Tonk Heroes* was to be released, Chet was still the titular boss at RCA Nashville, and he had doubts about some of the songs on the album that were cowritten by Billy Joe Shaver, a Texas-born pal of Willie's who had crashed into an Atkins session in the '60s just to meet Waylon. Shaver had a down-home dialectic to his lyrics that would come to define the modern country outlaw, but Chet hesitated to release the album at all, fueling the need in New York for the big bosses to approve rolling it out over Chet's objections—a real rarity but the correct decision; the LP sprinted to number fourteen, establishing the best anthemic representation of the outlaw movement. Waylon carried on as RCA's sometimes bent backbone, working with Shaver and other producers like Ronny Light and Danny Davis, gradually producing his own work.

Like Willie, he would have a storied and stoned future, branching into acting and narrating, but he nearly cashed in several times due to cocaine addiction. And also like Willie, he never really crossed Atkins publicly, even after Chet was no longer in the corporate beehive. As with literally everyone else in country, and certainly in Nashville, both outlaws would still have a loose and sometimes uneasy relationship with him, and in 1976 Atkins would produce *Wanted! The Outlaws*, a compilation of the early trail left by Waylon, Jessi, Willie, and Tompall Glaser, which was the first country music album to go platinum. And Waylon's 1979 *Greatest Hits* album, with two Willie duets, went five times platinum. As the "Ramblin' Man," Waylon's progression into a new country prophet reclaimed country music from the too-slick, L.A., soft country-rockers and provided the undercoating of rebellious and youthful dreaming and simple storytelling, aided by a little reefer. Still, he always walked a delicate line when speaking of Chet. And when an unauthorized biography of Jennings in 1983, written by R. Serge Denisoff, dissected the past rocky times between the two, Waylon was irate. Disavowing the book, he put out word that Denisoff

> said some things that there was no need talking about, like about Chet Atkins. I like Chet and I always have. We didn't get along on a lot of things . . . but I was wrong, we were both wrong, trying to do right. I just couldn't work the 'system' way. . . . When I'm recording, I don't want to see no guy sittin' there lookin' at numbers. I didn't feel what they felt. . . . You know, it's hard for an ole country boy to get into big business so fast.

Of course, that could have been Chet's own self-written epitaph. And Waylon, who was given an add-on section in a future edition of the book to at least publicly set things straight, went on his way, he and Willie both stretching the limit for self-indulgence and self-destruction—Willie to remarkable depths, being busted for coke and owing $32 million in back taxes, and being forced to record his 1990 album *The IRS Tapes: Who'll Buy My Memories?* while in prison, the profits going straight to the IRS. Improbably, Willie would defy age, and Waylon also lived longer than most figured he would, making it to sixty-five years. Outlawism made it to old age as well, its bone and marrow having been nurtured by Chet Atkins back in the turbulent '60s at a time when such country diversion might have been a passing fad. But then, anything in Nashville that was ever truly worth keeping was traceable to the Country Gentleman.

Having to call shots for brilliant but not entirely stable men was just part of the job, which was to increase the label's profit, but the toll of it all created more stress and strain than he figured was worth it, and it was compromising his work. As he told *People* in 1974, "I'm really just a guitar picker, and I'm ashamed of anything that takes me away from my music," adding speciously that he stayed in the job "only because of the security and the hospitalization insurance." Years after his death, his long-unpublished interview with Tony Bacon included the admission that "I was recording everybody in Nashville and killing myself with stress and everything, and my guitar playing suffered. But I managed to still sell an awful lot of records. . . . I'd write some, and I'd record an album in about three or four days. Now, if you listen, you can hear that I'm out of tune, you can hear mistakes and everything . . . but at the time there were mistakes on everybody's records."

While not specifying which albums he meant, one he may have regretted was another turn with Hank Snow, with whom he had connected for the 1969 *C. B. Atkins & C. E. Snow by Special Request* album, which gave Hank a new, younger audience. Their 1974 project, Snow's *Hello Love* album, aimed even higher, with fifty-year-old Chet and fifty-nine-year-old Hank leaning hard into a new song for Snow,

"Hello Love," cowritten by country-gospel singer, writer, and TV host Betty Jean Robinson and Aileen Mnich for an album with the same title. Recorded at the still-extant Studio A, the tracks would hover on homey, Hallmark-card-style sentimentality, covering Jud Strunk's "Daisy a Day," the much-recorded Stonewall Jackson song "I Washed My Hands in Muddy Water," and Kris Kristofferson's "Why Me," which the latter had recorded for Monument Records a year before. But the big play was "Hello Love," a poppy, steel-backed romp tickling Snow's thick drawl.

As Paul Yandell recalled it, "Chet called me to play rhythm. . . . About the second song, Hank was having trouble coming in after the intro. Chet pushed the talkback from the control room and said, 'Hank, you have to wait a couple of beats before you come in.' Hank Snow was his own biggest fan and didn't like to be corrected. Hank replied something disrespectful of Chet. And Chet didn't say a word. He just gathered up his papers and walked out and went home. We had to finish the session with just the engineer. A day or two later I was over at Chet's office and he said Hank had written him a letter apologizing for what he said. Chet said, 'I'll never produce him again.'"

He meant it, to the point of letting Ronny Light produce the rest of the album, which despite the kerfuffle soared to number four country on Chet's production of "Hello Love"—an instant meteor that went to the top of the country chart, Snow's first number one in twelve years, making him the oldest singer to have a number one until Kenny Rogers beat him by two years in 1999. The song was also adopted by Garrison Keillor as backing music on *A Prairie Home Companion*, the forum for Keillor's droll radio monologues about life large and small, which began on July 6, 1974, broadcast from the Fitzgerald Theater in St. Paul. It also led to Chet's guest spots on the show, playing whimsical acoustic rimes periodically for years to come as the two populists became close friends, and for Keillor, it was a deeper tap into prairie Americana, feeding off Chet's homespun tales of life in the hills during the Depression. Indeed, Keillor, a notorious loner who called himself a high-functioning autism victim, seemed to be able to make easy conversation with few people, one being Chet Atkins, to whom he owed a lot.

For Snow, however, the lack of Chet's guidance meant the virtual end of his relevance in a country world that, like rock, was programmed on radio by young program directors and being surmounted by the FM dial, which was dominated by hip disc jockeys playing long, druggy album tracks. Chet of course knew how the radio game worked, and had never expected any of his songs to have ever gotten radio coverage, partially explaining why even his best works were long guilty pleasures rather than mass-scale products. He thus made it his business to solidify country legends before they were deemed dinosaurs, including himself. In 1971 he recorded *Chet, Floyd & Boots*, produced by another beautiful dinosaur, the then fifty-year-old Ethel Gabriel, who had been at RCA since 1940 and overseen the label's light pop releases since 1959. Chet also made plenty of time for the new breed, recording the first of his three LPs with Jerry Reed. In 1972 came *World's Greatest Melodies*, a side project under the name of the Nashville String Band—which he and Homer and Jethro had conceived in 1968 as a three-man unit—that ran off five more albums in three years, the final one joined by Cramer, guitarists Ray Edenton and Jimmy Capps, steel picker Jerry Byrd, and mandolinist Johnny Gimble, along with a string section and backing vocals by the Jordanaires. It seemed Chet could take the country calling uptown or downtown, to the most granular essentials. His regret was that the Nashville Sound had become wrapped around what sold the best, and that was not native country but the whipped cream topping of country-rock.

That beat went on in 1974 with *Chet Atkins Picks on Jerry Reed*, Chet playing ten songs by Reed and one they cowrote, "Baby's Coming Home," and Jerry coproducing with Chet and Ferguson, writing the liner notes, and dueting on two tracks, "Squirrely" (cowritten with Paul Yandell, who also played on the album) and "Mister Lucky." Then Chet enlisted his hero Merle Travis for a one-off meant to braze their longtime interlocking, *The Atkins–Travis Traveling Show*, for which Chet traveled to L.A. to record, to catch up with the still quite active Merle's schedule. It was actually a three-man show, with Reed coming along as a third picker of distinction on eleven diverse tunes, two of which Chet and Merle cowrote, "Down South Blues" and "Boogie for Cecil," along with Travis's "Cannonball Rag," "Dance of the Golden Rag," and "Nine Pound Hammer," plus another by Shel Silverstein, a fetching tribute to them called "Mutual Admiration." Two pop tunes helped fill it out: "I'll See You in My Dreams" and "Who's Sorry Now."

Although Chet had looked forward to the historic collaboration, the leathery Travis demanded that the three of them had to play only acoustically, as it came right after his *Folk Songs of the Hills* album, and he had no intention of getting on Chet's level of electric wizardry. Less than gung ho about it, Chet would recall that "we were trying to duplicate that record, I guess," and that since he hadn't played pure acoustic for a while, "I don't know what I played on that album. I never listen to it." The work is indeed a picker's feast, a three-tone acoustic buffet, its CD release by BMG in 2002 only staking out how harmonic three different styles can sound, the shifting bass notes from one to the other almost visually darting across the stereo field. It rose to number thirty on the country chart and won the Grammy for Best Country Instrumental album—which Chet had lost the previous two years after winning Best Country Single for his cover of "Snowbird."

Staying within the fold of heavenly collaboration, he was compelled to put out a dream album—uniting with the estimable and even more imperious Les Paul, who was now in his sixties, divorced from Mary Ford, and semiretired, producing albums made in his home studio. Chet, who of course had played his first real guitar when Jimmy gave him that Paul model Gibson so long ago, invited Les to Nashville to record no-frills country-pop and jazz. The tracks would glide from Duke Ellington's "Caravan," Hammerstein's "Lover, Come Back to Me," Isham Jones's "It Had to Be You," Al Jolson's "Avalon," Johnny Green's "Out of Nowhere," and Lew Brown's "The Birth of the Blues." Although there was a tight A-Team crew, Chet and Les would essentially carve them into shape in Studio A over two days, May 6 and 7, eschewing any overdubbing. It was a nice idea but, clearly, Chet took it more seriously—did he ever not?—than Les, who may have felt overshadowed by the younger god, with cause. Paul Yandell recalled that while the two guitar gods played with gusto,

> Chet outplayed him at every turn. . . . Chet and Les would work out the intro and ending and then play the tune about once and then record it. It sounds to me that Les was trying to outdo Chet. But Chet was amazing. I don't think he fixed anything later. Everything was off the top of his head. On "Avalon," I sat in front of Chet on the floor and adjusted the old EchoPlex that he used back then. You can hear him [on the record] give me instructions. Les was playing a white Les Paul with low impedance pickups and all those switches on it. In the end, though, I think it was some of Chet's finest playing ever.

Naturally, Chet's competitive drive was in part due to Les. When Atkins looked back on his career, he admitted that it was really Paul's example that forced him to turn up his own attitude to nuclear levels. "I keep telling Les Paul," he said in 1976, "I'm gonna slip up behind him and kick his ass, because it's all his fault," meaning the rise of multitracking, which Chet had done well before he ever fiddled with tape. Still, for all of Chet's obsessive perfectionism, he could let stand mistakes if they accidentally struck the right tone and mood. Although he knew all the studio secrets, he still believed making records was a matter of emotion. He could demand take after take, but insisted that spending "30 minutes finding the right chord was time wasting overkill." A bigger problem was that new producers came along who, he said, "don't know a damn thing about music, can't hum you a tune, but they're so enthusiastic. That's a quality I've never had because I'm a bit of a pessimist." In his grim mindset, "you got a lotta strikes against you and the odds are that it *won't* be a hit."

All these factors added strike-dodging intensity in producing up to around forty artists at a time. And even after lightening that load, the competitive instinct remained, especially so when Les Paul was shredding away ten feet from him. That Les conceded was clear when he backed off and, as Yandell noticed, "clowned around most of the time." Still, the album, *Chester & Lester*, was a masterful blend that took off, rising to number eleven on the country album chart and winning the Grammy for Best Country Instrumental Performance and sparking a follow-up album two years later, *Guitar Monsters*, a rock-derived honorific that in the 1970s defined country guitar every bit as much as the rockers, to Chet's chagrin, as his native country persona seemed to ebb. Whenever that happened, whatever country-based honor awaited him, he leaped at it.

In '73, he went into the Country Music Hall of Fame at forty-nine, the youngest to ever make the grade, and won yet another Instrumentalist of the Year Grammy. Yet the cracks in the country wall were showing. While country crooner Charlie Rich won a Grammy, so did the Australian thrush Olivia Newton-John, and the latter seemed to offend the Country Music Association, which promptly invented a separate but equal category—Natural Country, which delineated native, more devout country singers from non-Dixie-based poseurs. This was intended as a protective measure for Nashville's hegemony but also reverse exclusion at a time when country music had reached its market peak. It might have done the country arc well had its king dismissed the CMA position and defended the natural evolution of an idiom that was in danger of becoming extinct twenty years before. Instead, Chet was now becoming more stuck in regret about losing the kith and kin of the "true" nature of the beast.

"I had a lot to do with changing country," he said with much chagrin in the December 16, 1974, *People*, "and I apologize."

19

PONTIFEX MAXIMUS OF NASHVILLE

The tensions with Les Paul notwithstanding, Chet came away from the album suffering another bout of the I'm-playing-like-shit blues, noting to Billy Reed of the Louisville *Courier-Journal & Times* in December 1974 that "the guitar is the most difficult instrument in the world to play. . . . You've got to have a good ear, good coordination, good taste, expression and emotions in your music. And there are very damned few who can do it." He of course was one who definitely could, but circumstances were making it harder. There were the business encumbrances, the suspicions about compensation, the cancer scares. And Atkins was right; the Gretsch endorsement had its potholes. The guitar maker had been bought in 1965 by the CBS Corporation for $13 million. Then, in 1967, the Ohio-based Baldwin instrument company bought Gretsch and moved the factory to Booneville, Arkansas, then to Cincinnati, where it kept building Atkins models, including newer ones like the Super Chet and Super Axe. But Chet was less than happy. One reason was that, under pressure and lacking legal representation, he had signed a new deal when the sale was made despite Gretsch refusing his request to be given stock in the company. Another was that the quality of the guitars had declined since the company left Brooklyn.

The more enlightened music crowd was nonetheless still hooked on the original-still-best wonder tool, the Country Gentleman, which Pete Townshend announced he had played on the Who's 1971 *Who's Next* album, calling it "the best guitar I've ever had" and "the loudest guitar I've ever owned," one that he never would have smashed to pieces onstage. But there would be a breaking point between Gretsch and Atkins that would seem linked to his burnout at RCA, which, because of his colon cancer surgery in 1973, made it seem physically related. In fact, the sharp-toothed country rock journalist and Jerry Lee Lewis biographer Nick Tosches described Chet in an August 1973 magazine piece as looking "more like an Exxon station grease monkey on his lunch break than the Pontifex Maximus of Nashville's Telecaster outlaws."

Chet himself detested what he sensed he had become and was in a foul mood in that *People* profile, in which writer Robert Windeler wrote: "Corporate administration embarrasses him. He isn't even sure of the name of his job: 'vice-president of somethin' or other.' He presses the intercom and asks, 'What is my title here anyway?' After several seconds of checking, the pretty blonde secretary responds, 'RCA Records division vice-president, country.' 'I'm ashamed of that,' says Chet." This would become a talking point he would push for years, another variation of it in 1987 being that "they give you titles like that in lieu of money. So beware when they want to make you vice president."

Indeed, before any of these quotes made it into the press, he was already gone from the job, with so little publicity that few even knew that late in 1973, he had informed the RCA brass that he was turning over the job he couldn't identify to Jerry Bradley. He said he would concentrate on his albums and cleared out his office. But remarkably, when the news dripped out, it had little practical relevance. Many of his fans hadn't ever paid much thought to his executive duties to begin with, and a good number of them would still believe he was running RCA Nashville—which in a strong sense was true. No matter his official role, he was the metaphoric godfather, and would be a voice as if from above when some important RCA decisions arose.

In 1976, for example, Waylon Jennings released *Are You Ready for the Country*, picking Los Angeles producer Ken Mansfield to produce the record. Jennings and the Waylors traveled to Los Angeles and recorded it with Mansfield. A month later, Waylon returned to Nashville and presented the master tapes not to Jerry Bradley but, perhaps out of habit, to Chet Atkins, who advised Jerry to green-light the album, which would climb to number one country and thirty-four pop, and become a gold record. Atkins may not have been a suit now, but he still haunted Studios A and B, tall and haughty as ever, and not a single Nashville singer or musician lost any of their conditioned infatuation for him. Willie and Waylon would periodically ring him up and discuss where their careers were going. Chet was often pursued to host country music TV shows, and if he or producers invited them to be guests with him, they would come running.

This was why even as Nashville changed with the times, he was up atop the power structure. The town itself was a product of his tenure, virtually all its producers having been put in place by him. Even so, there were now new Turks in a coterie of high-tech independent studios, the most buzz created by the Creative Workshop studio opened in 1970 by Buzz Cason, who had led Nashville's first rock band, the Casuals, before singing backup for Elvis and Kenny Rogers, and cowriting Robert Knight's "Everlasting Love." His first client at Creative was a young Jimmy Buffett, and country stars like Dolly Parton, Emmylou Harris, and Merle Haggard followed. Elvis planned to record there too, having duly kept his Nashville appointments for years at Studio B, produced by Felton Jarvis and still causing a ruckus as women clamored for him in the parking lot. But "Fat Elvis" cut back on work while drugging up on God knows what and on August 16, 1977, died in his bathroom at Graceland at forty-two—an epistle that the new country he had reformatted with "Heartbreak Hotel" was now old, and out of time.

That meant Chet Atkins, a man with gifted timing, had made the right move getting out of the executive suite before he could be asked to leave it. Because for all the influence he would still have, the game would focus on what was new; even the best left from the past would have no home. Indeed, it was that year when RCA was ready to undo the knot it had tied. Business at Studio B had slackened, and even Studio A had lesser demand. This came as the younger rock generation had found its own "greatest" guitarists within the gene pool of fully formed country-rock, men like Duane Allman—who before his fatal 1971 motorcycle crash in Macon, Georgia, had struck up a friendship with Merle Atkins in Nashville, where more hip and cheap studios were now on Music Row, such as Glaser Sound Studios, Sound Stage Studios, and House of David. The old guard that had been synonymous with Chet and Owen Bradley made way for the new breed—Dolly, Barbara Mandrell, the Judds, Ronnie Milsap, Eddie Rabbitt, Dottie West, Johnny Lee, Reba, the Statler Brothers, Amy Grant, et al. The main holdovers, Willie, Waylon, and Charley, found new home ground at Chips Moman's American Studio, which had moved from Memphis to get in on the shakeout, and Charley went in time to the Music City Hall studio. As much as country may have been working by habit on the Chet Atkins / Nashville Sound stylebook, their producers were unbound to labels. Moreover, studio personnel were demanding more money and more control over their work, in the mold of the now-aging Waylon Jennings.

Taking stock, RCA in 1977 was about to close its once-heralded Nashville studios—the ones it had never actually owned—as well as its studios in L.A. and New York, having decided to use the cheaper independent studios. This put into question the fate of the twin studios sitting nearly side by side on Roy Acuff Place. Studio B had the easier path. Its owner, Dan Maddox, quickly leased it to the Country Music Hall of Fame and Museum, which began marketing it as a tourist haven, preserving the studio as it was, with cables snaking around the room, folding chairs with RCA stickers, and Floyd Cramer's old Steinway still sitting in the corner. The museum ran endless buses to and from the famous studio, which in its first year as a shrine was visited by nearly eighty thousand people, leading Maddox to donate it to the museum, in partnership with a foundation run by West Coast music executive Mike Curb, who dressed up the property and renamed it 30 Music Square West. That the landmarks would survive pleased Chet, though a sometimes-torturous drama would envelop the forsaken Studio A, which would lead him and Owen Bradley to buy the building to save it from destruction, an odyssey that would take more than four decades to resolve, though neither of them would live to see it.

Still only fifty-three in 1977, Chet Atkins was ethereal enough to be somewhat sketchy. Few outside of Jerry Reed and Ray Stevens really knew what made him tick. For example, there were his political indulgences, which seemed to stretch across the spectrum.

Back in '72, the holy triad of Atkins, Cramer, and Randolph had performed at the governor's mansion at the inauguration of Republican Winfield Dunn. Yet Chet's political affiliations were never obvious and became something conjectural when Richard Nixon, desperate for dependably conservative Southerners to prop him up as he was being engulfed by the Watergate scandal, came to Nashville in March 1974 to dedicate the Grand Ole Opry's move to anodyne fairgrounds three miles up the Cumberland River on the new Briley Parkway, in the Pennington Bend section of East Nashville. Stars like Johnny Cash, Roy Acuff, Hank Snow, and Bill Anderson did their part to fawn over the man who would resign office within five months. But someone was missing—Chet Atkins.

He was scheduled to play that night and was in the newly christened Opryland during the afternoon rehearsals with Rick Foster, who took some pictures of him mingling with some of the acts. "Each star had his or her own dressing room and invited us in," said Foster. "Chet always introduced me like I was important, calling me a great classical guitarist or something along those lines. It seemed like I'd met every living legend in country music and then some." Yet when the show went on, Chet was conspicuously absent. That was such major news that even the *New York Times* mentioned it in an April profile of Atkins titled "You Can't Take the Country Out of Chet," with John S. Wilson writing that "the man who epitomizes the change in country music more than anyone else in Nashville . . . missed the last Grand Ole Opry at Ryman and the first show at Opryland. Chet Atkins was giving a performance in Mobile at the time." The explanation was good enough. But what about the timing, since the Nixon appearance had been in the works for some time? Was it a snub of a corrupt president who would soon be in purgatory? Only he knew, and he wasn't saying.

At the same time, being above the political fray certainly helped objectify him as damn near pristine. Which is why Nashville artist Brett de Palma created an acrylic and photo emulsion painting called *Home of Chet Atkins*, with Chet's Lynnwood house nestled pastorally in snow, a work that was put on display at the Martin Wiley Gallery. And just as Chet had figured, with the yoke of RCA business off his shoulders, his own work objectively improved as he pared back the dizzying toll of records he had produced and/or played on in the '70s—a toll that, in retrospect, seems humanly insane and physically impossible, not only the 200-plus each that he had produced for Willie and Waylon but, as other examples, 304 for Don Gibson, 145 for Dottie West, 69 for Skeeter Davis, 66 for Al Hirt, 57 for Bobby Bare, and 39 for Charlie Rich. Moreover, he now pared back his own records in order to put more time into each that he did, his singles output falling to one in '76, "Frog Kissin'," and two in '77, "Me and My Guitar" and a year-end "Jingle Bell Rock" redo.

On the other hand, he was more entwined in collaborative albums, recording the second one with Les Paul in one of the last projects at Studio A. But it was another rough go. Les was less committed to the pairing and Chet grew more impatient with him, and the vibe between them was more toxic than it was on *Chester & Lester*. The classics on the playlist this time included evergreens like "Lazy River," "Over the Rainbow," "It Don't Mean Thing (If It Ain't Got That Swing)," "Brazil," "Limehouse Blues," and "I Surrender Dear," and Chet wanted to ease the pressure by having Bob Ferguson produce the album. Ferguson also cowrote with Chet another track, "I'm Your Greatest Fan," something both giants had heard endless times. With all the precautions, though, Chet's impatience with Les boiled over. Paul Yandell, again in the crew, remembered that Les had a bad cold at the time "and didn't feel like playing. I don't think the tunes were as good either." Yandell, who was on rhythm guitar, approached the all-timer during a lull and affably said, "Say Les, play the intro to 'How High the Moon,'" Les's biggest hit and what Yandell calls "the greatest record ever made." His response made Yandell blanch. "Les coldly replied, 'I only play that when I get paid [for it].'" As well, Yandell hinted that the resentments ran deep between the two "monsters." "I'm not trying to cut Les," he said, "but there were other things that happened during those sessions and afterward I haven't told and don't intend to." It was a promise he kept, never explicating those things before died in 2011. He did say a bit more about it in a Les Paul ninetieth-birthday documentary, but his remarks were excised by producers.

The repeat collaboration was nevertheless another can't-miss Atkins album, any static in the sessions smoothed over by the two most brilliant and mellow guitars in history. It was also a hit, going to number twenty-seven country and nominated for the same Grammy the first album had won. Even so, only one single came off each of the Atkins-Paul albums, and neither charted. Not that this mattered much to Chet now that he was essentially out of the hit-single game. And the wider slack he had given himself let him work on side albums, the most novel being *First Nashville Guitar Quartet*, a chamber-style melding of four acoustic guitars played by Chet and younger musicians John Knowles, John Pell, and British Canadian Liona Boyd, who had played at Carnegie Hall. The smoothly injected string parts for violins and cellos were easily merged into a country-style format, making the album a highly overlooked piece of work that is today available in two more must-hear CD rerelease packages.

There was also *Chet, Floyd & Danny*, reuniting the two old confreres with trumpeter Danny Davis, who with fellow Nashville Brass horn players turned peaceful fodder like "Kentucky," "I Saw the Light," "Wabash Cannonball," "When You Wish Upon a Star," Cramer's "Last Date," and a tune written by the trio, "Four in the Morning," into a quite lovely country R&B, daring even to horn up Al Hirt's trumpet rendition of "Java." The album made the country top fifty and earned a

Best Country Instrumental Grammy nomination in 1978, which again pitted Chet against himself, competing with his *Me and My Guitar* album, the title tune a cover of the 1974 James Taylor song. The playlist also included Chet's own pulsating, emotionally wrought version of "Vincent," Jerry Reed's "Struttin'," and a song he cowrote with John Knowles, "My Little Waltz." He lost both Grammys, but by then he had a new favored guitar man to usher along: Lenny Breau.

The Maine-born, Canadian-raised fingerstyle jazz picker had raised quite a stir hosting a radio show on the CBC, and as it happened, Chet had known Breau's parents, country singers Hal "Lone Pine" Breau and Betty Cody, having produced a few sessions for them back in the '60s. Their son, an elfin-like beatnik type, idolized Atkins and played with a thumbpick and four fingers, using his little finger for high notes and pinkie nail to hit higher, brighter tones. Chet would later call him "one of the great players of this world" who "had taken some of my fragmentary ideas, and gone on and on into musical areas I had never dreamed of." He brought Breau to Nashville, signed him to RCA, and produced two albums that displayed Breau's sad, tender licks, which he played on feel without looking at any sheet music, but the albums were little noticed, and Lenny didn't record again for ten years. By 1977 he was living in a small flat on Music Row, nearly broke and hooked on alcohol and either heroin or methadone, looking like a Skid Row bum. Chet dropped in on him during the recording of *Me and My Guitar*, taking him into the studio, which was crowded with A-Teamers like Yandell, Cramer, and Ray Stevens, to play on two historical tracks, the 1833 "Long, Long Ago," by the English politician Thomas Bayly, and Cole Porter's jazzy "You'd Be So Nice to Come Home To," which Breau loved to play.

Chet reckoned that giving Lenny work was tantamount to saving his life, and he even talked him into recording an on-the-fly clutch of songs in Chet's basement studio while staying with Chet and Leona in order to keep him clean. The songs would become a low-key album released on a sidelight label—Sound Hole Records, operated by John Knowles—in 1979, sold only through mail-order ads in guitar magazines, and though hardcore fans loved Breau's jazzy treatment of songs by McCoy Tyner, Hank Williams, and Cole Porter, it would soon become a loss leader that has never been rereleased. But for Chet, it was cause to keep trying to get Breau into the studio for RCA, a task that seemed nearly impossible, though there was nothing Chet thought was beyond his ken. As it was, he too was gravitating to jazz.

In '78, PBS united him in an hour-long segment of the public network's *Soundstage* series with jazz/pop guitarists George Benson and Earl Klugh. He brought a coterie of A-Teamers, including Paul Yandell, to the show's home at the Chicago PBS station's Grainger Studio. The opening number had all three guitar gods jamming in full jazz mode as an integrated audience grooved. After Benson played his mellow guitar with his backup band, he brought on "two very good friends of mine, and probably yours also," whereupon Chet and Earl again flanked Benson, and Chet, clad in an all-white, open-necked suit, laid into a springy take on "Oh, Lonesome Me," Benson and Klugh merrily vamping slick asides, the latter on an amazingly funky, Latin-flavored acoustic.

During the heavily edited show, Chet was then seen in a floral shirt with his own backup, who came with him from Nashville, delivering more hot sauce and then showing off his wry wit. "My name is Chet Atkins, like the man told ya," he said. "I mention that because sometimes I get confused with Tom Jones." Hearing scattered laughs, he went on, "I usually get a few laughs right there." Then, with his newest find, bushy-haired harmonica cat Terry McMillan, they played the Melanie Safka folk tune "Look What They've Done to My Song, Ma" and a bouncing "Cherokee," before Chet and Yandell played an acoustic "Stars and Stripes Forever" as the crowd rhythmically clapped, Chet throwing in at the close, "Well, you may think this is the end . . . Well, it is." The three combined again for remarkably coherent harmonics, and then the network was running *The Fall and Rise of Reginald Perrin*. The grin on Chet's face during the show was worth watching, and the shame was that no album of the show would be released—nor would the episode even be seen again until the backwash of such performances in the Internet age—but Chet would relish the memory, and the notion of a jazz album would soon lead him into a new turn of life at already six decades old.

In late 1979 he went off to Paris with Paul Yandell, Henry Strzelecki, pianist and songwriter/arranger Randy Goodrum, and drummer Larry Londin to record his second live album, *And Then Came Chet Atkins*, a major upgrade from the first one, as the 1975 *In Concert* was essentially him alone strumming, as he did in that year's CMA awards show. This time, at the famed Olympia Theater, he and the band glided through two dozen songs of divergent genres, including two medleys, one of Beatles tunes ("If I Fell," "For No One," "Something," "Lady Madonna") and one of some of Chet's singles ("Trambone," "Hello! Ma Baby," "I'll See You in My Dreams," "The Poor People of Paris," "Mister Sandman," "Freight Train"), others of which were played fully, such as "Yakety Axe," "Snowbird," and "Vincent."

There was also Jerry Reed's "Drive In," and the free flow, easy vibe, and warm redemption in the Parisian hall not only had RCA release the work as a double album—a rare commodity for country—with liner notes by Atkins, but the excess of material carried over to a third live LP a year later, *The Best of Chet on the Road . . . Live*, filled in by tracks recorded in Nashville, one of which, "Blind Willie," was written and produced by Ray Stevens, with strings conducted by Goodrum, creating an album that would go top fifty on the country chart.

As handsome a return as these projects were, they occupied only a fraction of Chet's time, as was always the case. Before the trip, he had made an appearance at the White House with the first modern-day Southern president, Jimmy Carter, the third chief executive who had beckoned him, with Chet noting they had "no heavy conversation. We didn't touch on any earth-shaking topics," though the embattled president needed such company as the Iran hostage crisis deepened. Chet wasn't so sure. "Mr. President," he told him, "you're not going to help your reputation by hanging out with guitar players." Said Carter: "I've been around worse people than guitar players." First Lady Rosalynn Carter had also beckoned, inviting him to appear with her at the restoration of the Palace Theatre in Lorain, Ohio, and as the new decade arrived, there seemed little else the man could do that he hadn't already done, age notwithstanding.

Because so many of his albums, even the ones that didn't sell much, seemed to have deep historical context, his Grammy and CMA nominations were as if by rote, seemingly more necessary than whether he won or lost—he lost for CMA Musician of the Year all through the '70s but then won it five times in a row in the '80s. There would also be the lifetime achievement awards, which were a must, as was, for Chet, compiling the collaboration albums with the now-also-aging country guitar heroes. The next one of those happened in 1980 with Doc Watson. Unlike the Les Paul psychodramas, this one was a breeze. "It was real easy to work with Doc," he said, "because I knew all the tunes that he knew. We're from about the same area of the country. He plays a lot of the old fiddle tunes that I heard from the cradle." In the name of simplicity, they recorded it in Watson's room at the Spence Manor Hotel just down the block from Studios A and B, the same hotel where Elvis had stayed during his Nashville stays, famous for its 80-foot, guitar-shaped swimming pool named for Webb Pierce.

The album, *Reflections*, its cover a near-blank monochrome with only an old-time Victrola speaker on the lower-right edge, included four songs written by the two old pros, the aw-shucks "Me and Chet Made a Record," a two-song bluegrass medley, "Black and White" and "Ragtime Annie," and "Flatt Did It," a bow to Lester Flatt, who had died the year before. There was also a cover of the Delmore Brothers' "You're Gonna Be Sorry," along with two more medleys—"Tennessee Rag" / "Beaumont Rag" and "Texas Gales" / "Old Joe Clark"—plus Karl Davis's rollicking "Don't Monkey 'Round My Widder," delicious flat-picking turns on the Ramblers' old "Goodnight Waltz," and the stomping finisher, "On My Way to Canaan's Land," with Chet and Doc intoning names of favorite country singers. No album ever meant more to either man, and they bonded so well they took to the road to promote it, most memorably on the Johnny Carson show. It also garnered a Grammy nomination for Best Country Instrumental Album and would be rereleased in 1999 on CD and subsequently on classic vinyl by Sugar Hill Records—one more must-have, its impressive sales on the Internet proof that Chet Atkins's country tableau just never seems to die.

If there was something underrated about him, it was his impishness. In 1980 as well, he was fronting the whimsically named Million Dollar Band, cadging Sun Records' famous Million Dollar Quartet one-off with Elvis, Johnny Cash, and Carl Perkins, when he was asked to be a part of the *Hee Haw* series during its eleventh season. Despite its crude stereotyping of Southern redneck culture—which may have been intended as satire but was taken as an act of faith by its regular audience—the show somehow endured, surviving the TV networks' purge of "rural" shows. And to its credit, the show had a good side, reviving the native country music Chet worried he had sold out. Putting together the cream of the Nashville session players—Randolph, Cramer, Danny Davis, Johnny Gimble, Henry Strzelecki, Charlie McCoy on harmonica, drummer Willie Ackerman, and banjoist Bobby Thompson—he first led them onto the show's set at Nashville's WLAC TV studio on October 13. In later years they would play on the Opryland stage, when the show moved there, seven seasons in all. And Chet's duets with the show's host, Roy Clark, himself a master picker, are an absolute treasure trove.

He had always made time for highly rated TV shows such as Perry Como's *Kraft Music Hall* and Ed Sullivan's show; had multiple appearances on the talk shows of Carson, Mike Douglas, David Frost, and Dinah Shore; and appeared on the newer-edge variety shows of Johnny Cash and Tom Jones, and of course on his bobo Jerry Reed's *The Jerry Reed When You're Hot You're Hot Hour*. Reluctant but a good sport, he even tried acting on Reed's subsequent, short-lived cop show *The Fallen Idol*. He was often the face of *Nashville Now*. But his RCA output was still his main focus. And perhaps only he could have reclaimed the tragic Lenny Breau, at least for one historic project.

Since their brief collaboration, Breau had been in a downward spiral, lost in a heroin haze. He did on occasion come to Chet's home or office and play riffs in the basement that had even Chet flummoxed. Lenny would play the same song a few times, each one totally different. "Playing a different single-string chorus each time you do a tune is something," Chet would remember, "but playing a completely different accompaniment as well is unbelievable." He described Breau as "a spiritual man" who wrote songs pleading for heavenly deliverance, yet he would never find it. When Chet finally got him in the studio to record a duet album that would be called *Standard Brands*, he would recall that the timing was less than optimal.

> Lenny was going through one of his worst times of methadone and alcohol abuse. The methadone left him lethargic and slow. In spite of it, he could astound you on the guitar, and he was still the best. I tried to keep him straight but it was a battle I couldn't win. Not long ago a friend confided to me that during that time Lenny always kept a bottle stashed in my garage. I had a good inward laugh at that, thinking, "You clever little Frenchman, you did it again!"

This was the kind of forbearance that Chet had not shown Waylon Jennings or Willie Nelson about their hard drug usage, and even with his favoritism for Breau, it would take over a year to record nine tracks and thirty-three minutes. Paul Yandell, who was in the crew, recalled that Lenny would drop in and out of rehab or vanish from sight. When he'd materialize, Chet would take him to his house and see if he could lay down a few minutes of informal recording. Chet would recede his own playing so that Lenny's sinewy guitar lines were more audible. The tracks bounded from jazz to country to pop, the incredibly gifted duo playing mainly by instinct rather than design on Rodgers and Hart's "This Can't Be Love," Rodgers and Hammerstein's "This Nearly Was

Mine," Luis Bonfá's "Batucada," Antonin Dvorak's "Going Home," Walter Gross's "Tenderly," Jerry Gillespie's "Somebody's Knockin'," and Tex Owens's "Cattle Call," with the last track a five-minute-plus jam on Jimmy Van Heusen's "Polka Dots and Moonbeams."

Released with a cover shot of Atkins in a cool leather jacket smiling easily as Breau mugged for the camera with horror-movie eyes, the album was treated with indifference. This left a bad taste in Chet's mouth, more so considering that the 1994 CD rerelease proved what Chet had in mind; a retro-review in AllMusic called it "a fascinating lesson in the old teaching the new and vice versa. Breau's debt to Atkins is obvious, but so too is the respect that the elder statesmen reciprocates." In sum, though, what Chet did was to present the work as the very sound of torture, a man going through a hell that Chet could only imagine, which made his own woes seem trivial. What one hears in every groove, then, is something Chet could relate to—that Lenny Breau's lone tether to reality was the call of his magical guitar strings.

Chet dared hope that it would jump-start Lenny straight. Tommy Emmanuel, who had come to Nashville and was taken into Chet's small world of trustees, also spent time at Chet's home jamming in the basement. "[Chet] said, 'You want to pick a little?' So one time I started playing 'Me and Bobby McGee.' By the time I got to the chorus he joined in and we were locked in. Then he said, 'Come up stairs, I want you to meet someone.' And there was Lenny Breau. The three of us played for three hours without hardly taking a breath. Can you imagine a kid from the sticks like me coming here and playing with them? And then I took Lenny to his gig that night."

But sadly, all efforts to rescue Lenny were doomed when he suddenly took up with a woman named Jewel, whom Chet was suspicious of and tried in vain to convince Lenny not to marry. He made Lenny promise to call him before he took the plunge. A few days later, when Chet returned from a gig, Lenny came to the office. "Well, Chet," he said, "I tried to phone you but you were out—so I went ahead and got married." Soon after, he moved to L.A. He would record once in a while, but on August 12, 1984, at forty-three, he was found dead, floating in a swimming pool. Coroners determined he had been strangled, but though Jewel was the prime suspect, no charges were filed and the case remains a mystery. As an object lesson, Breau and Hank Williams were essentially the same person, though Breau's demise was more personally scabrous for Chet. On a select plane, it robbed music of what might have been the best guitar player ever born—or at least second best to the aging king of Nashville. A Canadian music award would be named for Breau, and Chet fondly remembered him with rare effusiveness as "my little friend that I loved and admired," yet with his blunt candor, he wouldn't pretend that Lenny got a raw deal. Rather, in an interview for the 1999 documentary *The Genius of Lenny Breau*, he avoided any sugar coating.

"Lenny," he said, "was one of those guys who was a genius at what he did, but that was all he could do. He could not take care of himself, and we all knew it."

20

OH YEAH, THE BOY CAN PLAY

The Breau album, one of the toughest hauls of his life, left a sour taste, and Chet would steer clear of doing another dual album for nine years. But he still went on winning Grammys. In 1981 he again reeled in two, his *Country After All These Years* album joining *Reflections* by winning Best Country Instrumental Performance. He was still the Godfather of the Guitar, as they called him on *Nashville Now*, and all around the town, he and his relations were thick in the music scene. His brother-in-law Roy Shockley, Billie Rose Atkins's husband, worked as an engineer at RCA, and his son, Mike Shockley, was an engineer, producer, and owner of Glaser Sound Studios, working with Willie Nelson, Waylon Jennings, Jerry Reed, Dolly Parton, and Ronnie Milsap, as well as engineering his uncle Chet's albums with Reed and Les Paul.

But even with all this sway, Chet chafed that RCA had seemingly cooled on him. And as it happened, the theme of starting another new era for himself was on his mind anyway. Early in the new decade, he had broken with Gretsch, a development that was big news indeed in the guitar subterrain. But if this seemed to be timed to making a dramatic personal change, in truth it was the result of factors not his doing. The company was mismanaging itself out of business. Problems first began after the Gretsch sale to Baldwin and the move of its factory to Booneville, Arkansas, and then to Cincinnati. As Chet attested, the quality of its high-end guitars suffered, and contact with Chet became sporadic. Then, in 1980, the company ended production of all Atkins models, a real slap in the face to the man who had put it on the map. Soon after, Gretsch then went out of business, a black day in the guitar world.

As this was happening, Chet's stretch with Doc Watson had led him to pick up his old Gibsons and play the same sort of Mother Maybelle / Rosetta Tharpe–style scratching and walking bass lines that had all but defined soul music generated at Motown and Stax. And so when Gretsch fell, Chet knew exactly where to go. As it was, Gibson had been trying to lure him for years. And so, his contract up, he called Bruce Bolen, who ran the artists relations department at Gibson and told him he was ready to make the move. Also providential was that he had pitched the idea to Gretsch to build a nylon-string solid body, with no success. Presenting the same idea to Gibson, the company did as he asked—the result being the newest Chet Atkins models, the Gibson CE and CEC solid-body classical acoustic originating in '82.

With eerie but immaculate timing, this came about only weeks before he ended his thirty-five-year run at RCA. Yet this was also not planned, and was prefaced by the sudden financial drift of the giant record label. Facing challenges to stay relevant, country stars had begun to go to other labels, costing losses in Nashville that spread label-wide. Jerry Bradley, feeling the heat that would have fallen on Chet had he stayed in the executive suite, quit as RCA Nashville chief to head the new Opryland Music Group in 1983, when the Gaylord Broadcasting Company purchased the Opry, its related properties, WSM, and Acuff-Rose Music. The label's new country music chief, Joe Galante, a thirty-two-year-old New York sharpie, had been a company man in Nashville for years learning the trade from Atkins, whom he revered like everyone else though he was focused on the new breed of country. That led RCA to take a gamble on this new breed in 1982 by signing Kenny Rogers, whose almost comatose country nature and high marketability cost them a jaw-dropping $20 million—taking country for more "uptown" than Chet ever imagined.

What's more, RCA Records brought aboard corporate bureaucrats who, for all their business degrees, couldn't do what Atkins had done every year as vice president—create profits. When a new president of the company took over, Bob Buziak, he openly complained about the company's "fast-moving and fast-talking guys who sounded like investment bankers and all wore gray suits, yellow ties and big smiles. And none of them wanted anything to do with the record business." In their collective swagger, they felt no real loyalty to men like Chet Atkins, who was about to turn sixty and was thus regarded as a fossil. The breaking point for him came when he took the idea of a purely jazz album to the new regime's A&R men only to be told the project was a nonstarter, though it is possible he had set up this rejection, knowing it would breach his heretofore freedom to record what he wanted—and give him a reason to walk, on his terms, rather than with a pink slip. This was exactly what happened over the summer of 1982, at which point he began making feelers to not just any label that would have him but the oldest and biggest label of all, Columbia Records.

He had stoked such potential ties for years, having nurtured a close relationship with Don Law, the label's Nashville chief, to whom he had tried to sell the primordial Everly Brothers so long ago. Law sadly had died in December, but Chet knew practically everyone in the business and that the Columbia Records stanchion and its main fulcrum, CBS Records International, owned more of contemporary pop and country than any other label would ever own, its monster-size stable including Bob Dylan, Bruce Springsteen, Simon and Garfunkel, and Pink Floyd, and the country ligatures of Willie Nelson, Kris Kristofferson, and Johnny Cash. In Nashville its studio—Owen Bradley's old Quonset Hut Studio, renamed Columbia Studio A—was still going strong. And Chet wanted in. On October 2, 1983, the move was leaked to the *Tennessean*, which ran a page-one story headlined CHET ATKINS, MR. RCA, READY TO SIGN WITH CBS, with CBS vice president Rick Blackburn confirming it, probably not knowing he was using the same gag line Chet had about Perry Como. "Chet Atkins is my idol," he said, "I have every LP Chet ever made and I'm a real fan. He is simply the best guitar player in the world . . . The signing will be soon, if I can get him off the golf course."

Within a week it was done, Chet giving his notice to Joe Galante, who knew he couldn't stand in his way even if he wanted to. Thankful for the decades of nobility he had been bequeathed by Steve Sholes, Chet was classy as always, with no rancor, leaving on a high note. His RCA swan song, the *Country After All These Years* album, was as perfect a title for the moment as was the Beatles' valedictory *Let It Be*. Indeed, the playlist had him covering Paul McCartney's "Let 'Em In," along with Blondie's "Heart of Glass," Willie Nelson's "On the Road Again," Jessi Colter's "Storms Never Last," and reworkings of the old country tune once recorded by the Carter Family "Wildwood Flower" and the traditional folk-country "I Can Hear Kentucky Calling Me." But if there was a parallel to the Beatles' final single, "The Long and Winding Road," it was his cover of Crystal Gayle's swollen torch song "Ready for the Times to Get Better," with him making sweet and profound music with just the right vibrato and no limit of inner emotion. As it only could have been.

He was no Springsteen or Paul Simon, and he would never aurally inhabit the dark side of the moon, but having him on board provided Columbia more credibility for its country stable, which only kept growing. The label smartly signed Dolly Parton in 1987, a move that would see her career explode and lead to a new deal for, *gulp*, $44 million. There was no reason to grieve for RCA, which restocked through its sale to Bertelsmann Music Group, upon which it finally paid to build office studio space, on Demonbreun Street, and the label would become a superpower in the global Sony Music Entertainment cartel, as would Columbia. Still, on his own distinct level, Atkins also prospered. The terms of the deal were kept quiet, but it was a red carpet, with Rick Blackburn saying, "If he wants to produce, he can. He'll get as much space as he needs here. It's people like Chet Atkins that built this thing."

And the Atkins effect was immediate. Country artist and producer Keith Stegall was persuaded to jump from Mercury, where he was also head A&R man, when a Columbia executive, Luke Lewis, told him, "Hey man, Chet Atkins did it, you can do it."

There were no yearly requirements for singles or albums. But once Chet was in the fold, Columbia was horning in on his space. Rather than signing off on a jazz album, the new suits steered him into something that would have probably driven him out of RCA if they had suggested it—a workout-themed album, to cash in on the craze stoked by Olivia Newton-John's bizarrely incongruous 1981 megahit "Physical." Though Chet could hardly believe it, the label wanted the playlist to be recorded as aerobic workout music, and he complied—but used his kingly standing to treat it as sly parody. When the bosses named the album—his fiftieth overall—*Work It Out with Chet Atkins*, he attached the self-mocking acronym of his CB radio handle and called it *Work It Out with Chet Atkins C.G.P.*, the cover of which hardly suggested sexy women in skin-tight leotards but instead had wrinkly men's workout clothes draped on a chair, sweaty towels, old sneakers, socks, and a Walkman on the floor, a sign of his deadpan humor, cautioning all listeners not to take the concept too seriously.

The tracks were nonetheless chosen for their chugging beats, and while Chet might have wondered why again he quit RCA, he didn't take it lightly. The sessions at Owen Bradley's old studio, taken over by Columbia Records, had just two other musicians, Randy Goodrum, who played keyboards and produced the LP, and David Hungate, the brilliant bass guitarist who had anchored the Grammy-winning Toto for four years before leaving L.A. for Nashville as a session cat. And they actually made this silly concept a nice, intimate country-rock jam, with "Warm Up," "Strolling," "Streakin'," and "Cross Country" medleys as decent country-pop. What could have been a crude embarrassment flowed from passage to passage, Hungate keeping a steady, pounding beat, and Chet and Goodrum delineating the tempos and mood changes on cornball tunes like "Bicycle Built for Two" and "Swanee River," soul fodder like "Bye Bye Blues," and Bach's "Bourrée" and John Denver's

"Take Me Home, Country Roads," with strings and pleasant vocals appearing here and there.

Columbia sprung for a promotional party at the Country Hall of Fame, a shindig at which Chet, according to the *Tennseean*'s Robert Oermann, "hid behind a partition" when Blackburn praised him in excess, then almost whispered into a microphone, "I'm not gonna make a long speech because I'm incapable of it, doncha know? But I appreciate this so much." The label also put some serious funds in ads, and *Work It Out* did well enough, the old boy hitting number sixty-four on the country chart, and the single of "Tara's Theme" was nominated for the Best Country Performance Grammy in '83. A year later, his holiday single "East Tennessee Christmas"—although a B-side to "Winter Wonderland"—was nominated for the same award. Clearly, the name Chet Atkins was still worthy of genuflection and some sort of nomination, and he was well paid for recording only that one album in '83, and only one single.

The latter was his and Goodrum's "Run Don't Walk" from *Work It Out*, the record billed to "Chet Atkins C.G.P.," which didn't chart. He finished the year with just one more release, as a guest musician on a one-off country-R&B duet by Ray Charles and George Jones, "We Didn't See a Thing," billed to "Ray Charles and George Jones (Featuring Chet Atkins)," which hit number six on the country chart. He then would go dark for a year, catching up on lost time to be with his grandchildren, Mandy and Jonathan, who lived in Elizabeth, New Jersey, where Merle and Will had moved. He made his only public music foray sitting in with the Washington Symphony in two concerts at the Kennedy Center. But when he resurfaced in 1985, it was for a major project that revolved around the odd couple of thumbpicking.

It happened after Mark Knopfler had taken a break from Dire Straits after the huge *Brothers in Arms* album. Knopfler had often praised Chet as the influence for his own insanely melodic and complex guitar riffs. Although he was left-handed, unlike Jimi Hendrix he didn't play holding a right-handed guitar upside down but with his right hand to emulate Atkins, with nearly the exact thumb and finger movements, though he used two off-thumb fingers, not three, which only Chet seemed to be able to fluently control. Having become aware of him through David Hungate, Chet believed it would be cool to have a finger-plucking rocker on an album. Calls were made to Knopfler's manager, Ed Bicknell, who told Chet to call Mark directly. He did, and when Knopfler picked up, having just gotten blitzed on bourbon, he thought it might be a phantasm. "It's not every day that Chet Atkins calls you up and asks you to play guitar with him," he recalled. He caught the next flight to Nashville. Chet met him at the airport and almost immediately, Knopfler was jamming with Atkins and Paul Yandell. And, Chet being Chet, he was already making refinements in Mark's technique, "something about moving my thumb," he said, laughing. "It was always good fun, and we just became friends," each so obsessed with their guitar that Knopfler remarked, "We both used to fall asleep" from pure exhaustion.

During the sessions on the album, *Stay Tuned*, the rail-thin, boyish-looking Knopfler, who had already won Grammys, still seemed in awe of Atkins, frequently looking over at Chet during songs to follow the intricacies on the fretboard. Their synergy came with not a speck of ego clashing, unlike the Les Paul album. Chet would recruit a holy communion of guest guitar greats to record one or two tracks each—Knopfler, Benson, Klugh, Hungate's former Toto bandmate, guitarist Steve Lukather, prime session man Larry Carlton, Paul Yandell, Dean Parks, and Brent Mason. Hungate was on bass, Boots Randolph on sax, and Jim Horn also played. Goodrum and Darryl Dybka, a regular in Earl Klugh's jazz band, were on keys, and a threesome of drummers included Toto's Jeff Porcaro. Mark O'Connor was on fiddle. Terry McMillan and the Brazilian samba percussionist Paulinho Da Costa furnished the rhythmic accents. The sessions ran over two months in the spring of 1985, rotating between the CA Workshop and the Sound Shop (where Paul McCartney recorded with Wings in the '70s) in Nashville, and in L.A. at the A&M Studio and the home base of Larry Carlton, Room 335, so named for the Gibson ES-335 guitar.

One can imagine the blast it must have been inside those walls as chords and beats from the crucibles of rock, country, and jazz danced about, and Chet only produced two tracks, one on which he dueted with Benson, "Sunrise," written by Benson and Randy Goodrum, and Wayne Moss's "A Mouse in the House." Hungate produced the other eight tracks, a nearly impossible task what with having to iron out so many different modes and idioms, as well as horns and strings, all mixed and remixed by Nashville engineers Mike Poston, Don Hahn, and George Butler—with Chet looming above them every step of the way. The pity was that the playlist was somewhat pallid, though three other songs were cowritten by Chet with Yandell, "Please Stay Tuned," "Some Leather and Lace," and, with some help from Knopfler, "Cosmic Square Dance," its opening fiddle run indeed launching into an airy double-guitar flight into the stars, with *Star Wars*–like computer speak and a fiddle ending.

This brought Chet Atkins into the blues-infused rock of a generally overproduced electro-pop and synth wave decade, and he nailed the soft edge of it as well as Chuck Mangione or the post-Brass Herb Alpert. However, despite being unsure if Atkins's longtime fans would reel from what struck some as formulaic elevator music, CBS sprung for another promotional event, at the Vanderbilt Plaza Hotel ballroom, with the Nashville bourgeois invited. Chet reeled in Benson, Klugh, Hungate, Carlton, and other big guns to play, and Blackburn made another nice speech about him. But while it was released as the first Nashville-centric album released on the CD format, it did only so-so, going to number sixty-four on the country chart, and the two songs released as singles—Dybka's "The Boot and the Stone" and "Please Stay Tuned," an upbeat, hard-rock turn with high-hat splashing and Lukather's torrid riffs nearly burying Chet's nuanced rhythm work—flat-out failed. The album missed the charts, although with his permanent country affiliation, the Grammy people again had an award ready, Best Country Instrumental Performance, for the ballyhooed "Cosmic Square Dance." At the awards, Chet and the equally reticent Knopfler humbly accepted their statues and said their alliance was nowhere near played out. And Chet, having done all that any human guitarist could, had the cushion of being able to duck in and out of any genre, old or new, and intended to do more of the same before anyone could dare say he was through..

For his next album, he enlisted Dybka to write six of the eight tracks, staying within the smooth, contemplative vein that these days is sometimes mockingly called yacht rock. Produced by Dybka and jazz/soul producer Ronnie Foster, who played organ in George Benson's backup group, the tracks swirled together into sometimes somnolent light jazz, only a few instruments in each song, the titles of which raised few pulse rates, such as the title tune "Street Dreams," "The Official Beach Music," "(Like a) Crystal in the Light," and the sole tune written by Chet, with John Knowles, "Honolulu Blue," rekindling the peaceful, intimate groove of the Nashville String Quartet but without any hard country tie-ins. The session men included jazz vets Lee Ritenour and Harvey Mason, and Chet gave a playing gig to Bruce Bolen, moonlighting from the artist relations office. Smooth as it was, *Street Dreams* was hard to swallow for Atkins buffs, and it came and went, with reviews wondering how in the world Chet Atkins became caught up in synthesizers that even his guitar couldn't cut through, rendering him something like Peaches and Chet.

He tried to move the goalposts a bit with his 1987 pseudo-island diversion *Sails*, coproduced with Hungate, a work similar to his past island-music diversion, but this too was a Dybka-dominated new age confection. The guitar echelon at the CA Workshop sessions—Klugh, Knopfler, Yandell, Eddie Rabbit's arranger Billy Joe Walker Jr.—was abutted by the Indian yoga guru Baba Ram Dave and bouzouki player Aristotle Onassid, and the songs brought an intriguing flavor to country and soft jazz. Chet wrote four of the ten tracks, "Wobegon (The Way It Used to Be)," a nimble acoustic nod to Garrison Keillor, "Waltz for the Lonely" with Goodrum, "Laffin' at Life" with Dybka and Hungate, and "On a Roll" with Dybka and Paul Yandell. Knopfler played with Chet and sang a Dylan-like lyric on the ballad "Why Worry," which had appeared in 1985 on Dire Straits' Grammy-winning *Brothers in Arms*. Rock & Roll Hall of Fame pianist Keith Jarrett contributed "My Song." The title track, a cover of the 1976 hit Orleans song by John Hall and his wife Johanna, was a beautiful yacht-rock trip with quietly swelling synth waves.

No singles would come off it, but Chet as ever seemed to be immune to the usual metadata. He had more than earned his place as a very selective artist whose arterial work was still reflexively bought by his fans, and he received invitations to highbrow TV venues. In 1987 he performed on the now-enshrined Cinemax special *Chet Atkins & Friends: Music from the Heart*, which like the PBS show was pure Americana, produced in Nashville as a Southern-fried dish of new country. And when Chet appealed to Willie Nelson and Waylon Jennings to appear with him, they were there, the rocky past notwithstanding. The other headliners on that show were Knopfler, the Everly Brothers, Emmylou Harris, and a new confidant, the unimaginably bluesy White singer/keyboardist Michael McDonald. Recorded live from Vanderbilt University's Neely Auditorium on May 2, Chet, jacketless in a tie and suspenders, appeared on camera, in character, in mid-strum, saying, "Hello out there, my name is Chet Atkins . . . and I'm a guitar player. Never wanted to be anything else." Then, just as Chet Atkins-like as ever, he called over to the orchestra, which included Knopfler, Yandell, Dybka, Londin, McMillan, and Ambrosia front man David Pack on guitar, and tersely ordered, "A little faster guys."

He opened with Knopfler, asking him if he'd rather sing or pick. "Well, Chet," he said, when you're in the presence of the world's number-one guitar player, you'd just rather pick and learn." With perfect timing, Chet said, "Just like I wrote it." The pair played "See You in My Dreams" and later "Lonely People" and John Lennon's "Imagine," and Knopfler did his band's "Walk of Life." Then the Everly Brothers came on. When Don said Studio B was now a museum, Chet said, "I don't know what that makes us." Don then nearly broke into tears recalling that "we wouldn't have been in Nashville without you, Chet." After Chet's normative teasing put-down, "Aw, shut up, Don, and sing," they did a medley of "All I Have to Do is Dream," "Bye Bye Love," and "Wake Up Little Susie," and the brothers sang "Why Worry." Waylon—who reminded everyone that he was still "fightin' the system"—did "Good Hearted Woman," joined by Willie, who segued into "Island in the Sea." Chet played mandolin as Emmylou sang "Precious Memories," then did three on his own—"Waltz for the Lonely," "Sunrise," and "I Still Can't Say Goodbye"—before the collective closing number, "Corinna, Corinna," with a walk-on by Ray Stevens.

Every minute of that hour-long show was timeless, with Chet letting it out to the point where his guitar at times had the whirl of a Wurlitzer organ. "Imagine" so affected him that when it was done, he patted Knopfler on the shoulder, a rare gesture for him. And before "Can't Say Goodbye," in a very postdated tribute, he dedicated the song to "my dad," his voice almost breaking as he sang lyrics like "I miss my dad tonight," bringing a long ovation from the audience. The hour was so engrossing that the pay TV network issued it as a CD on its own Roadshow label as part of its Cinemax Sessions series, and later on DVD as *Cinemax Sessions: A Session with Chet Atkins (Certified Guitar Player)*, an absolute must-see-and-hear.

Chet would return the favor to Knopfler by touring with him in England, the pair putting on another rousing show at the London Palladium, a benefit show staged by Bob Geldof's Amnesty International cause under the name of the Secret Policeman's Other Ball. The Cinemax show would also lead to other TV team-ups, with Dolly Parton and Jerry Reed, and the convergence with Knopfler was quite helpful to Chet. Their mutual admiration was clear, though Knopfler, who had reached the peak of success, was not one to sublimate before any other guitarist, not even Chet Atkins. "I learn from him," he said. "He's got a few little licks I've lifted, and I've shown him a few. Musicians do that . . . 'Show me a lick.'"

Chet liked him for that very reason, saying later that "you play at a higher level when you're playing with somebody else because you try a little harder, maybe to impress the guy you're playing with. And you try to impress him to play licks off what I've played. He doesn't think he's a great player, but he is." To be certain, Atkins's continued stream of albums was propelled by the fact that Knopfler was there to provide a challenge to him, or a crutch, either being something he now needed. Not incidentally, Knopfler knew when to concede. "Chet," he said, "loved the simple stuff, the stuff he would play in his kitchen, with two chords. And that's where we met. The simple stuff. We part company when it gets more complicated."

In 1988 Chet again plied on the "greatest guitar player" gag with an album simply called *C.G.P.*, again with Knopfler among the high-top crew Chet assembled for sessions to be produced by Atkins, Hungate, and Dybka. There were also brass players, horns, more keyboards and synthesizers, Londin on drums, Terry McMillan on percussion, and Steve Gibson, who played steel guitar on Dave Loggins's searing "Please Come to Boston" and Lynn Anderson's "(I Never Promised You a) Rose Garden." The ten tracks were homegrown, with Chet cowriting five, including one with Johnny Gimble ("Put Your Clothes On") and two with Dybka ("Chinook Winds" and "Jethreaux"), who also wrote "Which Way del Vecchio?"—a sly guitar-pickin' reference, as was another Chet cowrote with John Knowles, "Knucklebusters."

He also teamed with Shel Silverstein on "Mockingbird Variations," arguably the best song on the album, its light salsa, hip-swaying beat with Chet's extended tremolos mirrored by Hungate's tangy bass and a zithering synth line a complete break from the Nashville Sound template, and Chet threw in a peppy vocal on the final track, the live Cinemax rendering of "I Still Can't Say Goodbye," his emotional tribute James Arlie Atkins. Adding a rock tie-in, there was a cover of John Sebastian's old Lovin' Spoonful hit "Daydream," Chet and Gibson jamming with a too-'80s synth. More captivating once more was the cover of "Imagine," featuring another precious Atkins and Knopfler collaboration of mesmerizing synchronicity, their acoustic guitars abetted by a gentle layer of synth strings, packing all of Lennon's emotional tiers. That would be the album's focal point, but Chet chose to release "I Still Can't Say Goodbye," which he projected as a creed to carry him through old age.

If he was in an emotional state in 1989, it had everything to do with the sudden intrusion of reality. In addition to his own aging, that same year he lost both his only surviving brother and his mother, who had been betrayed by James Arlie back in Smoky Top, and whom Chet had returned to Luttrell several times a year to visit. Twelve years after Jimmy Atkins died at sixty-four in his post-career home in Nebraska City, Nebraska, Lowell died on January 23 in Clinton County, Indiana, at sixty-seven; then, at year's end, on December 15, the hardy Ida Ella Sharp Strevel passed in Pegram, Tennessee, at ninety-two, leaving Willie Strevel to outlive her by one year. Chet's only living sibling now was Billie Rose Strevel Shockley, who would make it to 2023 and age ninety-one. Chet would spend that turbid end-of-decade year essentially burying his past. He again went dark, neither recording nor releasing any records until another new decade rang in.

He seemed to be especially depressed. In a letter to Rick Foster, he grumbled that "I have been suffering with a bronicial [*sic*] problem, taking pills that make me irritable," not knowing that the problem was that the decades he had been a chain smoker had led to the beginning of lung cancer. For extended periods, he was so disinterested in music that, as he wrote to Foster,

> I haven't learned a new lick in so long. I don't hear as well now that I am on the back nine of life and music just doesn't sound as good and consuquently [*sic*] there is not the overwhelming desire to practice.

Whether it was boredom or medication, he also had latched onto a strange cause, adding that "I think we should start a drive to free Jim Bakker," the venal televangelist cohost with his frowzy, makeup-caked wife Tammy Faye of the *PTL Club*, whose high-money payoff to a church secretary turned into a mistress opened a morass of other illegal financial schemes and tax cheating that sent him to prison for five years. "I think the little dude was given a raw deal. All he did was over book and seperate [*sic*] a few folks from their pay check," suddenly forgiving about paycheck shorting after years of snorting about it in the music business. However, when he reverted back to his music, he was still as sharp as ever. Steve Wariner, who had been playing in Chet's touring band for years, came by to work out some songs with him. And as he recalled,

> Chet would bust your chops. If you didn't know every song known to man, he would bust you for it. He would name songs from the '30s and knew every word of them. I heard him once backstage when he sang "On Top of Old Smokey"—and he sang every verse. He knew every song. Show tunes, pop standards, big band, Hawaiian music, you name it. [But] he always wanted to learn. I'd go to his office, and he'd be working on a guitar lick, and he'd say, "Man, check this out." And I'm thinking, "Here's Chet Atkins. He's sixty-something and he's still excited about a lick."

In 1990 he seemed to have shaken off his blues and delusions about Jim Bakker, cowriting the wonderfully acrid "Did Jesus Wear a Rolex?" about shysters like Bakker, and jammed again with Knopfler on their collaborative gem *Neck and Neck*, a tour de force often submitted by Atkins fans as the best work of his life, and the one most relevant to the now-common junction of country and rock. Knopfler judged the album to be in the same deep vein as Chet's dual LPs with Merle Travis and Les Paul, two of Mark's favorites, which were, he said,

> nice and loose, quite happy records, and fairly rootsy, not too much in this easy-listening jazz thing Chet would be attracted to every now and again. . . . I was interested in Chet's country roots much more than this jazz thing and I didn't mince my

> words about that. . . . I couldn't stand it then and I can't stand it now.

Knopfler wanted to do one-finger playing, the "Travis stuff—that's where the roots of Chet's playing are." For example, "I'll See You in My Dreams," an old tune that just spilled out.

Knopfler believed he had gotten to the root of why Chet had never quite gotten the hang of old-time jazz. He was always melodic, always improvised melody and harmony," he explained, contrasted with jazz, in which "there's always more than one note playing, with some interesting chords." Thus, Knopfler could deduce that Chet was "not really a jazzer." Chet agreed to that limitation, and knew Knopfler could see into his soul enough to trust him to nominally produce the album, which wound through two Nashville studios and one on Mark's home ground, London, at the magnificently out-of-character Hillbilly Heaven studio, in an area harboring British country fans and Tobacco Road-like attractions such as Bubba's Garage and Grandma's Greasy Spoon Diner.

They wove through ten tracks, none written by Chet and one by Knopfler, his stab at rootsy country on the last cut, "The Next Time I'm in Town." And Chet covered his own hit "Yakety Axe" as a dual guitar melding that he had Merle Travis arrange, making it a three-generational finger-plucking effort, and Chet summoned up the ghost of Django Reinhardt by covering his jazz standard "Tears." Contributions were also made by Vince Gill, Floyd Cramer, Steve Wariner on bass, Mark O'Connor on fiddle and mandolin, and steel guitarist Paul Franklin, and Chet picked out two Don Gibson covers, "Sweet Dreams" and "Just One Time," along with the evergreens "I'll See You in My Dreams" and "There'll Be Some Changes Made," Randy Goodrum's "So Soft, Your Goodbye," and "Poor Boy Blues." The latter, the traditional country rag, had new lyrics by British guitarist Paul Kennerley, Emmylou Harris's then-husband, and its chugging blues, with vocals shared by Knopfler, Chet, and Gill, sounded much like the Dire Straits smash "Walk of Life." Chet also dueted, quietly, with Knopfler on the vocals of Knopfler's album-closing track, "Next Time I'm in Town."

This time the mix was just right, a lily-soft country bonbon, and the album—with Chet almost slyly hidden behind a massive Gibson L-10 on the cover, which pictured him and Knopfler—made it to number 27 on the country chart and number 127 on the pop chart, and did far better in England and, of all places, Scandinavia. The single of "Poor Boy Blues" reached the top hundred on the Canadian chart, and Chet would begin using "Next Time" as his closing number in concert. He and Knopfler also took bows at the Grammys again, when *Neck and Neck* yielded winners two consecutive years, the singles of "Poor Boy Blues" and "So Soft, Your Goodbye," both released in late 1990, winning, respectively, Best Country Collaboration with Vocal and Best Country Instrumental Performance—the former beating, among others, the Willie Nelson, Waylon Jennings, Johnny Cash, and Kris Kristofferson second joint album for Columbia, *Highwayman 2*, produced by Chips Moman.

Atkins and Knopfler were an odd couple with beautiful results. However, while the collaborations would continue here and there, they would not again share billing on an album. As the '90s moved in, Knopfler plunged into a Dire Straits farewell tour, while Chet, nearing his seventies, proceeded as always, moving forward as more honors and tributes accumulated. But even for a king with an unstoppable inner spring, the clock was running out of time.

21

LAST LICKS

In 1991 Chet traveled to Paris to play in concert with the French fingerpicker Marcel Dadi at the latter's Dadi festival. Dadi, France's answer to Mark Knopfler, emulated Chet's style right down to the thumb-pick and had journeyed to Nashville, in the '70s, to meet Atkins, and the two became long-distance friends—and for Chet, Dadi was another ally who would suffer a tragic end. Five years later, after he had been inducted into the Country Music Hall of Fame, he died when a plane he was on en route to Paris exploded off Long Island, killing all on board.

Tragedies like that always shook Chet but never deterred him, and probably helped stir a constant need to work lest he die a professional death. As it was, his past moved along with him, refusing to wither. "The word is out how I don't hanker to produce anymore," he said, yet his undimmed status in Nashville had kept more generations of hopeful country fame-seekers coming to see him, or at least sending demos to the office he kept on Music Row, though he was rarely there. Almost making light of the carryover, the old ogler said, "People still come with tapes, but I usually don't see 'em unless it's a shapely girl."

But he was hardly through yet. When he returned from Paris, he spent some time working on a new challenge, writing with John Knowles the score for the Tennessee Dance Theatre called *Midways*. It was, he said, "the first time I've tried to do this, but . . . the music community needs to overlap some with the local arts community. The dancers heard something on an old album that they liked, titled 'The Night Atlanta Burned.' They said, 'We could choreograph a tune like this,' so we got started." Working with the troupe's artistic directors Andrew Krichels and Donna Rizzo, the show, performed at the Polk Theater, was a critical success.

He then doubled back to the now-aging gonzo Jerry Reed, recording the last duet album with his old confrere at Buzz Cason's Creative Workshop studio. He asked Knopfler to play on two lighthearted-sounding songs—Wayne Simmons's "Gibson Girl," a reversion to Chet's long-ago quirk of equating a precious guitar with a precious woman, and a sly instrumental cover of Doug and Rusty Kershaw's raucous "Cajun Stripper," his fey vocal a homespun artifact that he, Reed, and Dybka, as coproducers of the album, sought as an Everyman touch. He and Reed cowrote the instrumental "Vaudeville Daze," an easy-listening stroll, with Chet on a warm, spacious-sounding fretless guitar, and Chet cowrote "Here Comes That Girl" with Darryl Dybka. Reed wrote three more in his playfully puckish mien: the touching, almost dainty "First Born," the kicky "Major Attempt at a Minor Thing," and a redo of his 1967 song "The Claw." Rocky Stone's "Nifty Fifties" and the first track, the Gershwins' "Summertime," the main guitar line played by Pat Bergeson, centered the traditional underpinning of the album—notwithstanding its title, from R. L. Kass's "Sneakin' Around," an under-the-sheets caper originally sung by Dolly Parton in the movie *The Best Little Whorehouse in Texas* but, here, the only verbal part being two overheated *ahhhh*s by Reed.

The LP hit number sixty-eight on the country chart when it was released in '92, and "Vaudeville Daze," released the year before, became another seemingly mandatory Grammy award for Best Country Instrumental Performance, with Chet and Jerry beating some very hip post-mod country nominees like Asleep at the Wheel's "Black and White Rag" and the Chieftains' "Cotton-Eyed Joe." Two years later, *Sneakin' Around* won the Best Country Instrumental trophy too. And the year in between, when Chet and Tanya Tucker presented the Best Male Country Performer award to Garth Brooks, that Best Instrumental award went to Chet's session man Mark O'Connor, for his *The New Nashville Cats* album. It was indeed a new order in country music, Nashville permanently its core, and sixty-nine-year-old Chet Atkins still at the top of it. During that '93 Grammys show, he was also given the Lifetime Achievement Award with Little Richard, Thelonious Monk, Bill Monroe, Pete Seeger, and Fats Waller. He, Richard, Monroe, and Seeger were still alive, and Richard was still rippin' it up in appearances, but only Chet was actively recording and in demand.

As such, he continued to broaden the CGP penumbra, which had now become a subject for interviewers. Chet went through a litany of reasons why it had come about, riffing that because he had no chance of ever attaining a PhD after dropping out of high school, it was *his* PhD. What's more, he himself seemed to forget or riffed on what those letters were supposed to mean. He had sent a letter to Rick Foster in 1989 in which he wrote, "C.G.P. means corny guitar player or certified guitar player, whatever you want it to be." Then, too, he never thought much about Grammy awards, even though he was an almost annual beneficiary of the National Academy of Recording Arts and Sciences (NARAS) member voting panels, no matter the quality or sales of the recordings. What's more, he felt the same about the Country Music Association's awards, even boycotting the show in 1988 when the CMA shoved the Musician of the Year honor out of the prime-time TV broadcast; he only found out he had won reading the papers the next day. When he accepted trophies, one could see his bemusement feigning excitement. And when universities offered him honorary degrees, he declined; instead, he boasted his CGP "degree," often wearing on his lapel a CGP pin crafted by Mark Pritcher, who ran the Chet Atkins Appreciation Society (CAAS), keeping a few in his pocket to hand out as gifts.

It was Yandell who suggested making the CGP into a private club with a king and a court—his cadre. The first entrant, at a CAAS event in a Nashville hotel, was Chet's court jester, Jerry Reed, then Steve Wariner, John Knowles, and Tommy Emmanuel, the latter of whom reached his Nirvana in 1993 when Chet called him in Australia and Tommy told him he was making an album. Chet asked, "You want me to play on a track?" That sent Tommy on another plane ride to Nashville.

> We recorded a track on my album "The Journey" [which went double platinum in Australia] called "Villa Anita." I'll never forget this. I'm flying between Denver and LA, 35,000 feet up and I call my mother and I say, "I'm having a sip of champagne in celebration of something magical . . ." Before I could say another word she went, "Don't tell me Chet's played on your album?" And I said yeah. She was so excited for me. She knew what it meant to me. That was a most wonderful experience. Each time we play[ed] together it [got] a bit better.

Being a CGP alumnus—something granted to Paul Yandell when Merle Atkins included him after Chet's death—is a royal cushion, so holy to Atkins fans that, like Chet, the members would make the three letters an appendage to their names. It was Nashville's not-so-secret society, and its president never stopped enjoying how much people could get impressed by the certification of a little inside joke. Indeed, before he died, he made sure to copyright the abbreviation and require permission for anyone to use it, a proviso his family has strictly maintained.

At the start of the decade, he was also back in Saint Paul to play on Garrison Keillor's PBS show. Keillor, who wrote and sang songs himself, owed much to him, not just for his guitar accompaniment but for material Keillor used in his monologues derived from Chet's winsome storytelling, which was a long tapestry of downhome Americana. "The other day in Cincinnati," Chet said at the time, "I told him about an affair I almost had at a hotel when I was a kid. He asked if he could tell that story." He and Keillor then hit the road together over the summer on an eighteen-city Keillor tour called *The Sweet Corn Show*, with Chet onstage chatting with Keillor during his monologues, dueting on songs, and at the end pointedly singing "Would God Wear a Rolex?" and "I Still Can't Say Goodbye." Still denying his own legend, though, he reiterated during the tour, "I'm still learning to play. I never stopped trying to learn. I never stopped trying to get the mediocrity out of my playing, and the predictability." As well, the almost-seventy Atkins now began to seem more like a rustic and melancholic character, sometimes scolding, sometimes defensive and needy. In one of his letters in 1992 to Rick Foster, he unburdened in a stream of consciousness:

> I have always known that I am a good person, I live too much by the golden rule, for my own good so what other people think has long ceased to concern me. It once did but after a lecture from my mentor Fred Rose (the best song writer and man I ever knew) I was freed from that. . . . Being a little square, I feel that most anything I like will appeal to the public also. To remain on a major label I must give them what they think they can sell but usually all that is changed is the background music. So I don't feel that I have pandered to the low instincts of people ever. When I was producing a lot of folks, it was the same. I deplore that type of content in the movies and songs of today. Ever since Kristofferson came on the scene, writers try writing sensuous songs in the same manner and it just doesn't work, they don't have the class.

He had even gotten a little ghoulish, thinking about his death and how his funeral memorial should go down.

> Thanks for offering to play at my finale. I would love that. Garrison Kellior has promised to come down or send down a nice taped eulogy. None of my brothers made it past my age (67) So, I don't do much planning ahead. I never buy to [*sic*] many guitar strings and sometimes don't even buy green Bananas. That's confidence in my future, isn't it. I'm sorry I didn't get back to you when you last called. I have had two

> really bad colds since Feb. and they laid me pretty low. I'm just getting over the last one. My best wishes to Wendy and the Chillun and LISTEN, make sure they get plenty of protein. I see so many vegetarians who look like they just escaped from Bergen Belson [*sic*].

When his mind turned to music, he reviewed a tape Foster had made, writing in 1993,

> The sound could be enhanced considerably if you had just a little digital reverb. There are some nice ones around now and they are not severely expensive. Well, I am still trying to play but it is less fun when the highs go. I have learned a couple of licks from a friend, now I must learn to utilize them . . . Anyhow, stay well and eat some beef once in a while. Moderation is the secret to good health. That is my opinion and it should be yours. That is a joak [*sic*] son.

By mid-decade, he was wearing tinted glasses, a white fedora, and arty suspenders, an elder growing old with grace and lingering hip-to-be-square élan—though he shocked everyone, and loved doing so, when doing a spot on the Nashville Network's *American Music Shop* with Reed. He came out in a black leather jacket and tight white pants, making Jerry look like his uncle in a gray cardigan. Chet had put on weight, his reedy frame looking fuller and well lived. But he still had the young, hungry look of a young man, one who had the security of a still-hectic workload and a reputation beyond the ability of anyone to fully appreciate. Typically, any recording was bound to win honors, and it happened again in 1993 when he sat in with the Texas country band Asleep at the Wheel for an instrumental cover of "Red Wing," the tragic Indian love song written in 1907 and adapted through the years by Woody Guthrie, Charlie Chaplin, and Bob Wills. The group had already won nine country Grammys, and this became their tenth and Atkins's twelfth. Then, in 1994, he and Hungate coproduced *Read My Licks*, the title tune being a nifty country blues riff about letting his guitar do his talking, written by Catesby Jones and David Roger Allen.

Chet shared guitar leads on it with Pat Bergeson and Steve Wariner as well as vocals with Wariner, who had become a big-ticket item at MCA Records, produced by another legendary producer, Jimmy Bowen. He also wrote one song, "Young Thing," a loosey-goosey stomp with groovy keyboard and harmonica licks, and cowrote three more, "Mountains of Illinois" with Bergeson, "Every Now and Then" with Randy Goodrum, and "Around the Bend" with Jerry Reed, on which Mark Knopfler made a guest appearance—as did George Benson on the old Johnny Mercer standard "Dream," which Benson produced and applied strings to, arranged by Bergen White. Chet finished the LP with another go-round on "Vincent." Without a beat lost, he was again accepting a Best Country Instrumental Grammy for the single of "Young Thing."

However, it was his teaming with a new entry into his world, Suzy Bogguss, on the old kicker "After You've Gone" by the late, great Black blues writers Henry Creamer and Turner Layton that charted his immediate future, giving him the idea to do about the only thing he hadn't yet—combining on an album with a female finger-plucker. He had met the Illinois-born singer-songwriter in the '80s and written in the liner notes for her debut album in 1989 that "her voice sparkles like crystal water." He also had introduced her on that *American Music Shop* telecast with Reed. She now had a mounting career and was signed to Liberty Records, and with her flaming red hair and smoothly bracing voice, she was suggestive of a harder Patsy Cline, as she went on to sell millions of albums and design a line of skin-tight, white leather garb.

Her influences were as diverse as the Ink Spots and John Hiatt, and she won a Grammy for a collaboration with Lee Greenwood. Working with her in periodic jams in his rarely used Music Row office, Chet had tempered her sometimes piercing soprano into subtle, emotionally spiked aureate, and chosen "After You've Gone" for her to sing. The up-tempo pace included Chet and Bergeson's dueling electric licks, seeming chemically soldered to the liquid-like vocal. The pity was that the song was not released as a single—which in general had become almost obsolete for him. Also of little concert for him was the fact that *Read My Licks* stagnated to number sixty-eight on the country chart. Yet the thirst for Atkins's newest release made for a sort of cottage industry, on a lower industry level but still profitable scale—which is why RCA in 1992 kept on issuing retro-Atkins albums, the sixth since he left, *The Atkins Years*, released that year. It's also why Amy Grant recorded a children's storybook for the small Rabbit Ears label, called *The Gingham Dog and the Calico Cat*, with Chet coproducing and composing the congenial acoustic backing score, played by him and Paul Yandell.

He could still pull in a hip crowd far from Nashville. On June 22, he and Reed played a dual concert in the Greenwich Village music club the Bottom Line. Chet's allure also explained the *Simpatico* album, which thrilled Bogguss to no end, much as Knopfler had been thrilled, because she could be an adjunct for even an elderly Atkins. It was a project Bogguss herself had suggested to her label and was basically in her hands, as coproducer with her engineer John Guess. In fact, Chet wasn't sure he should do the album, not knowing if he belonged on someone else's album. As Bogguss recalled, he worried that, as an "older person," he might take her from her younger audience and even "drag my career down." She assured him otherwise, and during the recordings at Nashville's Emerald Sound Studios, they easily teamed. Chet reminded her to stay "in the pocket," and she instructed him how to sing a low-note counterpoint on the song they cowrote with Doug Crider, "One More for the Road."

They drew upon a rich supply of material, inculcating some notable covers—Elton John and Bernie Taupin's "Sorry Seems to Be the Hardest Word," the old brakeman Jimmy Rodgers's "In the Jailhouse Now," Johnny Cash's "I Still Miss Someone," and Randy VanWarmer's "Wives Don't Like Old Girlfriends"—and adding originals like the pointed album closer, "This Is the Beginning," by Pat Donohue, another brilliant fingerpicker who had a regular gig with Garrison Keillor and whose fealty to Atkins was such that in '95, his *Back Roads* album would feature the tribute song "Stealin' from Chet," who played on it. Bogguss also cowrote, with Crider and Steve Dorff, the buoyant "You Bring Out the Best in Me," and added R. L. Kass's "Forget About It" and Michael Johnson's easy-listening "When She Smiled at Him."

The album was easy-listening catnip, the backing vocals again including Vince Gill as well as Beth Neilsen Chapman, Harry Stinson, and jazz singer Carl Atkins. But for most reviewers, the other Atkins was what pushed the low-key work to number fifty-five country. Both singles released were Bogguss's vocal duets with him, the other being on "Sorry Seems to Be the Hardest Word," which didn't make the chart but stood out to the keen ears of *Washington Post* critic Geoffrey Himes as "music worthy of her talent." About "You Bring Out the Best in Me," Himes added that it "summarized Atkins's effect on Bogguss . . . the no-fuss elegance of Atkins's guitar work forced Bogguss to curb her tendency to oversing and concentrate instead on the lyrics. When they finally went into the studio, the result was the most restrained and most effective vocals of her career."

The Liberty flacks contrived a whole new category for it—New Traditionalist Country—which must have tickled Chet, being involved in another new country format at an age when he might have been spending his time on his porch. Indeed, when the album was released in the fall of 1994, he had hit seventy, although the cover shot of them made him look decades younger, Suzy's arms wrapped snug around his shoulders behind him. When a video was made for "One More for the Road" for country music TV shows, he wasn't simply playing as he previously had next to Mark Knopfler on "Poor Boy Blues" and Jerry Reed on "The Claw," but playing in a period piece set in a busy 1940s hotel lobby with a band, Bogguss in a slinky black dress, he in suspenders, vest, and spats. He still didn't move around much and looked a tad nonplussed, but he tapped his foot as he played and exchanged adoring glances with her. As painful as it might have seemed to some, if anyone doubted times had changed, a look at the '90-hip, New Traditionalist Chet Atkins helped change their mind.

He and Bogguss seemed joined at the hip in '94 and '95. In May of the latter year, he made his fourth presidential gig, this time as the sole male performer and host of the PBS *Women of Country* broadcast recorded live on the South Lawn of the White House. Bill Clinton touted him for his "well-earned reputation for nurturing and encouraging country talent, and for a little country homespun wisdom." He introduced him as "probably the best-known guitarist in the world," whereupon Chet and a small Nashville band accompanied Bogguss, Alison Krauss, and Kathy Mattea, who had won a Grammy for their anti-AIDS benefit album *Red Hot + Country*. Natty in a tuxedo vest, he also dueted with Bogguss on their *Simpatico* song "This Is the Beginning" and did a solo instrumental on "Mark My Word." Stepen Stills joined the trio on the closing number, his "Teach Your Children," which Bogguss, Krauss, and Mattea recorded with Crosby, Stills & Nash, reeling in a Grammy nomination. Chet then slid into another duet with Bogguss on a Liberty celebrity album that brought him back to the concept he had begun in 1965, a country Beatles tribute. This one, called *Come Together: America Salutes the Beatles*, codifying the Fab Four a quarter century after they disbanded, had a John Lennon pencil sketch on the cover and seventeen covers by headliners such as Willie Nelson, Kris Kristofferson, Tanya Tucker, Randy Travis, Huey Lewis, and Delbert McClinton. Chet's track with Suzy, "All My Loving," produced by longtime country producer Jerry Crutchfield, laid slick contours on her emotional wailing. The album hit number thirteen country and made the top one hundred pop, and the Atkins-Bogguss single, on the B-side of Tucker's "Something" cover, was nominated for the Best Country Vocal Collaboration Grammy.

Never seeming to idle, Chet had another comfortable pocket to slide into, using the CGP emblem again to sell his next album, *Almost Alone*, billing himself as Chet Atkins CGP. As if needing to step back from a world of big-budget music videos, he stripped away glitz and glamour and just played some old, unadulterated country corn pone. Producing it himself, he wrote seven new songs and it was mainly just him on his acoustic Gibson, embellished by Paul Yandell on one of the new tunes, "Maybelle," a salute to Mother Maybelle, who had died in 1978. He had fiddler Randy Howard on another, "Sweet Alla Lee," and Randy Goodrum on keys on the jokey "I Still Write Your Name in the Snow," which Chet wrote with Billy Edd Wheeler, who had written "Jackson" for Johnny and June Carter Cash. The balance of the work was made up of old go-tos like Jerry Jeff Walker's "Mr. Bojangles," Irving Berlin's "Cheek to Cheek," Cole Porter's "You Do Something to Me," and an extraordinarily moving rendition, as the closer, of Schubert's "Ave Maria," which Chet had first played with lesser precision on his 1967 *Class Guitar* album. For this version he dipped it into a dream string arrangement by Bergen White.

The LP was slated for release in May 1996, with the single release of "I Still Write Your Name in the Snow"—a song with a notable gender twist about being cheated on, with the sneakiest put-down ever, Chet singing about catching his woman "messin' around" and boogying out of town in a pickup, whereupon he leaves her name etched in the snow, by "tinklin' in the wind . . . dotting the eyes and crossing the *t*'s," which he explained as something he and Billy Edd used to do off a porch in wintertime. Singing it on the country TV shows, he brought the audiences to hysterics, and though it didn't chart, another song from the LP, "Jam Man," became the latest, and last, boost into permanence. The song, played with an old-time Western swing groove, was, like the other cuts, deceptively simple, with Chet having supervised acoustic and electric multitracking, mixing, and mastering. It won him his fortieth Grammy nomination, and fourteenth win, in the category he all but owned, Best Country Instrumental—beating, among others, Steve Wariner's "The Brickyard Boogie." However, by the time that award was given out on February 26, 1997, at Madison Square Garden, it had become quite possible that the album might be not only his last recording but a posthumous one.

In March 1996 he had begun to cough up phlegmatic mucus. He had given up smoking years before, but the damage had been done.

He grudgingly went to a surgeon friend, Dr. James Coleman, who also played guitar as a sometime member of his sessions, for an examination. Coleman diagnosed it as lung cancer, yet another form of the disease he had battled through, but it was still early enough to be removed and be done with. And so for the third time in his life, he had cancer surgery, now performed by Coleman, who determined that it had not spread. Yet as if sworn to secrecy, none of the few who were aware let word slip as Chet quietly entered and then left the hospital, fedora pulled down over his face.

Superman yet again, he resolved to keep his scheduled appearances and activities, which were many. Looking ahead to 1997, there would be the annual Chet Atkins Appreciation Society fete and a new yearly event, Chet Atkins Musician Days, a weeklong street fair featuring musicians from around the world, an idea taken from the Fête de la Musique festival he had attended while in Paris. The planning was just beginning for it, and as early as August of 1996, he was back in action at the sold-out gig he had on Monday nights at Nashville's ritzy Caffe Milano, sardonically telling the audience, "I always wanted to play in a room full of friends. I guess you should be careful what you wish for." Then, in November, he went back to Washington, DC, with executives of TomKats Hospitality, a Nashville showbiz catering company, to meet with representatives of twelve countries, and plans were set for the first in a continuing series of Atkins Musician Days at Riverfront Park in June 1997, the profits going to a Chet Atkins Music Education Fund supporting young local musicians.

Moreover, during the festival there would be two massive tribute concerts to celebrate him in late June, one at the Nashville Arena Tower that would bring no less than ninety country acts to the stage. The other, called the Witness History Concert, would be at the Ryman Auditorium, where tickets would run from fifty to a hundred and seventy-five dollars. Another honor waiting for him was the *Billboard* Century Award in December 1997. With all this on his plate, he wanted to be able to have a new album to sell, and early in '97 he gathered a crew at CA Workshop for a mission of blues and bluegrass. Tommy Emmanuel, who at Chet's urging had been signed by Columbia two years before and had recorded several top-ten albums released in his native Australia, was given the choice plum of being his newest dual recording partner.

The album, *The Day Fingerpickers Took Over the World*, billed on the cover as that of "Chet Atkins with Tommy Emmanuel," had a tight rhythm section with Paul Yandell, new guitarist Clark Hagan, Randy Goodrum, Johnny Gimble, Terry McMillan, and drummer Giles Reeves. But the work was essentially a two-man band, Chet and Tommy playing off each other's distinctive chord structures through a wonderfully cohesive and compelling thirty-six minutes. Chet wrote three songs—"Tip Toe Through the Bluegrass," "News from the Outback," and "Smokey Mountain Lullaby"—and cowrote "Ode to Mel Bay," an inside joke using the music publisher's name to playfully rag string players, and the title tune, changing the lyrics of the Dave Pomeroy and Emily Kaitz gentle put-down on bass players into a mock horror flick, the carnage leaving only the pickers. Tommy also contributed "Dixie McGuire," a new arrangement of the Australian folk tune "Waltzing Matilda," and a personal curtsy to Chet, "Mr. Guitar."

However, during the sessions it was clear that Chet was a sick man. Emmanuel would recall that "Smokey Mountain Lullaby" started as a solo piece but Chet "came to me and said why don't we make it a duet." But they had to get it done in a hurry because, as Tommy learned, Chet was now suffering from brain cancer, and was less coherent during the recording sessions due to radiation treatment. Chet, he said, was playing a Ramirez classical guitar in keys different than what had been charted, with Tommy having to make changes on the fly. "We only had a short time, it was all then and there, and that was his last piece he ever wrote, which is why it meant so much to me. And I recorded it myself later on."

Anticipating that it might indeed be Chet's grand finale, the Grammy nabobs made the song his fortieth, and last, nomination, as Best Country Instrumental, though it lost to Alison Krauss & Union Station's "Liza Jane." And, despite the new hurdle, Chet made a remarkable comeback, keeping his commitments. When rumors of his lung cancer surgery began to circulate, he casually announced that "I've had my battle with cancer and won. Now it's behind me." Though he didn't disclose the nature of the latest cancer, he said it was "low malignancy," "minor," and in remission. However, this was wishful thinking. In a May 1997 letter to Rick Foster, he wrote that he'd had "two bouts with cancer, lung and brain." (He omitted the long-ago colon cancer.) I will be through with radiation next Tuesday, then some MRI to see if it did any good. I can't play now. The left hand is pretty useless. A rough technique may return with some practice." The letter ended, "Thanks for caring. Chet A."

On June 25, which Governor Don Sundquist named Chet Atkins Day, he darted from event to event, as he would all week, dutifully introducing acts onstage at Riverfront Park and the CAAS shindig, and at another concert at the Nashville Arena, where Rick Jordan played John Loudermilk's "Windy and Warm" and Mac Davis's "Hooked on Music." At the nighttime Ryman Auditorium tribute, which was called the Witness History Concert, Chet arrived looking exhausted as he sat in the front row in his hat and open-necked shirt, with Leona and their grandson Jonathan, as a carousel of performers entered and exited the stage, the big names being Knopfler, Bogguss, Wariner, Eddy Arnold, Kitty Wells, Johnnie Wright, Larry Carlton, Travis Tritt, Clint Black, Marty Stuart, Pat Boone, and the Jordanaires, along with lesser-known names like Peter Ostroushko, Dean McGraw, Bernd Steidl, the Nikolai Schuishou Electra Acoustic Band, Ronnie McDowell, Jerry Bradley's son Harold with the Nashville String Machine, and Hank Williams III, who played and sang his granddaddy's "Kaw-Liga," one of Hank's songs Chet had accompanied him on way back when.

Leona had told the promoters that Chet wouldn't be up to playing, but he did get onstage when Knopfler presented him with a Chettie, a new award named for him shaped like a guitar neck. They sang "The Next Time I'm in Town." He then tipped his hat, took the microphone and, typically Chet, deadpanned, to laughter, "I'm just so sick of hearing how great I am." But he was dead serious when he added, "What burns me up, I haven't heard Owen Bradley's name mentioned one damn time," which was even more outrageous given that Owen was in ill health as well and would die only months later, on January 7, 1998, at eighty-two, leaving behind a brood that all worked in some capacity in the music business. The closing act was rockabilly singer Bekka Bramlett, who then told the audience, "Chet has an open heart and mind, enough that what everyone said was too wild, he said was just wild enough."

Some might have assumed that the tribute was more of a premature memorial, which of course in some ways it was. Late in 1997, he was given royalty treatment on the PBS country-rock series *Austin City Limits*' "Legends" spot, when segments of his five appearances on the show were compiled. And yet, with down time to get stronger and practice again, he made occasional appearances. On June 12, 1998, he felt well enough to go out on a gig with Jim Coleman and accordionist LynnMarie to Knoxville's Tennessee Theatre. Shortly before, Dr. Coleman had examined him and diagnosed a stroke in his left big toe. As Coleman said, "The people in his band didn't want him to play this show, because they didn't think he was up to doing it. But he played so great. He did the song 'Vincent' on solo guitar, and it was one of the greatest things I ever heard. The house was packed. It was $26 a ticket, and it was sold out. All his family was there and his oldest friend, Buster Devault, from Luttrell." But what Coleman, who recorded an album tribute to Atkins called *Guitar Made America Great*, most remembered was a revealing side trip that Chet took him on back to Smoky Top.

> His step-father is still living and was there. We went to his house. We also went back to the little farm where Chet and his mother and father had lived. The people who were living there now said, "I guess this is really great for you to come back here." But Chet said, "No.'" He said, "Coming back here is one of the most painful things that I could ever do,

> because this is where my father left me and my mother when I was six years old."

The most painful thing he had to live with now, however, was that he could really only play the role, not the music, of Chet Atkins. When seen in public, the regal old king was frail but, as always, Chet. Appearing on the *Ryman Country Homecoming* TNN series in 1999, he was in the center front of three columns of country legends, seated beside Roy Clark and B. J. Thomas and a few seats from Willie, Waylon, Bobby Bare, Porter Wagoner, and Glen Campbell. While the others sang and played on acoustic guitars, Chet held a guitar but never played it. He did, however, join in when Thomas preceded "Raindrops Keep Falling on My Head" by running through all the stars who had rejected recording it. Chet, who of course had a story for every occasion, leaped up to reveal that Wagoner was one of those. Porter, clad in his Nudie suit, bellowed in laughter. "Chet Atkins turned down 'Busted' for me!" he said, referring to the huge hits recorded instead by Johnny Cash and Ray Charles in 1962. Busted himself, Chet leaned back in mock pain and shame. Oh, the stories they could tell.

Just after the new century arrived, when Russell Faxon's brass, life-size statue of him playing a guitar was dedicated on the lower level of a Bank of America plaza on Fifth Avenue North and Union Street, Chet made sure to be there. Needing a cane to walk, his face bloated by the effects of radiation therapy and pain-killing drugs, he still looked regal in his fedora, black jacket, and brightly colored scarf as he sat on the bench that Faxon had made part of the statue to allow "wannabe pickers," as he put it, "to come down and play with Chet Atkins." With Leona and Eddy Arnold at his side, he stared at his own sculptured face and said, "I think it looks a lot like me, even the big ears." After Sundquist and Mayor Bill Purcell spoke, and Vince Gill and Suzy Bogguss vamped a few songs, he was on the way home.

His last recorded music would be a duet he made with Pat Donohue, called "Stealin' from Chet," for Donohue's live *Radio Blues* album compiling his performances from *A Prairie Home Companion.* Otherwise, he hinted that he might recover his strength and skills. When Paul Yandell came by one day to visit him, Chet told him he was doing "not bad." Rick Foster, who telephoned him regularly, remembered that "we had a long phone conversation during which he told jokes and said he was watching too much TV but would soon be playing again—no complaints or self-pity."

Foster knew better and wanted his idol to know one thing. "I told him that there were three people in the music business who were so far above their competition that they really didn't have any competition—Segovia, Elvis, and Chet Atkins." Chet said nothing for a few moments. Then a smile.

"You know, you're right," he said.

Epilogue

THIS IS HOW CHET PLAYED IT

Chester Burton Atkins had made it into a new millennium fraught with new tensions, new wars, national schizophrenia, and acceptance of odious con-men politicians he likely would have been terrified by had he lived fifteen years longer. Perhaps it was with some sense of relief that he knew the end was near. In 2000 he finished writing a 182-page billet-doux to his collection of some sixty guitars, the glossy cocktail table book *Chet Atkins: Me and My Guitars*, with an introduction by Jerry Reed, who called the collection Atkins's "arsenal." The final page, essentially Chet's last words, reflected on the unresolved anxieties and comforts those instruments had brought him:

> I've had a great life [but] I could have done better. . . . Now that I've retired from performing, I don't practice anymore, but I still like to sit and hold my guitar. It's a familiar comfort to cradle it. . . . I pray for the safety of my family and friends, for a good night's sleep, and that I'll wake up the next morning in good health. Beyond that, it's all in the Lord's hands because I know I've done the best I could. And now, it's about time to wrap up my story. We wish it could go on and on, but I've reached the point where it has to end. . . . The players

> come and go, but the music lives on, and eternity will take care of the rest.

Nashville shared that long view, and the sad reality that it would soon lose him. Over the summer of 2000, the Nashville Network prepared a documentary produced by Gregory Hall called *Chet Atkins: A Life in Music*, culling interviews with him and others with a wide range of contemporaries dating back to Glen Campbell and including Dolly Parton, Les Paul, Mark Knopfler, George Benson, Vince Gill, Willie Nelson, and Waylon Jennings, who walked a tightrope praising Chet while still sniping at the Nashville "assembly line" that he begat. The documentary ran on September 16, winning a Primetime Emmy nomination, and was released on home video. (A DVD release, *Legends of Country Guitar*, with classic clips of Chet jamming with Merle Travis, Mose Rager, and Doc Watson, would appear in 2004.) Of course, his music had long since been in the musical scores of TV shows and movies, and he'd appeared on other shows as an actor, sort of, playing himself, as far back as 1966 in the potboiler movie *Nashville Rebel*. He also rang up late-night TV gigs with Jay Leno and Conan O'Brien.

On May 30, 2001, Leona, who had conditioned herself to expect this moment, could not awaken him from a deep sleep. She called an ambulance, but when it arrived, he was pronounced dead, his seventy-seven years filled with conquests and wonder, his genius inarguable but elusive to fully explain. When the heartbroken Leona released a simple statement that day announcing his death, an insoluble pall hung over Nashville the way it had when John F. Kennedy was murdered, and it seeped across the nation and the globe. Garrison Keillor got word during a live *Prairie Home Companion* broadcast from the Tanglewood music ravine in Massachusetts. Announcing Chet's death, to moans from the audience, he called him "a beautiful man who grew up feeling strange and awkward" and "for whom the guitar was his great consolation and his great love."

The *Tennessean*'s page one headline on July 1 was 'Mr. Guitar'

Chet Atkins Dies, with two staff writers assigned to the story. The Associated Press coverage was page-one news in papers in hundreds of cities elsewhere, and the bigger papers' music writers wrote personal encomiums. The long *New York Times* obituary by Ben Ratliff pronounced him the "Architect of the 'Nashville Sound.'" Martin Weil's *Washington Post* recitation was subtitled "Style Inspired Variety of Musicians." Other missives came in as Leona and Merle arranged his burial. Fans would be able to file past his casket for three hours on July 2 at Roesch-Patton Funeral Home on Broadway. The service was held on the third at the Ryman, the elegies not mainly in words but in music. Garrison Keillor would deliver the eulogy and brief musical selections, performed on a stage bare except for Chet's casket and a spotlight shining on a symbolic display of Chet's white fedora propped behind a bright orange Gibson electric guitar.

It seemed all of Nashville turned out. A sickly Johnny Cash and June Carter Cash paid respects at the funeral home, and the next day thousands filled the old redbrick building that had engendered Chet so many mixed emotions. In choosing pallbearers, Leona chose as the active ones who would carry his casket out of the hall to be led by Ray Stevens, Vince Gill, Steve Wariner, Paul Yandell, Harry Warner, David Conrad, Jonathan Russell, and his father, Dr. Will Russell. The honorary pallbearers numbered over fifty, including Harold Bradley, Jerry Reed, Les Paul, Waylon Jennings, Mark Knopfler, Don and Phil Everly, John Knowles, Charley Pride, Boots Randolph, Garrison Keillor, Don Gibson, Suzy Bogguss, Dolly Parton, Pat Bergeson, Porter Wagoner, Bob Ferguson, and Joe Galante. (A preposterous Google AI Overview note claiming Elvis was a pallbearer even seems possible on some paranormal level.) Overflow crowds shut out of the hall's two tiers formed a phalanx outside, and the hour-long service was carried on loudspeakers outside the hall to those gathered on opposite sides of Fifth Avenue.

Eddy Arnold began the service by saying, "We won't ever see the like, the talent, in one man. If you ever heard of any man—anywhere—who had it all, it was this man." Connie Smith then came to the stage and sang "Further Along," accompanied by a foursome including David Hungate.

Then Yandell, Wariner, and Gill played a four-song fingerpicking medley, one being the old Carter Family tune "Wildwood Flower." Keillor, his hair tousled and his face drawn, delivered his frank and perceptive eulogy, which included some harsh truths about the enigma of the man, though his grief was affecting. "He had a natural reserve to him," he said, "but he overcame it so he could tell people he admired them. If Chet Atkins was a fan of yours, you really didn't need another one."

A final performance by mandolinist Mary Stuart re-created the almost morbid "The End of the World," which had recast Skeeter Davis's pain and shadowed her own premature death, and now seemed to frame that of Chet Atkins. His casket was taken out to a hearse, with Vince Gill unashamedly weeping, and driven to Harpeth Hills Memory Gardens cemetery on Highway 100. He was buried in a small plot in an open area of the grounds, and a simple oblong headstone would mark it only with ATKINS on the bottom and on the upper left CHESTER BURTON, his birth and death dates as well as KNOWN TO THE WORLD AS "MR. GUITAR" engraved under it in small letters. The upper right was left blank for when Leona would be added. A bench a few feet away would have ATKINS carved into it. Having predetermined these details himself, he was self-effacing to the end, though his existential notion that he was driven by "some unknown force . . . a desire to be accepted, I guess," would have been at least quelled a bit if he only knew how many tourists sit on that bench seemingly every day and remember what he meant to them.

When Chet passed, Pat Donohue's *Radio Blues* was about to go on the market. But Pat wouldn't let it be released until he could write his own elegy as a liner note—"What can I say? The most exciting three minutes of my life. We miss you Chet." The sense of loss, though, was transitioned into the need to continue what he had started. Chet Atkins Days would go on, uninterrupted, as would the Chet Atkins Appreciation Society dinners and concerts. A major Chet Atkins day came a year later when he went into the Rock & Roll Hall of Fame, an institution that came into being when he was sixty-two. Leona and Jonathan represented him at the March 18 rites of industry self-congratulation in New York's Waldorf Hotel ballroom, when the other inductees were Tom Petty and the Heartbreakers, Talking Heads, the Ramones, Issac Hayes, Gene Pitney, and fellow Nashvillian Brenda Lee. Chet was inducted by bluegrass singer Marty Stuart and the proto-punk-country front man of the Stray Cats, Brian Setzer. "There's every other guitar player," said Stuart, "and then there's Chet." After Jonathan accepted the award, Setzer fingerpicked a few Chet-style passages on a Gretsch Country Gentleman.

Leona was herself given a marker of sorts when in 2006 Garrison Keillor adapted his Wobegon monologues on *A Prairie Home Companion* into a rustic musical comedy directed by Robert Altman and named three characters the Johnson Sisters, a fictitious singing act memorializing Leona and Lois Johnson's aboriginal act back when Chet met Leona, who made it to 2009, when she died at eighty-five (Lois had died, as did her husband and old Atkins crony Jethro Burns, in 1989). Among her pallbearers were Don and Phil Everly, Ray Stevens, Paul Yandell, Garrison Keillor, Harry Warner, Pat Bergeson, David Conrad, and Vince Gill. Leona was buried in the same plot as Chet at Harpeth Hills cemetery, her name on the upper right of the headstone, just as they had planned.

One detail that had been left to be settled was the messy afterlife of Studio A, which for years was leased by the Atkins and Bradley families. However, one of the early lessees of the building, a musician named Ben Folds, publicly fought prospective sales, renewing his lease twenty-four straight years and subleasing space to others, one being country singer James Johnson. The place was eventually sold in 2014, but Folds made a public cause out of saving it from demolition, whereupon eighty-eight-year-old Harold Bradley insisted that "the architecture of Nashville's evolving sound is a synergy of creative energy. That's still here, and it has nothing to do with this building." Although Chet himself had made similar statements downplaying the divination of the Nashville Sound, it may have been just as well that Chet Atkins and Owen Bradley weren't alive to hear that.

The battle ended amicably when Studio A was leased in 2015 to Mike Curb for a dollar a year, integrated with Studio B into the Music Square West complex, and named as a national landmark, still active as a studio for John Hiatt and the ageless Bobby Bare, and as the home of the Low Country Sound label owned by producer Dave Cobb. Those legendary studios, just down the block from Chet Atkins Place, are permanent markers, and outside the city, a stretch of Interstate 185 in southwest Georgia is named Chet Atkins Parkway. But the real marker is that some thirty million people worldwide own a guitar, including for many those storied Atkins Gretches—which, as if by fate, were reclaimed as Gretch property when Gibson stopped making their versions after Chet's death, and Gretsch was reborn as an arm of Fender.

There is, however, that one piece of Atkins landscape that sits uneasily—his inexplicable place on the mysterious FBI "dead list" of former "suspects" of undetermined offenses, which the FBI defines very loosely as "a list of notable or [deceased] famous individuals for whom there are FBI files (usually) or cross references to FBI files." A devil's advocate might note that as apolitical as he was—his only such activities were $500 payments to moderate Republican presidential candidates Fred Thompson and Lamar Alexander in the mid-'90s, and campaigning for Tennessee senator Howard Baker. Presented with engraved cufflinks by Ronald Reagan during a White House visit, Chet wore them only a couple times before stashing them in a drawer. Yet he was a strong union man and advocate of Black talent in the pit of the South during Jim Crow, which could have demonized him to some FBI pencil pusher or another. As well, the FBI's response to this author's FOIA—"We were unable to identify [any relevant] records."—comes with the itchy disclaimer that "this response neither confirms nor denies the existence of your subject's name on any watch lists."

Yet with no crumbs of supporting evidence or even a hint of anything amiss, it might be well advised to take to heart the testimony of a DOJ inspector general named Glenn Fine, who in 2011 testified to the House Committee on Homeland Security about a terrorist watchlist that "numerous complaints had been filed by persons complaining that they are included . . . by mistake," and that the list had "significant weaknesses [and] is not . . . fully accurate." If that warning applies here, this Atkins mystery is just another government secret or screwup. But one cannot stop a little voice inside the head that whispers, *What the hell did Chet Atkins ever do to be put on such a list?*

Fortunately, Atkins probably never knew anything of it, since he was bothered enough by the mysteries of his fame, musing:

> [Sometimes] I think, "Why have I been so successful?" and I can't figure it out. But then I might listen to one of my old performances and I think, "Maybe I did have something. Maybe no one else was doing it at that time." . . . But at the time it meant nothing. I thought it all stunk. I didn't like to hear myself play, and I still don't. I remember I went up to Knoxville to one of Christopher Parkening's concerts—this was 15 or 20 years ago—and he said, "I was nervous out there." I said, "Why?" and he said, "Because you were out there." I said that it shouldn't make any difference, and he said, "It does."

Point agreed, though the most subjective issue anyone can ever indulge in is who the best guitarist of all time is, or was. For what it's worth, *Rolling Stone*'s 2010 rankings of the "100 Greatest Rock Guitarists" placed him at number twenty-one, between Carlos Santana and Frank Zappa—a fair verdict for a country music figure uninterested in hard rock or fame who recorded instrumentals, though it's reasonable to believe all those ranked ahead of or behind him mutually idolized him. This unresolvable argument aside, we can stipulate that Duane Eddy's elegy that Atkins "influenced everybody who picked up a guitar" is also sufficient. Because it explains why Atkins's many varied albums are still being rereleased in countries worldwide, some in beautiful vinyl as they had been first issued, and with a completeness that would have stunned even Chet, such as the two-CD set from Australia's Raven Records, Chet Atkins's *Four Master Class Albums 1978–1997*. Guitar classes still give lessons about how to play in the Chet Atkins style. One tutor is Chet's nephew, Jimmy Atkins III, who can get everyone's attention in class by saying, "This is how Uncle Chet played it."

Down in Printer's Alley, where grizzled regulars meet at Tootsie's Orchid Lounge and Skull's Rainbow Room, people point out the tables in the back where he used to sit, chugging bourbon and inhaling cigars. The lifelike metallic incarnation of him remains a public attraction and has even become a sort of hat rack, as when people put ski caps on the king's head in winter so that homeless Nashvillians can take them. When the area was bulldozed in 2023 for a new shopping center, the statue was moved to the sidewalk outside the Musicians Hall of Fame, where people still sit on that inviting chair, feeling his presence. Nor have those precious Atkins guitars faded away. Right back where they started from, Gretsch sells plenty of new model 6120s, and the originals that he collected are exhibited at the Country Music Hall of Fame—where even Chet's old cluttered workshop bench (which despite his expertise as an electronics wiz in the studio never included a home computer; rather than e-mail, he kept writing letters longhand and using his old CB radio even after that fad had all but vanished) has been displayed—or auctioned at lofty prices by the estate, which also governs tributes such as periodic stage musicals.

Tommy Emmanuel, Steve Wariner, and John Knowles, the first two in their seventh decade and the latter his eighth, carry on as CGP survivors. Wariner's 2009 album *My Tribute to Chet Atkins* was billed to "Steve Wariner, C.G.P.," and it spawned the hit single "Producer's Medley"—a re-creation of the medley Chet used to perform in concert, culling segments of songs he had produced for Perry Como, Jim Reeves, Al Hirt, Jerry Reed, and the Everly Brothers—for which Steve was nominated for the Best Country Instrumental Performance Grammy. In 2011, when Suzy Bogguss played at the Country Music Hall of

Fame, it was to reprise the *Simpatico* album and tell stories about her and Chet's collaborations. In 2024 a CD set called *We Still Can't Say Goodbye* was released with re-creations of Chet's best-known songs by Emmanuel, Ricky Skaggs, Brad Paisley, James Taylor, Alison Krauss, and Eric Clapton.

As for his few remaining prominent contemporaries, Ray Stevens owns the CabaRay Showroom dinner theater. Willie Nelson in his nineties was still high as a kite and scoring number-one country hits, and Dolly in her late seventies now sings ersatz rock while squeezing into a peekaboo cheerleader outfit—the very kind of progress Atkins warily envisioned back in '56 when Elvis wore his pink britches. Atkins, in fact, nicely and typically and accurately summed up the newest new era of country music, saying late in his life, "We get so pop [that country] fans turn away. . . . To young fans right now, country music just means some guy with a tight ass and a white hat."

The proof is the Country Music Awards show, its non-country-based producers determined to imitate MTV vibes, and more supporting evidence is that some of Chet's riffs have been sampled by rappers with names like Evee, DJ Hush, and Blockhead, which might have sent Chet Atkins into toxic shock if he were still here. Moreover, as Nashville has broadened its musical palate and its millennial influx, including hard rock and metal heads, the doppelgänger hangs heavy in the air. AAron Camaro—easily identifiable in his Old Glory head wimple, endlessly dangling hair, goggle shades, and glittered MC jacket, who hosts a podcast called *Decibel Geek* with fellow headbanger Chris Czynszak—admits to having no country music expertise, yet just being in Nashville led him into the Atkins mythos. With pride, he said:

> I've never worn a cowboy hat, and I don't think Chet did either. But I've been here about twenty years now, got here after Chet died, and I now know why my dad talked about Chet Atkins. You just learn how important he was. Like when you go to a music store downtown and the 6120 Fenders are all up on the walls. And that statue of him. He's lookin' right at

> you. You walk into a honky tonk at midnight and somebody's bustin' a Chet Atkins song. You hear "Yakety Axe" and you stop and listen, because it kicks ass.
>
> It's funny you asked about Chet, because I was just thinking I'm gonna go down to Studio B and dig that vibe. I haven't gotten there yet, but it's something I really think I have to do. Because once you know about Chet Atkins, you know that he was the Eddie Van Halen of his time!

To be sure, country music still monopolizes Nashville, but as a money-snorting cash cow that, with great irony, rules in a town that has lost much of its simple communality reflecting the old-time country ethic. Once, Nashville could boast about its reasonably priced property, from which Atkins made some nice turnover cash. Today, it has been grabbed up by modern corporate avarice. Nashville had to fight off economic downturns for years, but when the software giant Oracle announced it would move its headquarters to Nashville in April 2024, the *Wall Street Journal*'s front-page story—headlined NASHVILLE IS BOOMING, LOCALS FRET ABOUT THEIR FUTURE IN MUSIC CITY—reported that corporate incursions had caused housing prices to rise so high that many residents had fled the city. One expatriate said, "It almost doesn't look like Nashville anymore. Whew Lord, I wish people would stop moving here."

This transition has made more fortunes for some but only magnified the country music dilemma, its consanguinity with its vanishing roots and opaque traditions. Still stuck in the past are decaying bootstraps like Jason Aldean and Kid Rock, serving up far-right blather as if it were a birthright of the genre, no matter the hip cosmetics. The counter-influences, though, also wear tight pants quite nicely—witness the irrepressible Texas diva Maren Morris, who has put on blast the country cartel's lingering racism and hypermasculinity, adding, "I'd like to burn it to the ground and start over. But it's burning itself down without my help."

The courtly, roving-eyed Country Gentleman might have enjoyed a good laugh at that dig, having engendered the slings of an industry he made filthy rich by selling around thirty-five million records bathed in its ambience. Rather than fight, Atkins opened new portals for a wheezing cultural morphon, doing it by, as he said with perfect metaphorical economy, taking the twang out of it. And for all his worrying about the unwanted consequences of strategic de-twanging and cultural upraising, he kept at that mission without ever turning back, or taking the easy way out with a chord that needed to be better. All the way or no way. That was how Chet Atkins played it.

NOTES

Introduction: A Country Gentleman

"Talking to Chet Atkins": "The Guitar Is More Than a Facade," *Billboard*, June 3, 1967.

"I still like to hold": "Chet Atkins Revisited," Bob Moore Online, accessed February 20, 2025, https://www.angelfire.com/tn2/bobloyce/chet3.html.

"I had that burning": Chet Flippo, "King Picker: The Rolling Stone Interview with Chet Atkins," *Rolling Stone*, February 12, 1976, 45.

"if people knew": Nicholas Dawidoff, *In the Country of Country* (New York: Random House, 1999), 19.

"a master of informality": Flippo, "King Picker," 45.

"felt a little sorry": Richard Harrington, "Chet Atkins' Guitar Enters the Smithsonian," *Washington Post*, September 20, 1980.

"an accident": Harrington, "Chet Atkins' Guitar."

"a little half-assed": Robert Windeler, "Bio: Chet Atkins Helped Country Music Move Uptown—and Now He Regrets It," *People*, December 16, 1974, 62.

"Chet's tone": Rick Foster, "Memories of Chet Atkins," Rick Foster Guitar, accessed February 20, 2025, http://rickfosterguitar.com/chetmem.html.

"I can play": Windeler, "Bio: Chet Atkins," 62.

"When I'm playin'": *The Week in Rock*, MTV, originally aired circa October 1990, via YouTube, https://www.youtube.com/watch?v=FegE0Df_Zl8.

"I lose confidence" and *"help[ed] me get"*: Windeler, "Bio: Chet Atkins," 63.

"I knew I could": Robert K. Oermann and Peter Cooper, "Mr. Guitar Chet Atkins Dies," *Tennessean*, July 1, 2001.

"despite being shy": Russ Cochran, *Me and My Guitars*, text by Chet Atkins and Michael Cochran (Milwaukee: Hal Leonard Corporation, 2003), 150.

"borrowed his voice": Lucy Harbron, "Five Musicians Who Clashed with Joni Mitchell," *Far Out*, November 15, 2023, https://faroutmagazine.co.uk/five-musicians-who-clashed-with-joni-mitchell/.

A few blocks east: Markus K. Dowling, "Chet Atkins Statue Restored, Unveiled at New Musicians Hall of Fame," *Nashville Tennessean*, June 11, 2023.

Atkins and Bradley: Jessica Nicholson, "Estates of Bradley and Atkins Release Response Regarding RCA Studio A," *MusicRow*, July 1, 2014, https://musicrow.com/2014/07/harold-bradley-releases-response-to-ben-folds/.

"Chet knew to buy": John S. Wilson, "You Can't Take the Country Out of Chet," *New York Times*, April 7, 1974.

"It's the sound": Ben Ratliff, "Chet Atkins, 77, Is Dead; Guitarist and Producer Was Architect of the 'Nashville Sound,'" *New York Times*, July 1, 2001.

the guitar is "like a universe": "Paul Simon Talks Losing His Hearing, Finding His Wife, and Breaking Up with Art Garfunkel," Howard Stern official website, September 22, 2023.

"Everything I've ever done": Bob Curtright, review of *America's Music: The Roots of Country* (TBS documentary), *Wichita Eagle*, June 2, 1996.

Harrison copied so melodiously: Tom Kolb, "Master the Mixolydian Mode Like Chet Atkins, George Harrison, Jimi Hendrix, Eddie Van Halen and Many More," *Guitar Player*, February 23, 2023, https://www.guitarplayer.com/lessons/master-the-mixolydian-mode-like-chet-atkins-george-harrison-jimi-hendrix-eddie-van-halen-and-many-more.

which George said: Liner notes for *Chet Atkins Picks On the Beatles*, RCA Victor, 1966.

Davies said his influences were: Arun Starkey, "Jimi Hendrix Once Picked the 'Greatest Band' He Had Ever Seen," *Far Out*, November 17, 2023, https://faroutmagazine.co.uk/jimi-hendrix-once-picked-the-greatest-band-he-had-ever-seen/.

"I just assumed it was": Mark Knopfler, "Chet Atkins Documentary," YouTube, October 26, 2015, https://www.youtube.com/watch?v=luQDdPtO904.

"I thank God": Michael Gray, "Chet Atkins Made Dreams Possible," CMT official website, July 3 2001, via Bob Moore Online, https://www.angelfire.com/tn2/bobloyce/chet3.html.

"label" or "sales tag": Wilson, "You Can't Take the Country Out of Chet."

"If it's good": Chet Atkins with Bill Neely, *Country Gentleman* (Chicago: Henry Regnery, 1974), 209.

"Don't try to hit": Tom Redmond, "Working with Chet Atkins: An Interview with Ray Stevens," MisterGuitar.com, August 8, 2009, https://misterguitar.us/news/raystevens4.html.

When recording an album: Jim Ohlschmidt, "The Acoustic Inventions of Chet Atkins, Certified Guitar Pioneer," *Acoustic Guitar*, August 27, 2020.

"went too far": Jack Hurst, "Dynamic Duo," *Chicago Tribune*, July 31, 1988.

"wasn't the most accomplished": Fred Dellar, "Chet Atkins: Mr. Nashville," *MOJO*, September 2001.

"Chet made it OK": Craig Havighurst, "Chet Atkins: The Lasting Influence of 'Mr. Guitar,'" NPR.com, December 16, 2011, npr.org/2011/12/17/143837702/chet-atkins-the-lasting-influence-of-mr-guitar.

"technical revolutionary who built": Bob Doerschuk, "Chet Atkins' Certified Guitar Players," *Guitar Player*, March 2018.

"Finding Chet Atkins": Music publisher Al Gallico to Steve Sholes, per *Billboard*, June 3, 1967.

"I feel like a damn prisoner": Flippo, "King Picker," 45.

"He was not a saint": Garrison Keillor, "Eulogy to Chet at His Funeral," MisterGuitar.com, July 3, 2001, https://misterguitar.us/news/eulogy.html.

His name appears alongside hundreds: "Updated Federal Bureau of Investigation Record/Information/Dissemination Section (RIDS) Dead List (Complete), 2011," governmentattic.org, January 9, 2012, https://www.governmentattic.org/5docs/FBI-DeadList-Update_2011.pdf, 27.

denying that any relevant records: US Department of Justice to the author, June 29, 2023.

1. Dust Bowl Blues

Chet Atkins once told: Nigel Patterson and Piers Beagley, review of *Elvis Studio Sessions '56: The Complete Recordings*, Elvis Information Network, accessed February 20, 2025, https://elvisinfonet.com/book_review_MRS-Elvis-The-Complete-Recordings-Studio-Sessions-1956.html.

"Elvis," he said: Alan Walsh, "The Day Elvis Split His Pink Britches," *Melody Maker*, March 8, 1969.

"really sensual" and "very spooky": Tyler Golsen, "Tom Petty on the Elvis Presley Song That 'Could Have Been the National Anthem,'" *Far Out*, August 23,

2023, https://faroutmagazine.co.uk/tom-petty-on-the-elvis-presley-song-that-could-have-been-the-national-anthem/.

Elvis perhaps a passing fad: Heather Hahn, "Elvis Presley's Methodist Moment," *United Methodist Insight*, January 8, 2018, https://um-insight.net/in-the-church/elvis-presley-s-methodist-moment/.

"don't want to analyze lyrics": Wilson, "You Can't Take the Country Out of Chet."

"excessively obsessed": Cochran, *Me and My Guitars*, 15.

census takers found the place: "Chester Atkins," US census form, Union County, TN, April 5, 1930, Ancestry.com, https://www.ancestry.com/search/collections/6224/records/66110568.

in the house, the owner: Dawidoff, *In the Country of Country*, 63.

"Cherokee blood": Atkins with Neely, *Country Gentleman*, 3.

"he would escape and come right back home": Atkins with Neely, 3.

his draft board registration: "James Arlie Atkins," US draft registration card, Luttrell, TN, June 5, 1917, Ancestry.com, https://www.ancestry.com/search/collections/6482/records/23085403.

"beautifully trained Irish tenor voice": Atkins with Neely, 6.

"a kind and tolerant woman": Atkins with Neely, 7–8.

"He always whistled when everyone else cried": Atkins with Neely, 10.

2. Silvertone

"would get drunk and come in late": Atkins with Neely, *Country Gentleman*, 17.

The first records he listened to: Atkins with Neely, 34.

"and broke it over my head": Atkins with Neely, 42.

the sound, he said, was "just beautiful": Cochran, *Me and My Guitars*, 19.

"Get the hell off": Atkins with Neely, *Country Gentleman*, 42.

"hit me like a bolt of lightning: Cochran, 14–15.

Bailey came on and performed: Myron Tassin, *Fifty Years at the Grand Ole Opry* (New Orleans: Pelican, 1975).

he did return to the Opry in the 1970s: Walter Carter and Randy Hilman, "DeFord Bailey, Grand Ole Opry's First Musician and First Artist to Record in Nashville, Dies at 82," *Nashville Tennessean*, July 3, 1982.

"using his fingers, trying to copy": Cochran, *Me and My Guitars*, 18.

"wanted to score": Dawidoff, *In the Country of Country*, 46.

"We were working down field": Dawidoff, 46.

"my health was failing": Atkins with Neely, *Country Gentleman*, 39.

"took me to hear blacks": Atkins with Neely, 39.

"In Georgia there wasn't" and *"My dad taught me"*: Dawidoff, *In the Country of Country*, 46.

"there were blacks all around us": Atkins with Neely, *Country Gentleman*, 46.

"it sounded so wonderful, lonesome": Atkins with Neely, 53.

"they treated us" through *"I was a stranger"*: Atkins with Neely, 53.

"in blackface, of course": Atkins with Neely, 48.

"I must have learned": Atkins with Neely, 53.

3. Django on the Go

Arnold Shultz, meanwhile, was left: Paul Kingsbury, *The Encyclopedia of Country Music* (New York: Oxford University Press, 1998), 484.

"invented my own way": Cochran, *Me and My Guitars*, 19.

"I never tried to play like Merle": Ohlschmidt, "Acoustic Inventions."

"I was beginning to find": Atkins with Neely, *Country Gentleman*, 61.

"a good and sincere man": Atkins with Neely, *Country Gentleman*, 61.

his registration card: "Chester Burton Akins," US Selective Service registration card, Luttrell, TN, June 30, 1942, Ancestry.com, https://www.ancestry.com/search/collections/2238/records/201345562.

"I felt numb": Atkins with Neely, 68.

"Chester, is that you?": Atkins with Neely, 69.

"Hire him": Atkins with Neely, 72.

4. Hire Him . . . Fire Him

"all the people I liked": Atkins with Neely, *Country Gentleman*, 81.

"This was when I first heard": Cochran, *Me and My Guitars*, 25.

"Everybody listens to it": Atkins with Neely, *Country Gentleman*, 80.

"You ought to hear my little brother!": Cochran, *Me and My Guitars*, 28.

Back home, Kitty Wells asked him: *Greenville (TN) Sun*, November 9, 1943.

Chester bought himself his first new axe: Cochran, *Me and My Guitars*, 22.

"blew my mind": Atkins with Neely, *Country Gentleman*, 83.

"I want to live so much": Atkins with Neely, 105.

"I will never forget the scene": Atkins with Neely, 106.

"I actually think he was proud": Atkins with Neely, 100.

"He had tears in his eyes": Atkins with Neely, 100.

5. "The Real, Fresh-Squeezed Thing"

"Yeah, Chet," he said: Wayne Bledsoe and Bradley Reeves, "Arthur Q. Smith: The Greatest Songwriter You Never Knew Finally Gets His Due," KNOX News, November 25, 2016, https://www.knoxnews.com/story/entertainment/music/2016/11/25/arthur-q-smith-greatest-songwriter-you-never-knew-finally-gets-his-due/94127112/.

not only scared but "damned depressed": Atkins with Neely, *Country Gentleman*, 89.

"the Junior Order hall": "Cumberland Mountain Ramblers Coming," *Morristown (TN) Gazette and Mail*, May 5, 1944.

"plenty of good old mountain music": "Merry-Go-Round Boys Coming Here Saturday," *Rogersville (TN) Review*, May 25, 1944.

"a fifteen-cent room": Atkins with Neely, 66.

"winos, weirdos, and rats": Atkins with Neely, 110.

"I can't play like you can": Atkins with Neely, 112.

"[Django] played the Civic Center": Flippo, "King Picker," 32.

"Did you know that Chester Atkins": Radio, *Daily Reporter* (Greenfield, IN), August 1, 1945.

"I was using the Vibrola": Cochran, *Me and My Guitars*, 29.

"the only time I ever": Atkins with Neely, *Country Gentleman*, 114.

"Ches, how would you like": Atkins with Neely, 114.

"The audience was noisy": Cochran, *Me and My Guitars*, 30.

"You're just what we've": Atkins with Neely, *Country Gentleman*, 121.

"and that's where we married 'em": Richard Harrington, "Twin Pickers," *Washington Post*, November 14, 1982.

"I didn't take [it] very well": Cochran, *Me and My Guitars*, 30.

6. Paging Chet Atkins

"Chester Atkins [the] champion": *Hopewell (VA) News*, September 24, 1946.

"my heart wasn't in it": Cochran, *Me and My Guitars*, 31.

"almost like a big employment agency": Atkins with Neely, *Country Gentleman*, 130.

"Chester Atkins wouldn't make it": Ron Sylvester, "100 Ozarkers: 'Si' Siman Impacted Country Music," *Springfield News-Leader*, October 10, 1999

the greatest guitar player in the world: Cochran, *Me and My Guitars*, 32.

his "cowboy period": Atkins with Neely, *Country Gentleman*, 135.

"I tried to cover all the bases": Paul Ackerman, "Sholes: Discoverer and Developer," *Billboard*, June 3, 1967.

"you just found out your laundry": Atkins with Neely, *Country Gentleman*, 134.

"Western maestro piping with a flair": Record Reviews, *Billboard*, November 1, 1947.

"corn right out of the West": Review of "I Know My Baby Loves Me" / "Canned Heat," *Richmond Times-Dispatch*, December 14, 1947, 12D.

"lively and spirited instrumental": Record Reviews, *Billboard*, November 1, 1947, 116.

"I would get in the studio": Cochran, *Me and My Guitars*, 35.

"using vibrabo and all that": *The Tonight Show*, NBC, originally aired July 18, 1973, via YouTube, https://www.youtube.com/watch?v=oBTpK8iEo-Q.

7. Galloping Guitar

"it was the last thing I wanted": Cochran, *Me and My Guitars*, 36.

"depressed about our careers": Cochran, 38.

"I felt everybody hated me": Atkins with Neely, *Country Gentleman*, 146–147.

"a music man like nobody": Ben Finley, "Sad Story Behind Elvis' First Hit," *Columbian* (Clark County, WA), July 11, 2024.

"does some nimble banjo-style rolls": Mark S. Reinhart, *Chet Atkins: The Greatest Songs of Mister Guitar* (Jefferson, NC: McFarland, 2014), 33.

8. Down on Music Row

saying the station's offer: John Carter Cash, *Anchored in Love: An Intimate Portrait of June Carter Cash* (Nashville: Thomas Nelson, 2007), 35.

"there wasn't enough work" and *"put on his serious business suit"*: Cochran, *Me and My Guitars*, 53–55.

a "damn machine,": Tony Bacon, "Chet Atkins Discusses His Relationship with Gretsch in Previously Unpublished Interview," *Reverb*, October 19, 2017, https://reverb.com/news/chet-atkins-discusses-his-relationship-with-gretsch-in-previously-unpublished-interview-bacons-archive.

"when I first came down here": Flippo, "King Picker," 32.

"You sorry son of a bitch": Amanda Petrusich, "We Can't Quit You, Hank Williams," *New Yorker*, April 5, 2016, https://www.newyorker.com/culture/culture-desk/we-cant-quit-you-hank-williams.

"two meters too long" through *"Hank said let's go"*: Flippo, "King Picker," 32.

"We used to record" and *"His ideas were great"*: Ackerman, "Sholes: Discoverer and Developer."

"Since hearing 'Galloping on the Guitar'": "Lowdown Hoedown," *Bristol Virginia Tennessean*, November 3, 1950.

Song reviews marveled: Dorothy Hamill, Spinning the Turn Table, *Press-Chronicle* (Johnson City, TN), May 30, 1952.

"brought gasps from the crowd": *Nashville Tennessean*, June 14, 1953.

"every song here": "Chet Atkins Albums Ranked," Return of Rock, October 6, 2020, https://returnofrock.com/chet-atkins-albums-ranked/.

9. "The Bourbon Would Almost Knock You Down"

"call his wife at two" and *"Men tend to fall"*: Mark Zwonitzer with Charles Hirshberg, *Will You Miss Me When I'm Gone? The Carter Family & Their Legacy in American Music* (New York: Simon & Schuster, 2002), 295.

"the bourbon would almost": Atkins with Neely, *Country Gentleman*, 176.

"went off the deep end": Roger Williams, *Sing a Sad Song: The Life of Hank Williams* (New York, Penguin, 2005), 155.

"God comin' down the road": Mark Ribowsky, *Hank: The Short Life and Long Country Road of Hank Williams* (New York, Liveright, 2017), 306.

"after each take": Flippo, "King Picker," 32.

"any religion has an answer": Atkins with Neely, *Country Gentleman*, 173.

"Right now he's a boy": *Grand Ole Opry*, WSM, originally aired January 3, 1953.

"The Chet Atkins Fan Club": Eddie, "Chet's Fans Plan Meeting Here," *Nashville Banner*, July 17, 1953.

David Cobb coined it: Norm Van Maastricht, *Paul Yandell, Second to the Best: A Sideman's Chronicle* (Arglen, PA: Schiffer, 2016), 91.

"a serious, restless young man": Vic Weals, Home Folks, *Knoxville Journal*, July 2, 1954.

"a lot of notes": Atkins with Neely, *Country Gentleman*, 202.

"modern ending" and *"You hit a sour note"*: Atkins with Neely, *Country Gentleman*, 166.

hadn't sung since 1947 through *actually destroyed the masters*: Wilson, "You Can't Take the Country Out of Chet."

10. A Gretsch in Time

"actively avoided being cast": Van Maastricht, *Paul Yandell*, 8.

"cried like a baby": Cochran, *Me and My Guitars*, 63–64.

"I never liked them": Bacon, "Chet Atkins Discusses His Relationship with Gretsch," https://reverb.com/news/chet-atkins-discusses-his-relationship-with-gretsch-in-previously-unpublished-interview-bacons-archive.

"was always coming up": Bacon, https://reverb.com/news/chet-atkins-discusses-his-relationship-with-gretsch-in-previously-unpublished-interview-bacons-archive.

he thought it was "hideous": Cochran, *Me and My Guitars*, 68.

recalled these designs as "junk": Bacon, "Chet Atkins Discusses His Relationship with Gretsch," https://reverb.com/news/chet-atkins-discusses-his-relationship-with-gretsch-in-previously-unpublished-interview-bacons-archive.

"mellow tone with brilliance": Van Maastricht, *Paul Yandell*, 43.

"Chet," he told him: Atkins with Neely, *Country Gentleman*, 186.

"built a bridge": Liner notes for *A Session with Chet Atkins*, RCA Victor, 1954.

"joyful, yet sophisticated": Richard S. Ginell, review of *A Session with Chet Atkins*, Allmusic.com, accessed February 20, 2025, https://www.allmusic.com/album/mw0000883184.

"I think if [Fred Gretsch]": Bacon, "Chet Atkins Discusses His Relationship with Gretsch," https://reverb.com/news/chet-atkins-discusses-his-relationship-with-gretsch-in-previously-unpublished-interview-bacons-archive.

11. That Do Make It Nice

"Ira was a little difficult": Van Maastricht, *Paul Yandell*, 39.

"As I was roaming" through *"I really didn't care"*: Van Maastricht, 36.

"We'd sit up until three": Van Maastricht, 51.

"I would watch his hands": Van Maastricht, 190.

"[Investments made by Chet]": Rick Sanjek, interview with the author, November 27, 2023.

12. Elvis Is in the Building

was too "regimented": Spencer Leigh, "The History of Heartbreak Hotel," *Independent* (UK), April 30, 2011, https://www.independent.co.uk/arts-entertainment/music/features/the-history-of-heartbreak-hotel-6105739.html.

"keep doing what you're doing": Andrew Hickey, "Heartbreak Hotel," episode 38 of *A History of Rock Music in 500 Songs*, recorded June 24, 2019, https://500songs.com/podcast/episode-38-heartbreak-hotel-by-elvis-presley/.

Elvis still couldn't keep still: Adam Victor, *The Elvis Encyclopedia* (London: Gerald Duckworth, 2008), 29.

"He had Lamar with him": Flippo, "King Picker," 34.

a "morbid mess": "Heartbreak Hotel," Elvis: The Music, accessed February 20, 2025, https://www.elvisthemusic.com/music/heartbreak-hotel/.

Guinness World Records says: "Best-Selling Solo Artist," Guinness World Records, accessed April 14, 2025, https://www.guinnessworldrecords.com/world-records/best-selling-solo-artist.

today "Hound Dog" ranks: Rob Copsey, "The Official Top 50 Biggest Selling Elvis Presley Singles Revealed," Official Charts, August 16, 2017, https://www.officialcharts.com/chart-news/the-official-top-50-biggest-selling-elvis-presley-singlesrevealed__10564/.

"a combination of country and skiffle": Rikky Rooksby, *Lyrics: Writing Better Words for Your Songs* (New York: Hal Leonard, 2006).

not that it appeased: Robert Fink, "Elvis Everywhere: Musicology and Popular Music Studies at the Twilight of the Canon," in *Rock Over the Edge: Transformations in Popular Music Culture* (Durham, NC: Duke University Press, 2002), 97.

"vomit a little": Serene Dominic, *Song by Song: The Ultimate Burt Bacharach Reference for Fans, Serious Record Collectors, and Music Critics* (London: Music Sales Group, 2003), 68.

"traditionalists resented the hedonism": Bill C. Malone, *Don't Get Above Your Raisin': Country Music and the Southern Working Class* (Chicago: University of Illinois Press, 1961), 80.

13. Oh, Lonesome Me

the indelible phrase: Bill C. Malone, *Country Music USA* (Austin: University of Texas Press, 1968), 253.

Musicologist Mark Reinhart: Reinhart, *Chet Atkins*, 71.

"did a lot of Chet Atkins stuff": Paul McCartney, *Many Years from Now* (New York: Henry Holt, 1998), 82, 273.

the "mighty Chet": Bill Maples, "Lucky Chet Atkins Has a Secret!," *Nashville Tennessean*, February 22, 1957.

"Some folk worthy": Knopfler, "Chet Atkins Documentary," https://www.youtube.com/watch?v=luQDdPtO904.

"I can still see them": Mark Ribowsky, *Crying in the Rain: The Perfect Harmony and Imperfect Lives of the Everly Brothers* (New York: Backbeat, 2024), 29.

"Don said, 'We just signed'": Ribowsky, *Crying in the Rain*, 38.

"We just experimented around": Flippo, "King Picker," 43.

he told Atlantic's producer: Jerry Wexler and David Ritz, *Rhythm and the Blues: A Life in American Music* (New York: Knopf, 1993), 109–110.

14. Theme from a Dream

"He would say": Bob Doershuk, "Chet Atkins' Certified Guitar Players," *Acoustic Guitar*, December 2, 2022, https://acousticguitar.com/chet-atkins-certified-guitar-players/.

"a great improviser": Wythe Walker, "'I Live My Life the Way I Play Music': A Q & A with Tommy Emmanuel," *Arkansas Times*, December 11, 2017.

"I think it was 1962" and *"I had reached"*: Mark Pritcher, "Tommy Emmanuel: A Great Guitarist Comes Up from Down Under," Tommy Emmanuel Official Australian Web Site, April 19, 1997, http://users.adam.com.au/donald/markinter.htm (site discontinued).

"I lost a lot of money": Calvin Gilbert, "Chet Atkins Exhibit Conjures Fond Memories for Steve Wariner," CMT official website, September 1, 2011, http://cmt.com/news/eeqi0j/chet-atkins-exhibit-conjures-fond-memories-for-steve-wariner (page discontinued).

"They would just steal": Bacon, "Chet Atkins Discusses His Relationship with Gretsch," https://reverb.com/news/chet-atkins-discusses-his-relationship-with-gretsch-in-previously-unpublished-interview-bacons-archive.

people claim his ghost: "Skull's Rainbow Room," Ghost City Tours, accessed February 20, 2025, https://ghostcitytours.com/nashville/haunted-nashville/skull-rainbow-room/.

"was a lot wilder": Atkins with Neely, *Country Gentleman*, 179.

"Chet was never a member": Van Maastricht, *Paul Yandell*, 49.

"the biggest hit ever": Maxine Brown, *Looking Back to See: A Country Music Memoir* (Fayetteville: University of Arkansas Press, 2005), 145–146.

"one of the great makeout": Richard S. Ginell, review of *Chet Atkins in Hollywood*, Allmusic.com, accessed February 20, 2025, https://www.allmusic.com/album/mw0000010760.

"one of the great songs": Ribowsky, *Crying in the Rain*, 89.

"like a dance": Jeff Thanki, "Historic RCA Studio B, 'Home of 1,000 Hits,' Turns 60," *Nashville Tennessean*, October 30, 2017.

15. "How the Hell Did He Come Up with That?"

"someone who sounds like": "January 12, 1964," Keith Flynn's Elvis Presley Pages, accessed February 20, 2025, https://keithflynn.com/recording-sessions/640112.html.

National Guardsmen had to quell: "Record Number of Arrests Made in City During Jazz Festival Riot," *Newport Daily News*, July 5, 1960.

"about fifty percent": Atkins with Neely, *Country Gentleman*, 190.

"a piano player imitating": Harry Bacas, "Top Tunes—'Last Date,'" *Washington* (DC) *Evening Star*, November 5, 1960.

"play me a Jim Reeves record": Doershuk, "Chet Atkins' Certified Guitar Players," https://acousticguitar.com/chet-atkins-certified-guitar-players/.

"tried to make good records": Flippo, "King Picker," 34.

"Country music used to be": Martin Hawkins, "Jack Clement: Everybody Loves a Nut," *Country Music People*, January 1980.

"I was at the studio": Michael Buffalo Smith, "Cowboy Jack Clement: Cash, Pride, Sun and Polka," Swampland.com, May 2006, http://swampland.com/articles/view/title:cowboy_jack_clement.

was guided by Atkins: Stacie Seifrit-Griffin, "The Everly Brothers :'Cathy's Clown,'" National Recording Registry, August 24, 2021, https://blogs.loc.gov/now-see-hear/2021/08/from-the-national-recording-registry-the-everly-brothers-cathys-clown-1960/.

"This is the lonely man's": David Halberstam, liner notes for *Chet Atkins' Workshop*, RCA, 1961.

"cascading arpeggiated harmonics": Ohlschmidt, "Acoustic Inventions."

"The damned guy finished": "Windy and Warm," episode of *The 1937 Flood Watch Podcast*, March 10, 2023, https://1937flood.substack.com/p/windy-and-warm.

"no more than hokey": Steven Cook, review of *Travelin'*, Allmusic.com, accessed February 20, 2025, https://www.allmusic.com/album/travelin-mw0000863275.

16. "But It's Chet Atkins!"

"It's a good manifestation": Tony Gonzalez and Nate Rau, "Revolution and Rebirth at Studio A," *Nashville Tennessean*, March 3, 2003, https://www.tennessean.com/story/news/local/2015/03/28/studio-a-nashville-50th/70463174/.

Atkins didn't hesitate: "Chet Atkins Though the Years," *Knoxville News*, September 12, 2019, https://www.knoxnews.com/picture-gallery/entertainment/2019/02/21/chet-atkinschet-atkins-through-the-years-through-years/2935492002/.

"the original country music": Waylon Jennings and Lenny Kaye, *Waylon: An Autobiography* (New York: Warner, 1996), 104.

"I sent for him": Rick Clark, "Jack Clement," *Mix*, December 1, 2003, mixonline.com/recording/jack-clement-365193,

"Clement never mentioned": Sanjek, interview with the author.

"When word got around": Julie Zauzmer, "'Cowboy' Jack Clement, Country Music Icon, Dies at 82," *Washington Post*, August 8, 2013.

Black musicians looked "bored": Sanjek, interview with the author.

"Friends, I realize": Charles K. Wolfe, liner notes for *Country Music* by Charley Pride, Time Life Records, 1981.

As Mark Reinhart notes: Reinhart, *Chet Atkins*, 116.

"gets far more": Liner notes for *Chet Atkins Picks on the Beatles.*

one calling it "disposable": Stephen Thomas Erlewine, review of *Chet Atkins Picks on the Beatles*, Allmusic.com, accessed February 20, 2025, https://www.allmusic.com/album/chet-atkins-picks-on-the-beatles-mw0000646915.

"But it's Chet Atkins!": Nicole Dotzenrod, "Vietnam Survivor Chet Shorten Will Lead Lincoln Memorial Day Parade," *Valley Breeze* (Lincoln, RI), May 2, 2018.

"I'm sure there are other": Redmond, "Working with Chet Atkins," https://misterguitar.us/news/raystevens4.html.

"We were consciously trying": Flippo, "King Picker,"34.

17. "Chit Atkins, Make Me a Star"

"most of the musicians": Van Maastricht, *Paul Yandell*, 186–187.

"I used to come to Nashville": Albert Cory, "Chet Atkins Making Art vs. Nurturing Artists," *Life Since the Baby Boom*, Substack, December 6, 2023, https://albertcory50.substack.com/p/chet-atkins.

"an ideal match": Jason Ankeny, review of *The Scene Changes*, AllMusic.com, accessed February 20, 2025, https://www.allmusic.com/album/the-scene-changes-mw0000845624.

"Jerry Reed is a whole": Liner notes for *The Unbelievable Guitar and Voice of Jerry Reed*, RCA, 1967.

"that redneck guitar player": Joel Whitburn, *The Billboard Book of Top 40 Country Hits, 1944–2006* (Menomonee Falls, WI: Record Research, 2006), 273

"the star-spangled home": Lillian Roxon, "The Town with the 'Fresh Sound,'" *Sydney Morning Herald*, June 19, 1966.

Comer got himself into hot water: Shultz v. Deane-Hill Country Club Inc., 310 F. Supp. 272 (E.D. Tenn. 1969), September 26, 1969, via Justia, https://law.justia.com/cases/federal/district-courts/FSupp/310/272/1382189/.

"Hundreds of guys": Redmond, "Working with Chet Atkins" https://misterguitar.us/news/raystevens4.html.

"because we fight": Windeler, "Bio: Chet Atkins," 64.

"a great guy": Sanjek, interview with the author.

"nothing stopped my girl watching": Atkins with Neely, *Country Gentleman*, 112.

"playin' guitar, playin' golf": Windeler, "Bio: Chet Atkins," 60.

"She grabbed me by the ass": Dawidoff, *In the Country of Country*, 42.

"I was only twenty-six": Sanjek, interview with the author.

"If I can ever help": Foster, "Memories of Chet Atkins," http://rickfosterguitar.com/chetmem.html.

twenty-five-page special insert: "A Salute to Chet Atkins," *Billboard*, June 3, 1967.

he lapsed into a coma: "Guitarist's Father, James Atkins, Dies," *Nashville Tennessean*, March 12, 1968.

"He sang me to sleep": "Atkins: Father Aided Career," Associated Press, March 12, 1968.

Sholes was pronounced dead: "Steve Sholes, Country Music Pioneer, Dies," Associated Press, April 23, 1968.

"I worked for Steve": Michael Streissguth, *Outlaw: Waylon, Willie, Kris, and the Renegades of Nashville* (New York: HarperCollins, 2013), chap. 1, digital ed.

"Yeah, I got pretty good": Bacon, "Chet Atkins Discusses His Relationship with Gretsch," https://reverb.com/news/chet-atkins-discusses-his-relationship-with-gretsch-in-previously-unpublished-interview-bacons-archive.

18. Outlaw Men

Chet get up and play: "Chet Atkins' Daughter Marries Irishman," Associated Press, January 11, 1971.

"we were saying 'okay'": Ribowsky, *Crying in the Rain*, 194.

"get Perry off his fishing boat": Windeler, "Bio: Chet Atkins," 62.

"They called the doctor": Van Maastricht, *Paul Yandell*, 179.

"had a good crying jag": Atkins with Neely, *Country Gentleman*, 216.

a good part of Nashville: "Guitarist Chet Atkins Has Colon Surgery," UPI, April 24, 1973.

its "human sound": Willie Nelson with David Ritz, *It's a Long Story: My Life* (New York: Little, Brown, 2015), chap. 16, digital ed.

"Whatever you do": Streissguth, *Outlaw*, chap. 1.

"If you're wired": Bill Conrad, "Waylon Jennings / Sex, Drugs & Rockabilly," part 3, *No Depression*, June 28, 2012, https://nodepression.com/waylon-jennings-sex-drugs-rockabilly-part-3/.

"Pills were the artificial energy": Andre Dansby, "Waylon Jennings Dead at Sixty-Four," *Rolling Stone*, February 14, 2002.

"Chet Atkins thinks": Streissguth, *Outlaw*, chap. 1.

was "too boring": Nick Tosches, "Waylon Jennings: Maybe They Don't Even Know I'm There," *Zoo World*, August 1974.

"the worst that could happen": Streissguth, *Outlaw*, chap. 1.

"That's the biggest": Streissguth, chap. 1.

"In the outlaw story": Streissguth, introduction.

"said some things": Robert K. Oermann, "Waylon: The Outlaw Who Went for Broke," *Nashville Tennessean*, November 5, 1983.

"I'm really just a guitar picker": Windeler, "Bio: Chet Atkins," 61, 62.

"I was recording everybody": Bacon, "Chet Atkins Discusses His Relationship with Gretsch," https://reverb.com/news/chet-atkins-discusses-his-relationship-with-gretsch-in-previously-unpublished-interview-bacons-archive.

"Chet called me": Van Maastricht, *Paul Yandell*, 174.

Keillor, a notorious loner: Dirk Sutro, "Chet Atkins, Garrison Keillor Bite into Some 'Sweet Corn,'" *Los Angeles Times*, July 23, 1990.

"we were trying": Ohlschmidt, "Acoustic Inventions."

"Chet outplayed him": Van Maastricht, *Paul Yandell*, 172–173.

"I kept telling Les Paul": Flippo, "King Picker," 34.

"I had a lot to do": Windeler, "Bio: Chet Atkins," 62.

19. Pontifex Maximus of Nashville

"the guitar is the most": Billy Reed, "Atkins, at 50, Continues Love Affair with Guitar," *Courier-Journal & Times* (Louisville, KY), December 22, 1974.

he had signed a new deal: Bacon, "Chet Atkins Discusses His Relationship with Gretsch," https://reverb.com/news/chet-atkins-discusses-his-relationship-with-gretsch-in-previously-unpublished-interview-bacons-archive.

"the best guitar I've ever had": Michael Brooks, "'I'll Never Be Able to Play the Kind of Leads I Want': Pete Townshend Discusses Guitar Solos, Gibson SGs and More in This Fascinating Interview From the 'GP' Vault," *Guitar Player*, August 2, 2023 (orig. publ. May 1972), https://www.guitarplayer.com/players/pete-townshend-may-1972-guitar-player-interview-extract.

"more like an Exxon station": Tosches, "Waylon Jennings."

"Corporate administration embarrasses him": Windeler, "Bio: Chet Atkins," 60.

"they give you titles": "Chet Atkins: Master Picker Jazzes It Up," *Nine-O-One*, December 1987, 10–11.

RCA in 1977 was about to: Max York, "RCA Reveals Plan to Close Studios Here," *Nashville Tennessean*, January 8, 1977.

"Each star had": Foster, "Memories of Chet Atkins," http://rickfosterguitar.com/chetmem.html.

"the man who epitomizes": Wilson, "You Can't Take the Country Out of Chet."

a toll that, in retrospect: Search for "Chet Atkins," finnishcharts.com, accessed February 20, 2025, https://finnishcharts.com/search.asp?cat=s&artist=chet+atkins&artist_search=starts&title=&title_search=starts.

"and didn't feel like playing": Van Maastricht, *Paul Yandell*, 173.

"one of the great players": "Chet Atkins, The Genius of Lenny Breau," *Frets*, July 1986, 46.

"two very good friends of mine": *Soundstage*, PBS, originally aired December 12, 1978.

"no heavy conversation": "Atkins Visits the White House," *Johnson City* (TN) *Press*, May 5, 1979.

"It was real easy": Ohlschmidt, "Acoustic Inventions."

"Playing a different": Atkins, "Genius of Lenny Breau," 46.

"Lenny was going through": Ohlschmidt, "Acoustic Inventions."

"a fascinating lesson": Robert Taylor, review of *Standard Brands*, AllMusic.com, accessed February 20, 2025, https://www.allmusic.com/album/standard-brands-mw0000111348.

"[Chet] said, 'You want to pick'": Pritcher, "Tommy Emmanuel," http://users.adam.com.au/donald/markinter.htm (site discontinued).

"Well, Chet," he said: Atkins, "Genius of Lenny Breau," 46.

"Lenny," he said: Ray Routhier, "Maine-Born Jazz Guitarist Lenny Breau Remains Influential 30 Years After His Killing," *Portland Press Herald*, April 12, 2016, https://www.pressherald.com/2016/04/10/maine-born-jazz-guitarist-lenny-breau-continues-to-influence-and-amaze-more-than-30-years-after-his-death/.

20. Oh Yeah, the Boy Can Play

Gibson had been trying: Bacon, "Chet Atkins Discusses His Relationship with Gretsch," https://reverb.com/news/chet-atkins-discusses-his-relationship-with-gretsch-in-previously-unpublished-interview-bacons-archive.

a jaw-dropping $20 million: Stephen Golden, "The Pop Life: RCA Gambling on Kenny Rogers," *New York Times*, July 28, 1982.

"fast-moving and fast-talking": William K. Knoedelseder Jr., "The Rap on RCA Records: The Original U.S. Record Company Is Back in Groove," *Los Angeles Times*, September 18, 1988, https://www.latimes.com/archives/la-xpm-1988-09-18-fi-3214-story.html.

"Chet Atkins is my idol": "Chet Atkins, Mr. RCA, Ready to Sign with CBS," *Tennessean*, October 2, 1983.

"If he wants to produce": "Chet Atkins, Mr. RCA," *Tennessean*.

"Hey man, Chet Atkins": James Rea, "The Producer's Chair: Keith Stegall," SongLink, https://www.songlink.com/20130307-the-producers-chair-keith-stegall.html.

"It's not every day": Knopfler, "Chet Atkins Documentary," https://www.youtube.com/watch?v=luQDdPtO904.

"Hello out there": "Chet Atkins: Certified Guitar Player," episode of *Cinemax Sessions* (a.k.a. *Chet Atkins & Friends: Music from the Heart*), Cinemax, originally aired September 6, 1987.

"I learn from him": Sutro, "Chet Atkins, Garrison Keillor."

"I have been suffering": Foster, "Memories of Chet Atkins," http://rickfosterguitar.com/chetmem.html.

"Chet would bust your chops": Calvin Gilbert, "Steve Wariner Talks About His Grammy-Nominated Tribute to Chet Atkins," CMT official website, December 15, 2009, http://cmt.com/news/8df578/steve-wariner-talks-about-his-grammy-nominated-tribute-to-chet-atkins (page discontinued).

"nice and loose, quite happy": Knopfler, "Chet Atkins Documentary," https://www.youtube.com/watch?v=luQDdPtO904.

21. Last Licks

"The word is out": Dawidoff, *In the Country of Country*, 42.

"the first time I've tried": Richard Schweid, "Atkins Scores with Tennessee Dance Theater," *Nashville Tennessean*, March 3, 1991.

Chet went through a litany: Van Maastricht, *Paul Yandell*, 194.

"C.G.P. means corny": Chet Atkins to Rick Foster, Rick Foster Guitar, accessed February 20, 2025, http://rickfosterguitar.com/chetlet.html.

"You want me to play": Pritcher, "Tommy Emmanuel," http://users.adam.com.au/donald/markinter.htm (site discontinued).

"The other day in Cincinnati": Sutro, "Chet Atkins, Garrison Keillor."

"I have always known": Chet Atkins to Rick Foster, http://rickfosterguitar.com/chetlet.html.

"her voice sparkles": Liner notes for *Somewhere Between* by Suzy Bogguss, Capitol Records, 1989.

As Bogguss recalled: Geoffrey Himes, "Bogguss Hits Mark," *Washington Post*, October 13, 1994.

"music worthy of her talent": Himes, "Bogguss Hits Mark."

"well-earned reputation": *Women of Country: In Performance at the White House*, PBS, originally aired September 27, 1995.

"I always wanted to play": Brad Schmidt, Brad About You, *Nashville Tennessean*, August 7, 1996.

"came to me and said": "Tommy Emmanuel@CAAS 2009—Smokey Mountain Lullaby & Story," YouTube, July 21, 2009, youtube.com/watch?v=g9hGE8KypHE.

"I've had my battle": Tom Roland, "Atkins' Cancer in Remission," *Nashville Tennessean*, June 11, 1997.

"two bouts with cancer": Chet Atkins to Rick Foster, http://rickfosterguitar.com/chetlet.html.

"I'm just so sick of hearing": Tom Roland, "Concert Honors 'Mr. Guitar,'" *Nashville Tennessean*, June 15, 1997.

"The people in his band": Ed Morris, "Friend Tells of Chet Atkins' Last Show," CMT official website, June 30, 2001, http://cmt.com/news/h42doz/friend-tells-of-chet-atkins-last-show (page discontinued).

"Chet Atkins turned down": *Ryman Country Homecoming*, part 1, TNN, originally aired October 9, 1999.

allow "wannabe pickers": Alan Bostock, "Grab a Seat Next to Chet," *Nashville Tennessean*, January 13, 2000.

was doing "not bad": Van Maastricht, *Paul Yandell*, 284.

"we had a long conversation": Foster, "Memories of Chet Atkins," http://rickfosterguitar.com/chetmem.html.

Epilogue: This Is How Chet Played It

"I've had a great life": Cochran, *Me and My Guitars*, 182.

"a beautiful man": Leon Alligood, "'Prairie Home Companion' Thanks Atkins for the Music," *Nashville Tennessean*, July 1, 2001.

pronounced him the "Architect": Ben Ratliff, "Chet Atkins, 77, Is Dead; Guitarist and Producer Was Architect of the 'Nashville Sound,'" *New York Times*, July 2, 2001.

"Style Inspired Variety": Martin Weil, "Master Guitarist Chet Atkins Dies," *Washington Post*, June 30, 2001.

"We won't ever see": Peter Cooper, "Pickers Play Their Last Respects on Ryman Stage, *Nashville Tennessean*, July 4, 2001.

"He had a natural reserve": Peter Cooper, "Friends, Fans Celebrate Atkins' Life and Music," *Nashville Tennessean*, July 4, 2001.

"some unknown force": "Chet Atkins: In His Own Words," *Nashville Tennessean*, July 1, 2001.

"What can I say?": Liner notes for *Radio Blues* by Pat Donohue, Prairie Home Productions, 2002.

"There's every other guitar": "Marty Stuart and Brian Setzer Induct Chet Atkins at the 2002 Hall of Fame Induction Ceremony," Rock & Roll Hall of Fame, YouTube, February 14, 2020, https://www.youtube.com/watch?v=qG52OpCt9UQ.

"the architecture of Nashville's": Nicholson, "Estates of Bradley and Atkins," https://musicrow.com/2014/07/harold-bradley-releases-response-to-ben-folds/.

mysterious FBI "dead list": "Dead List (Complete), 2011," https://www.governmentattic.org/5docs/FBI-DeadList-Update_2011.pdf, 27.

engraved cufflinks by Ronald Reagan: Van Maastricht, *Paul Yandell*, 262.

"We were unable to identify": US Department of Justice to the author, June 29, 2023.

"numerous complaints": "Statement of Glenn A. Fine, Inspector General, U.S. Department of Justice before the Committee on Homeland Security, U.S. House of Representatives Concerning 'The Terrorist Screening System and the Watchlist Process,'" US Department of Justice Office of the Inspector General, November 8, 2007, https://oig.justice.gov/node/664.

"[Sometimes] I think": Ohlschmidt, "Acoustic Inventions."

"influenced everybody": David Fricke, "100 Greatest Guitarists," *Rolling Stone*, December 3, 2010, https://www.rollingstone.com/music/music-lists/100-greatest-guitarists-david-frickes-picks-146383/.

"This is how Uncle Chet": Bruce Keener in "Jimmy Atkins with Jerry Reed's 6120 Guitar," The Chetboard, February 3, 2011, MisterGuitar.com, https://misterguitar.us/forum/viewtopic.php?f=6&t=632.

"We got so pop": Dawidoff, *In the Country of Country*, 50.

"I've never worn": AAron Camaro, interview with the author.

the Wall Street Journal's front-page story: Cameron McWhirter and Mariah Timms, "Nashville Is Booming, Locals Fret About Their Future in Music City," *Wall Street Journal*, April 28, 2024.

"I'd like to burn it": Mikhael Wood, "Maren Morris Is Getting the Hell Out of Country Music: 'I've Said Everything I Can Say,'" *Los Angeles Times*, September 15, 2023.